NORTH OF THE LIFFEY
Pages 64–75

FEY

FEY

SOUTHEAST DUBLIN

SOUTHEAST DUBLIN
Pages 30–49

0 kilometres   100

0 miles   100

EYEWITNESS TRAVEL GUIDES

DUBLIN

INTRODUCING
DUBLIN

Putting Dublin on the Map

Dublin is the capital of the Republic of Ireland, which takes up 85 per cent of Ireland, an island that lies in the far northwest of Europe. Dublin sits on the eastern coast of Ireland, on the Irish Sea, which separates Ireland from Great Britain. The Liffey is the main river running through the city. Dublin and its surrounding county have a population of just over one million, and good international communications.

Europe

Most visitors to Dublin come either by air or on the ferry to Dun Laoghaire or Dublin Port. The main ferry routes are from Wales, Scotland and England. There are international flights to Dublin airport. Many European flights are routed via Amsterdam or Great Britain, but flight times are only around an hour from British airports.

0 kilometres 100

0 miles 50

KEY

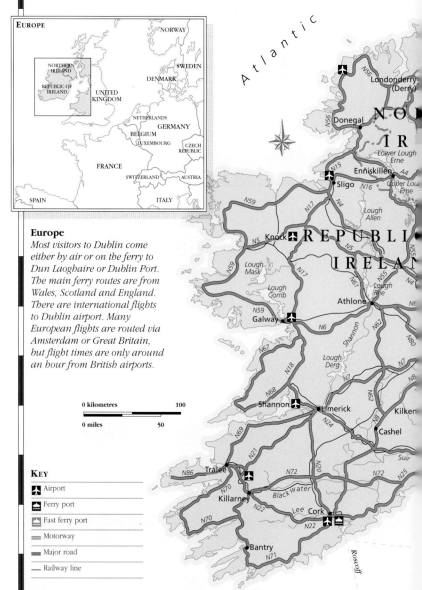

✈	Airport
⛴	Ferry port
⛴	Fast ferry port
▬	Motorway
▬	Major road
—	Railway line

Interior of Avondale House, the home of Charles Stewart Parnell

Dublin dish of oysters, often consumed with Guinness

Sheep on the farm at Newbridge Demesne, north of Dublin

Bookcases of rare books in Marsh's Library

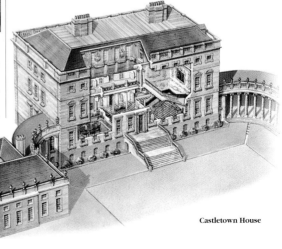

Castletown House

EYEWITNESS TRAVEL GUIDES

DUBLIN

Main Contributor: TIM PERRY

OBEDIENTIA FELICITAS

CIVIUM URBIS

LONDON, NEW YORK,
MELBOURNE, MUNICH AND DELHI
www.dk.com

PROJECT EDITOR Claire Folkard
ART EDITOR Jo Doran
EDITOR Freddy Hamilton
DESIGNERS Paul Jackson, Nicola Rodway
EDITORIAL ASSISTANT Sophie Warne
DTP DESIGNERS Samantha Borland, Lee Redmond, Rachel Symons
PICTURE RESEARCH Victoria Peel

PHOTOGRAPHERS
Joe Cornish, Tim Daly, Magnus Rew, Antony Souter,
Alan Williams

ILLUSTRATORS
Stephen Conlin, Gary Cross, Claire Littlejohn,
Maltings Partnership, Robbie Polley, John Woodcock

Reproduced in Singapore by Colourscan
Printed and bound by South China Printing Co. Ltd., China

First published in Great Britain in 1999
by Dorling Kindersley Limited
80 Strand, London WC2R 0RL
Reprinted with revisions 2000, 2001, 2002, 2003, 2004, 2006

Copyright 1999, 2006 © Dorling Kindersley Limited, London
A Penguin Company

A CIP CATALOGUE RECORD IS AVAILABLE FROM THE BRITISH LIBRARY.

ISBN 1-4053-1200-9
ISBN 978-14053-1200-4

**The information in this
DK Eyewitness Travel Guide is checked annually.**
Every effort has been made to ensure that this book is as up-to-date
as possible at the time of going to press. Some details, however,
such as telephone numbers, opening hours, prices, gallery hanging
arrangements and travel information, are liable to change. The
publishers cannot accept responsibility for any consequences arising
from the use of this book, nor for any material on third-party
websites, and cannot guarantee that any website address in this
book will be a suitable source of travel information. We value the
views and suggestions of our readers highly. Please write to:
Publisher, DK Eyewitness Travel Guides, Dorling Kindersley,
80 Strand, London, Great Britain WC2R 0RL.

Government buildings at dusk

Façade of St Teresa's Church

CONTENTS

INTRODUCING DUBLIN

**View across the tombstones of
Glasnevin Cemetery**

Greater Dublin

Nearly one third of the Republic's population lives in Dublin. Nevertheless the city is relatively uncongested and access to the centre from the ports and airport is easy.

ADDRESS TO

Chas S. Parnell, Esq.

President of the Irish National Land League

Sir — We tender you on behalf of the tenant farmers of Ireland a hearty céad míle fáilte home again to the country you have so nobly served during your brief sojourn in the United States. Short as your stay has been in that mighty Western Republic it has nevertheless been signalised by the most splendid and opportune services to the present wants of our starving people, while being at the same time pregnant with encouraging hope for the future welfare of our fatherland. While thousands of families, pauperised through the operation of an infamous land system have been saved by your wondrous and indefatigable exertions from the fate which befel our famine-slaughtered kindred in '47 and '48, the heart of Ireland has followed in the wake of your triumphal progress among a generous and sympathetic people, and throbbed with expectant joy as they pledged you the moral support of America in our struggle against felonious landlordism.

As the representative of the Irish People and delegate of the National Land League, you and your colleague Mr. John Dillon, have had extended to you honours and manifestations of encouragement surpassing any yet conferred by the land of Washington, Franklin and Carroll upon the champions of oppressed nationalities; and your country felt proudly raised once more to the dignity of a recognized nation when the House of Representatives bestowed upon you the proud privilege of advocating the cause of Ireland before the most representative assembly of the greatest Government in the world. From the St. Lawrence to the Potomac — from the Atlantic seaboard to the plains of Minnesota — the landlord-banished portion of our people have pledged anew their fidelity to Ireland and their vows for her deliverance, when by those enthusiastic greetings immense demonstrations and military parades they welcomed you as the ambassador of their resurgent Ireland while their munificent contributions and promised continued cooperation infuses a spirit of sanguine expectation into our impoverished people that the felt cause of their poverty and humiliation will soon fall beneath the united efforts of our entire race.

You are landing in Ireland at a time which may be deemed a momentous period in the history of that coercive and infamous Union which has been such a political scourge to our country and when the spirit of Irish nationality is endangered by the virulent attacks of a truculent and unscrupulous Government. We sincerely hope that you have sped across the waters like another Perseus to save the Andromeda of nations from the political monster now threatening her with national destruction and that her deliverance from immediate danger achieved you will return to the assistance of your colleagues to complete the mission you were sent on by the body of which you are the honoured and trusted head.

Signed

Patrick Egan,   J. F. Grehan,   Thomas Sexton,
A. J. Kettle,   R. J. Donnelly,   Michael Davitt.

PARNELL ADDRESSING THE UNITED STATES HOUSE OF REPRESENTATIVES IN SESSION.
WASHINGTON, FEBY 2ND 1880.

THE HISTORY OF DUBLIN

THE CITY OF DUBLIN *first took form in the early 9th century when Vikings founded one of their largest settlements outside Scandinavia on the site of the present city. Since then, it has suffered wars and conflict over many centuries. In the 20th century Dublin has established its own identity and today it is a thriving, modern city, rich in history and proud of its past.*

Archaeological digs show evidence of civilization in the Dublin area as early as 7500 BC. The 4th millennium BC saw the influx of Neolithic farmers and herdsmen who built monumental tombs such as those found at Newgrange *(see pp112–13)*.

The Celts arrived around 700 BC and things changed little for 1,000 years. When St Patrick arrived in AD 432 bringing Christianity with him to Ireland, the Celts were quick to embrace the religion. During the golden age of Celtic Christianity the Dublin area was home to several churches and it is said that the present-day St Patrick's Cathedral (built in 1192) is where the saint baptized converts around AD 450. This era produced high levels of Christian scholarship, resulting in such treasures as the elaborately decorated Book of Kells *(see p38)*.

The city's modern Gaelic name of "Baile Atha Cliath" derives from a Celtic settlement on the north bank of the River Liffey. Known then as Ath Cliathe ("the ford over the hurdles") it was the only crossing over the river and lay at the junction of four major roads. It was the community at Ath Cliathe that bore the brunt of the island's first planned naval invasion by the Vikings.

Engraving showing St Patrick banishing snakes from Ireland

THE VIKINGS

Norse Vikings established their first harbour in Dublin in AD 841 and left in AD 902, under pressure from local chieftains. They returned 15 years later and built a stronghold situated between the present location of Dublin Castle and Wood Quay. It was here that the rivers Liffey and Poddle converged in a body of dark, still water which the Vikings called *Dyfflin* or *Dubh Linn* (or "black pool").

In 919 at the Battle of Dublin the Vikings fended off the King of Tara and by the mid-1100s they started to intermarry with the Celts. The Vikings were then defeated at the Battle of Clontarf in 1014 by Brian Ború, the Irish High King. Under King Sitric the Silkbeard, Dublin became a Christian vassal state. He oversaw the construction of a wooden cathedral (later rebuilt as Christ Church). By this time Dublin's population was around 5,000.

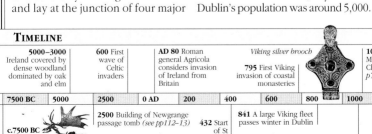

TIMELINE

5000–3000 Ireland covered by dense woodland dominated by oak and elm	**600** First wave of Celtic invaders	**AD 80** Roman general Agricola considers invasion of Ireland from Britain	*Viking silver brooch* **795** First Viking invasion of coastal monasteries	**1096** St Michan's Church *(see p74)* built

7500 BC	5000	2500	0 AD	200	400	600	800	1000	1200

c.7500 BC First inhabitants of Ireland *Extinct giant deer or "Irish Elk"*	**2500** Building of Newgrange passage tomb *(see pp112–13)*	**432** Start of St Patrick's mission to Ireland	**841** A large Viking fleet passes winter in Dublin **1014** High King Brian Ború of Munster defeats joint army of Vikings and the King of Leinster at Clontarf	**1147** St Mary's Abbey *(see p74)* built

◁ **Address to Charles Stewart Parnell by the Land League**

ANGLO-NORMAN CONQUEST

Feuds in Ireland led to Dermot Mac-Murrough, the King of Leinster, asking Henry II of England to send an army to aid him. This resulted in the appearance of Richard de Clare, better known as Strongbow, in 1169. Within a year he had taken control of Dublin and married MacMurrough's daughter. He was also the instigator of the construction of Christ Church Cathedral *(see pp62–3)*.

When MacMurrough died in 1171, Strongbow was in line to succeed him. Henry II sent an army to Ireland to check his ambitions, in part by recognizing Strongbow's suzerainty over the province of Leinster. Henry then spent four months in Dublin establishing control.

The Marriage of Strongbow and Aoife, by Daniel Maclise (1854)

Under Anglo-Norman control, the structure and size of the city grew. Fortified walls and watchtowers were built, and in 1205 construction on Dublin Castle started. St Patrick's was made a cathedral in 1220 and underwent massive expansion while, in its shadows, the Liberties, the city's earliest suburbs, were growing in strength. The city became overcrowded and in 1348 was struck by the terrifying plague known as the Black Death.

TUDOR AND STUART RULE

Like the Vikings before them, the Anglo-Normans had entwined themselves in Irish society through marriage and religion. Some of them, such as the Fitzgeralds, the Butlers and the Burkes, effectively controlled dynasties. One of them, "Silken" Thomas Fitzgerald, son of the 9th Earl of Kildare, staged a revolt against London in 1534. This was defeated by King Henry VIII who, in 1541, passed the Act of Supremacy that made him King of Ireland and the head of the Church which, under the English Reformation, had broken from Rome. All land was the property of the English crown and, by dissolving the monasteries and sentencing to death all men of the Fitzgerald family, he indicated the start of a strongarm rule and the introduction of Protestantism to Ireland.

The reign of Elizabeth I witnessed the development of the island into a British colony, with plantations set up throughout Ireland. In 1592, on the site of a dissolved monastery near Dublin, she founded Trinity College as a seat of Protestant learning: a status it retained well into the 20th century.

Henry VIII with Bishop Sherbourne by Lambert Barnard (1519)

TIMELINE

1166 Dermot MacMurrough, King of Leinster, flees overseas	**1297** First Irish Parliament meets in Dublin	**1366** Statutes of Kilkenny forbid marriage between Anglo-Normans and Irish	**1471** 8th Earl of Kildare made Lord Deputy of Ireland
1172 Pope affirms King Henry II of England's lordship over Ireland			

1200	**1250**	**1300**	**1350**	**1400**	**1450**

1169 Strongbow's Anglo-Normans arrive at invitation of exiled King of Leinster, Dermot MacMurrough	*A section of Strongbow's tomb*	**1348** The Black Death: one third of population dies within three years	**1394** King Richard II lands with army to reassert control; returns five years later but with inconclusive results	**1487** Kildare crowns Lambert Simnel, Edward VI in Dublin

London's grip over Ireland intensified in 1649, when Oliver Cromwell arrived in Dublin. His infamous campaigns left several thousand dead or deported and he forced the Irish from their fertile lands in the east to the barren western province of Connaught.

The Rotunda Hospital in 1795, Dublin's first maternity hospital

THE PENAL LAWS

In 1690, the Catholic ex-king of England, James II, was defeated by the Dutch Protestant William Prince of Orange (King William III) at the Battle of the Boyne. In the years following, religious persecution was formalized into a Penal Code. Catholics were prohibited from voting, trading, buying land, holding elected or state office, or entering professions.

THE PROTESTANT ASCENDANCY

While William III's Penal Laws were spelling hard times for the Catholic population in the rest of Ireland, Dublin's middle classes and aristocrats (many of them absentee landlords who came to Ireland during the entertaining season) enjoyed a very comfortable existence.

William of Orange at the Battle of the Boyne

Throughout the 18th century they commissioned ostentatious homes such as Leinster House and Powerscourt House. The owners of the grand town houses employed master craftsmen from around the world, such as the German-English architect Richard Castle and the Swiss-Italian stuccodores Paolo and Filippo Francini.

Among the desirable addresses at the time were St Stephen's Green, Marlborough Street to the north of the Liffey and Ely Place on the southside. If they were ill, the Royal Hospital at Kilmainham attended their needs. Dublin also boasted the Rotunda Lying-In Hospital, the first maternity hospital in the British Isles. Much of the funding for this venture came from the adjacent and ornate Rotunda Gardens (no longer in existence), where members of high society frequently met and attended concerts. In Georgian times the privileged Protestants were able to patronize the arts: Handel premiered the *Messiah* in the city in 1742. Eleven years earlier, the still extant Royal Dublin Society was founded to promote the arts, science and agriculture. Many great academics and novelists also emerged from Trinity College, including the philosopher Edmund Burke, and Jonathan Swift, author of *Gulliver's Travels* and the Dean of St Patrick's Cathedral *(see p59)* from 1713 to 1745.

PUBLIC WORKS IN THE 18TH CENTURY

Many of the most impressive sights in Dublin today were built during the Protestant Ascendancy, in the Georgian era.

Among the most splendid structures of this period are Castletown House (1722–32), the Custom House (1791) and the Four Courts (1786–1802). The two latter buildings were both designed by James Gandon. Dublin was also one of the first cities in the world to enjoy planned development with the inauguration of the Wide Streets Commission in 1751. Further improvements came with the National Botanic Gardens in 1789.

Commerce also helped shape the city. In the 1760s the Grand Canal was built and Ireland's most famous company began in 1759 when Arthur Guinness opened his brewery.

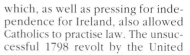

Lacquer cabinet, Castletown House

CATHOLIC EMANCIPATION AND RESISTANCE

Despite lengthy protests by pamphleteers and orators, the first real hint of relaxation of the penal laws came in 1782 when the Irish Parliament, led by Henry Grattan, passed a Declaration of Rights which, as well as pressing for independence for Ireland, also allowed Catholics to practise law. The unsuccessful 1798 revolt by the United Irishmen, led by Dublin Protestant Wolfe Tone, may have been instrumental in convincing the Westminster government to impose the 1800 Act of Union. This dissolved the Irish Parliament and saw the introduction of direct rule from England.

The first 19th-century revolt against British rule was led by Robert Emmet in 1803, who attempted to seize Dublin Castle. The most effective protest of the early part of the century was led by Daniel O'Connell, a Catholic lawyer, who later became known as "The Liberator" as a result of his efforts on behalf of the people who shared his religious beliefs. He supported mass peaceful protests and was elected an MP in 1828 but, as a Catholic, was unable to take his seat. In response to O'Connell's mass rallies and protests, the Emancipation Act of 1829 was passed. O'Connell was the first Catholic to be elected Mayor of Dublin in 1841 but, when he later called for a repeal of the Act of Union, he was jailed.

James Gandon's impressive Custom House, on the north bank of the Liffey

TIMELINE

1750	1775	1800	1825

1751 The Rotunda Lying-In Hospital *(see p70)* is first maternity hospital in the British Isles

1791 James Gandon's Custom House *(see p68)* is built

1800 Act of Union: Ireland legally becomes part of Britain

1817 The Royal Canal *(see p83)* is completed

1838 Father Mathew founds temperance crusade – whiskey production is reduced by half

1759 Arthur Guinness buys the St James' Gate Brewery *(see pp80–81)*

Guinness Brewery Gate

1828 After a five-year campaign by Daniel O'Connell, Catholic Emancipation Act is passed, giving a limited number of Catholics the right to vote

1845 Start of Great Famine, which lasts for four years

THE GREAT FAMINE AND FURTHER REBELLIONS

The history of 19th-century Ireland is dominated by the Great Famine of 1845–8, which was caused by the total failure of the potato crop. Although Irish grain was still being exported to England, around one million people died from hunger or disease. By 1900, the pre-famine population of eight million had fallen by half. Many of the poor moved into Dublin and the middle-class Dubliners moved out to the suburbs. Rural hardship fuelled a campaign for tenants' rights that evolved into demands for independence from Britain. Great strides towards "Home Rule" were made in Parliament by the charismatic politician, Charles Stewart Parnell.

O'Connell Street shortly after the Easter Rising

Ration card from Famine period

SUPPORT FOR HOME RULE GROWS

In 1902 Arthur Griffith founded the Sinn Féin newspaper; its name, meaning "We, Ourselves ", expressed their central policy thrust and it soon gave rise to a political party of the same name. In 1913 the Irish Volunteers (the forerunners of the Irish Republican Army) were formed. Political freedom was increasingly important at this time of stark poverty and violent clashes between workers and employers. One of the leaders of the workers' side, James Connolly, would soon broaden his political agenda to Republicanism.

WORLD WAR I AND THE EASTER RISING

Although the Home Rule Bill made its final passage through the British parliament, its implementation was suspended due to the outbreak of war. A small contingent felt that the best time to launch an attack on British rule was when Britain was at its weakest. Hence, on Easter Monday 1916, Patrick Pearse and other members of a provisional government proclaimed the Declaration of Independence from the General Post Office (see p69) in O'Connell Street. The band of rebels occupied several buildings in the capital. The Easter Rising was put down within a few days but only after 300 citizens were killed and much of the city centre razed to the ground. The British forces lost patience with the Irish cause and the rebel leaders were shot for treason at Kilmainham Gaol. This overreaction made those executed into martyrs and renewed resentment towards Britain.

Daniel O'Connell, "The Liberator"

View of O'Donovan Bridge which links the north and south sides of modern Dublin

INDEPENDENCE AND CIVIL WAR

The years after World War I were some of the busiest and bloodiest in Dublin's history. The resentment over the treatment of the Rising leaders, and a plan to bring in conscription in Ireland, helped the cause of the Sinn Féin party, which won three-quarters of Irish seats in the 1918 election. These new MPs refused to take up their seats and instead met at a newly formed Dáil Éireann (Parliament of Ireland) at the Mansion House *(see p39)*. The Dáil's Minister of Finance was Michael Collins, who was also head of the Irish Volunteers' campaign of urban guerrilla warfare. On the morning of 21 November 1920, Collins ordered the assassination of 14 undercover British officers in Dublin. That afternoon British forces retaliated in what soon became known as Bloody Sunday, when they shot 12 spectators at a big Gaelic football game at Croke Park stadium. Other small skirmishes continued throughout

the city, including the burning of the Custom House *(see p68)* in May 1921. Soon after this the British government instigated a truce and both sides signed the Anglo-Irish Treaty.

The treaty gave limited independence to what was to be called the Irish Free State, but six Ulster counties were to be excluded and members of the Free State parliament (the Dáil) would have to swear allegiance to the British monarch. A faction of the Dáil led by Eamon De Valera opposed the treaty and in June 1922 Civil War broke out. Anti-treaty forces occupied the Four Courts building *(see p74)* but this was bombed (as was much of O'Connell Street) by the army under Collins. The Free State government proved ruthless in its imprisonment and later execution of anti-treaty rebels, but Collins himself finally became a victim when he was ambushed and shot. In May 1923 De Valera ordered an end

Eamon De Valera, a major figure in modern Irish politics

TIMELINE

1918 Sinn Féin sweeps election; Countess Constance Markievicz elected first woman MP		**1947** A statue of Queen Victoria is removed from the front courtyard of the Irish parliament buildings		*The Irish flag*
1920 First "Bloody Sunday" at Croke Park				

1920	**1930**	**1940**	**1950**	**19**

	1922 Michael Collins killed		**1941** German air raid on Dublin		**1963** John
1921 Anglo-Irish treaty signed; leads to Civil War		*Michael Collins, the leader of the Irish Volunteers*		**1954** Brendan Behan's *The Quare Fellow* is published	Kennedy, the fir US President Irish descer visits Dubl

THE HISTORY OF DUBLIN

to the fighting by anti-treaty rebels and left the Sinn Féin party.

RECENT HISTORY

Within three years De Valera had formed a new party called Fianna Fáil, which translates as "Warriors of Ireland". By 1932, his party had ac-

Young Irish dancers

quired power after claiming the majority of votes. With only two short periods of time out of office, De Valera held the post of Taoiseach

European City of Culture doorway

(prime minister) until 1959, when he became president for a further 14 years. His policies were largely insular and mirrored the Catholic Church on social issues. During World War II De Valera kept Ireland neutral and as a result Dublin only experienced one major bombing incursion from the Luftwaffe.

After the war, Fianna Fáil were beaten in the election by Fine Gael. Though they were the descendants of the pro-treaty side, it was Fine Gael who oversaw the creation of the Republic of Ireland in 1949, which severed all ties with Britain by leaving the Commonwealth.

Dublin remained relatively immune to the political situation in Northern Ireland, as it does today, though in 1966 the IRA bombed the huge Nelson Column (even larger than the one in London's Trafalgar Square). Its only remaining piece, the massive head, is

now on display in Dublin's Civic Museum *(see p58)*. Then in 1972, the British Embassy in Dublin was petrol-bombed, in retaliation for the shooting of 13 civilians on a protest march in Derry, in Northern Ireland, on what became known as Ireland's second Bloody Sunday.

DUBLIN INTO THE MILLENNIUM

In 1991 Dublin was named European City of Culture and this spurred the rejuvenation of Temple Bar *(see pp56–7)* into a world-class cultural quarter. The majority of new development was in the wealthier areas south of the river, though the divide between north and south has narrowed since the late 1990s and the economic boom hailed as the Celtic Tiger. Dublin is now a lively, modern and cosmopolitan city. Progress made under the forward-thinking presidency of Mary Robinson is continuing under her successor, Mary McAleese.

Grafton Street in modernized southwest Dublin

1970	1980	1990	2000
1972 Ireland joins European Community	**1988** Dublin engages in millennium celebrations to boost its image although most historians trace its founding to an even earlier date	**1991** Dublin is the European City of Culture	**1998** Peace talks between the British and Irish governments, and parties in Northern Ireland, result in the Good Friday Agreement
1976 British ambassador assassinated in Dublin	**1979** Pope John Paul II celebrates mass in front of more than one million people	**1990** Mary Robinson is the first woman elected as President of Ireland	**1996** Anti-drugs campaigner and investigative journalist Veronica Guerin murdered

President Mary Robinson (1990–97)

DUBLIN AT A GLANCE

ALTHOUGH IT IS a fairly small city, Dublin offers a wealth of different attractions which draw in millions of visitors each year. Those in the city centre or a short way outside Dublin are covered in the *Area by Area* section of this book. Sights further out of the city include the elegant stately homes of Castletown House and Powerscourt. In central Dublin, Temple Bar offers shopping, eating and drinking and the arts in a trendy, relaxed environment. Alternatively the glittering treasures of the National Museum or the liquid treasures of the Guinness Storehouse may lure you inside. A selection of Dublin's most popular sights is given below.

DUBLIN'S TOP TEN ATTRACTIONS

National Museum
See pp42–3

Guinness Storehouse
See pp80–81

Trinity College
See pp36–7

Castletown House
See pp98–9

National Gallery
See pp46–9

St Patrick's Cathedral
See p59

Powerscourt
See pp106–7

Temple Bar
See pp56–7

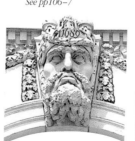

Custom House
See p68

Christ Church Cathedral
See pp62–3

◁ **The bell tower in Trinity College**

Celebrated Visitors and Residents

F OR MANY CENTURIES Dublin has produced some of the greatest literary names in history. However, Dubliners are also famous for music, philosophy and politics. Edmund Burke, widely considered to be the father of British Conservatism, was born to the north of the Liffey. Writers such as Yeats, Beckett and Wilde lived in the city intermittently, having been born in Ireland. Jonathan Swift began the tradition of brilliant Irish writing at around the beginning of the 18th century. Great Irish writing continues to this day, with such prize-winning authors as Seamus Heaney, William Trevor, John Banville and Roddy Doyle.

The Duke of Wellington
Wellington was born in Dublin, close to what is now Wellington Quay, in 1769. He became one of the most successful generals and politicians in British history.

G F Handel
The German-born composer decided to première his most famous oratorio, the Messiah, *in the new Music Hall in Fishamble Street in 1741.*

NORTH OF THE LIFFEY

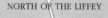

SOUTHWEST DUBLIN

Jonathan Swift
Famous as the author of many literary works, including Gulliver's Travels, *Swift became Dean of St Patrick's Cathedral in 1713.*

Bram Stoker
The author of Dracula, *one of the most famous horror stories ever written, was born in Dublin in 1847 and lived on Harcourt Street just off St Stephen's Green.*

James Joyce
Quite possibly Dublin's most famous author. Two of his greatest works, Ulysses *and* The Dubliners, *are set in Dublin. Many of the characters and places in* Ulysses *are based on reality.*

William Butler Yeats
Born in Sligo, in northwest Ireland, Yeats was one of the founders of the Abbey Theatre. The poet spent much of his adult life in London but returned to Ireland frequently.

Samuel Beckett
The playwright was born south of Dublin and studied at Trinity College (see pp36–7). One of his most famous and enigmatic works is Waiting for Godot.

SOUTHEAST DUBLIN

Oscar Wilde
This flamboyant author and playwright was born in Dublin – his family home can still be seen on the corner of Merrion Square. He enjoyed great success with such plays as The Importance of Being Earnest.

| 0 metres | 200 |
| 0 yards | 200 |

Dublin's Best: Pubs

EVERYONE KNOWS that Dublin is famous for its vast number of drinking establishments but, on arrival in the city, the choice can seem overwhelming. All the pubs are different – they range from vibrant, trendy bars to traditional pubs. Whatever your choice of environment and beverage, you can be guaranteed to find it in Dublin. These pages offer just a taster of the most popular pubs in the city and what they are famous for, but for a more complete listing, turn to pages 132–3.

Slattery's
Once a popular music pub just north of the Liffey, Slattery's has recently been totally modernized and is just as much of a success in its reincarnation as a trendy bar.

NORTH OF THE LIFFEY

The Stag's Head
This gorgeous Victorian pub has a long mahogany bar and has retained its original mirrors and stained glass. Located down an alley off Dame Street, this atmospheric pub is well worth seeking out.

SOUTHWEST DUBLIN

The Brazen Head
Reputedly the oldest pub in Dublin. The present building, still with its courtyard for coach and horses, dates back to 1750. The interior is full of dark wood panelling and old photographs of Dublin.

Hogan's
A café bar rather than a pub, Hogan's is a stylish establishment serving excellent drinks, and is popular with a young, trendy crowd. It is centrally situated on George's Street.

Oliver St John Gogarty

This famous old pub in the heart of Temple Bar is renowned for its live music throughout the day, and good food. It is named after the poet and friend of James Joyce. The atmosphere is relaxed and it is popular with visitors keen to sample a part of traditional Dublin.

O'Neill's

Just round the corner from Grafton Street, O'Neill's is one of the best places in the city for pub food. Its cosy atmosphere and location close to Trinity College make it a favourite with Dublin's student population.

LIFFEY

SOUTHEAST DUBLIN

0 metres 200

0 yards 200

McDaid's

Playwright Brendan Behan downed many a pint in this pub, which dates from 1779. Though on the tourist trail, McDaid's retains a bohemian charm, and bars upstairs and downstairs provide space for a leisurely drink.

O'Donoghue's

A good mix of locals and tourists, young and old, frequent this pub in the heart of Georgian Dublin which has been a city favourite for years. Famous as the pub where the Dubliners folk group began in the 1960s, it is known today for its live traditional music.

DUBLIN THROUGH THE YEAR

Revellers at the
St Patrick's Day parade

THE CITY IS at its busiest in July and August, which are the most popular months for visiting Dublin. June and September can be pleasant but don't count on the weather, since Ireland's lush beauty is the product of a wet climate. Most Dublin sights are open all year round but, in the low season (generally November to March), some of them have limited opening hours or close completely. In summer, events are held in honour of anything from gardens to James Joyce, but a common thread is music, and few festivals are complete without it. Dublin is at its best when celebrating and is thus a treat at Christmas or New Year. Look out for the word *fleadh* (festival) in the city, but remember, too, that the Irish are a spontaneous people: festivities can spring from the air, or from a tune on a fiddle.

Trinity College rowers competing on the Liffey (April)

SPRING

AFTER THE QUIET winter, spring sees a flurry of festivals and events. St Patrick's Day is often said to mark the beginning of the tourist season. This national holiday is celebrated with music and carnival-style abandon throughout the city. Accommodation is often in short supply around this time so do book in advance.

Annual parade through the streets of Dublin
to celebrate St Patrick's Day (March)

MARCH

Celtic Flame *(14–17 Mar).* A national festival of contemporary and traditional music, song and dance culminates at various Dublin venues.
St Patrick's Day Festival *(around 17 Mar).* Numerous street theatre acts fill the city during colourful celebrations that centre on a parade on St Patrick's Day itself (17 March).
Temple Bar Fleadh *(around 17 Mar).* Three-day festival of traditional music in honour of St Patrick in the Temple Bar area.
Irish Kennel Club Show *(mid-Mar),* Cloghran. Annual championship dog show.
Poetry Now Festival *(last week).* Held in Dun Laoghaire, the events include readings, masterclasses and children's activities.

APRIL

Colours Boat Race *(first weekend).* A rowing race along the Liffey between University College Dublin and Trinity College.
Howth Music Festival *(Easter weekend).* This pretty fishing village on the outskirts of the city *(see p88)* plays host to three days of popular music.
Feis Ceoil *(mid-Apr),* various venues around Dublin play host to one of Europe's oldest and most prestigious classical music festivals.

May Day Parade in central Dublin

MAY

May Day Parade *(1 May)* Celebrations and colourful parades through the city streets on this national holiday.
Dublin Garden Festival *(late May or early Jun),* RDS Ballsbridge. Large, four-day horticultural show.
Laytown Beach Races *(late May or early Jun).* Horse races on a beach north of Dublin.

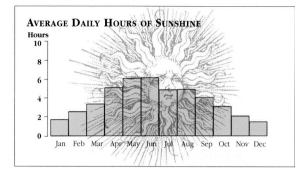

AVERAGE DAILY HOURS OF SUNSHINE

Hours

Jan Feb Mar Apr May Jun Jul Aug Sep Oct Nov Dec

Sunshine Chart
Hours of sunshine in rainy Dublin are few and far between for most of the year. In summer, however, the days are often long, hot and very sunny. As in the rest of the country, the weather is notoriously unpredictable, so skies can cloud over in minutes.

SUMMER

SUMMER REPRESENTS the height of the festive calendar for the visitor and the Dubliner alike and is the city's busiest time of year. There is a succession of outdoor music, arts and community festivals of all kinds, culminating in the city's top social event, the annual Dublin Horse Show.

JUNE

Diversions *(May-Aug, see pp56–7).* Free open-air entertainment at various venues throughout Dublin's Temple Bar district.
Music in the Park *(Jun–Aug)* Various city parks hold free open-air concerts at lunchtime on weekdays, and on Sundays.
County Wicklow Gardens Festival *(all month).* Held at private and public gardens south of Dublin, including Powerscourt *(see pp106–7).*
Bloomsday *(16 Jun).* Walks, lectures and pub talks across

Bluesman Eric Bibb performing at Temple Bar Blues Festival (July)

the city to celebrate James Joyce's greatest novel, *Ulysses.*
Maracycle *(mid-Jun).* Thousands of cyclists race each other from Dublin to Belfast and back again.
Scurlogstown Olympiad Celtic Festival *(mid-Jun),* Trim *(see p114).* Traditional Irish music, dance, fair and selection of a festival queen.
Music in Great Irish Houses *(second and third weeks).* Classical music recitals in grand settings at various venues.

JULY

Dun Laoghaire American Week *(first week, see p88).* US-themed jamboree with bluegrass music, a barn dance and Fourth of July fireworks.
Docklands Festival *(third week).* A community festival that centres on Pearse Street and City Quay, with shows and activities for all ages.
Anna Livia International Opera Festival *(second week).* Opera performances staged around the city.

The Dublin Horse Show (August)

AUGUST

Summer Music Festival *(all month),* St Stephen's Green *(see p39).* Free lunchtime concerts, and sporadic open-air Shakespeare performances.
Dublin Horse Show *(second week),* RDS Ballsbridge *(see p83).* Dublin's premier sporting and social event includes showjumping, dressage and a chance to show off your hat.
People's Photographic Exhibition *(last weekend),* St Stephen's Green *(see p39).* Local photographers' work hung on the green's railings.
Festival of World Cultures *(late Aug).* Dun Laoghaire *(see p88).* A celebration of multiculturalism with arts, music, crafts, and more.

Powerscourt Gardens, part of the County Wicklow Gardens Festival (June)

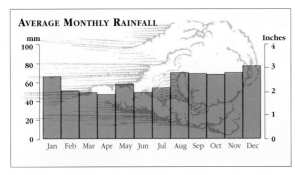

AVERAGE MONTHLY RAINFALL

Rainfall Chart
Ireland is one of the wettest countries in Europe, with rainfall distributed evenly throughout the year. Fortunately, Dublin is situated in the drier eastern half of the country, but visitors should still be prepared for rain at any time of year.

Revellers on Hallowe'en (October)

AUTUMN

AUTUMN KICKS OFF with the Liffey Swim, a race along Dublin's river attempted only by the strong hearted. Later the traditional sports of Gaelic football and hurling, the latter a kind of aerial hockey, hold their popular national finals in the city. The theatre festival held in October is world class.

SEPTEMBER

The Liffey Swim *(first Sat)*. Since 1920, Dubliners have turned out to watch swimmers brave the Liffey's murky waters from Watling Street Bridge to the Custom House *(see p68)*.
Dublin Fringe Theatre Festival *(mid two weeks)*. Great variety of shows held at various venues all over the city.
All-Ireland Hurling Final *(second Sun)*, Croke Park.
All-Ireland Football Final *(fourth Sun)*, Croke Park. Popular Gaelic football final.

Carpets at the annual Irish Antique Dealers' Fair (September)

Irish Antique Dealers' Fair *(last week)*, RDS Ballsbridge *(see p83)*. The country's most important antiques fair.

OCTOBER

Dublin Theatre Festival *(first two weeks)*. Features new works by Irish playwrights, plus many foreign productions.
Dublin City Marathon *(last Mon)*. Starting and finishing on O'Connell Street, the route takes in many Dublin landmarks, including Phoenix Park and Trinity College. Every year several thousands participate.
Hallowe'en (Shamhna) *(31 Oct)*. On the night when spirits rise, children wear fancy dress and celebrations include a parade and fireworks.

NOVEMBER

Opera Ireland *(a week in Nov)*. Autumn run at the Gaiety Theatre. Another short season is put on in April.
Toy and Train Collectors' Fair *(last Sun)*, Rochestown Lodge Hotel, Dun Laoghaire *(see p88)*. Model cars, dolls, comics and teddy bears. Other fairs in April and September.

Large field of runners competing in the Dublin City Marathon (October)

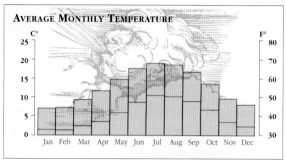

AVERAGE MONTHLY TEMPERATURE

Temperature Chart
This chart gives the average minimum and maximum temperatures for the city. Extremes of temperature are rare: the winter is mild, with the mercury seldom falling below zero. In summer, however, the occasional day can be very warm.

WINTER

ALTHOUGH WINTER is a quiet time for festivals, there is a range of entertainment on offer, including sporting and theatrical events. Christmas is the busiest social period and there are plenty of informal celebrations. There is also a wide choice of National Hunt (steeplechase) race meetings, especially at Leopardstown, south of the city centre.

Glendalough *(see p102)* in the snow

Christmas scene at Mansion House

DECEMBER

Pantomime Season *(Dec–Jan)*. Traditional pantomime performed at theatres in Dublin and throughout Ireland.
Christmas *(24–25 Dec)*. Christian celebrations include going to midnight mass on Christmas Eve.
St Stephen's Day *(26 Dec)*. On the day after Christmas, Catholic boys dress up as Wren boys (chimney sweeps with blackened faces) and sing hymns to raise money for charitable causes.

Leopardstown Races *(26–29 Dec)*. This four-day meeting is the biggest in the country at this traditional time for horse racing.
New Year's Eve *(31 Dec)*. Celebrations around the city to welcome in the New Year.

JANUARY

Salmon and Sea Trout Season *(1 Jan–Sep)*. Start of the season for one of the most popular pastimes in Ireland.
Irish Champion Hurdle *(late Jan)*. Major horse race at Leopardstown *(see p97)*.

Hurdlers at Leopardstown (January)

FEBRUARY

Six Nations Rugby Tournament *(on various weekends Feb–Apr)*, Lansdowne Road. Ireland, England, Wales, Italy, Scotland and France compete; two/three matches in Dublin.
Malahide Food and Drink Affair *(late Feb, see p87)*. A festival of Irish food and drink, plus cultural activities.

PUBLIC HOLIDAYS

New Year's Day (1 Jan)
St Patrick's Day (17 Mar)
Good Friday
Easter Monday
May Day (1 May)
June Bank Holiday (first Mon in Jun)
August Bank Holiday (first Mon in Aug)
October Bank Holiday (last Mon in Oct)
Christmas Day (25 Dec)
St Stephen's Day (26 Dec)

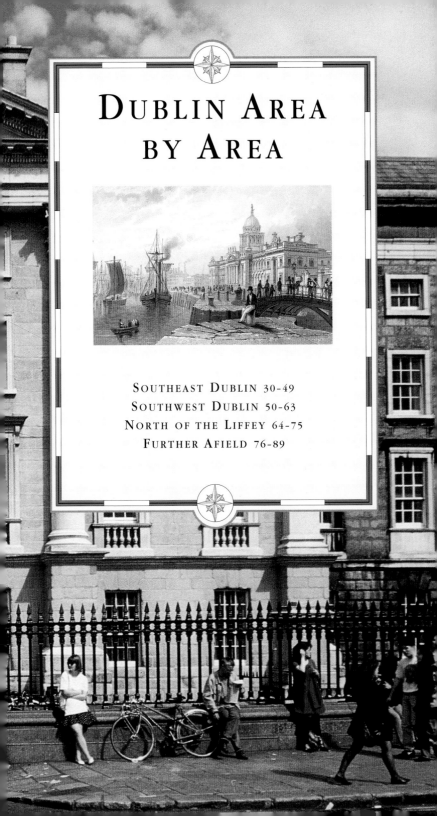

DUBLIN AREA BY AREA

SOUTHEAST DUBLIN

THIS PART OF Dublin was virtually undeveloped until the founding of Trinity College in 1592. Even then, it was almost a hundred years before the land to the south was enclosed to create St Stephen's Green.

The mid-18th century saw the beginning of a construction boom in the area. During this time, public buildings such as the Old Library at Trinity College and Leinster House were built. Many of the

Window in the Government buildings

buildings in Merrion Square still have their original features. Today, visitors are attracted to Southeast Dublin by the shops on Grafton Street and by the museums in the area, among them the excellent National Gallery and the National Museum with its displays of Irish Bronze Age gold treasures. The "Dead Zoo", as the fascinating Natural History Museum is known, has preserved its wonderful Victorian interior.

SIGHTS AT A GLANCE

Museums, Libraries and Galleries
Heraldic Museum ❺
National Gallery pp46–9 ⓲
National Library ⓱
National Museum pp42–3 ⓮
Natural History Museum ⓯
Royal Hibernian Academy ⓴

Historic Buildings
Bank of Ireland ❶
Government buildings ⓭
Iveagh House ⓫
Leinster House ⓰
Mansion House ❼
Newman House ❿
Number 29 ㉑
Royal College of Surgeons ❽
Trinity College pp36–7 ❷

Historic Streets
Ely Place ⓬
Grafton Street ❹
Merrion Square ⓳

Churches
St Ann's Church ❻
St Teresa's Church ❸

Parks and Gardens
St Stephen's Green ❾

KEY

▨	Street-by-Street map *See pp32–3*
🚉	Railway station
🚇	DART station
🚊	Luas stop
🅿	Parking
ℹ	Tourist information

GETTING THERE
Buses 5, 7A, 8, 10, 13, 14A, 15A, 45 and 46A go along Nassau Street which is in walking distance of most of the sights in this area. If you are coming from further afield, both the Luas and the DART serve the area.

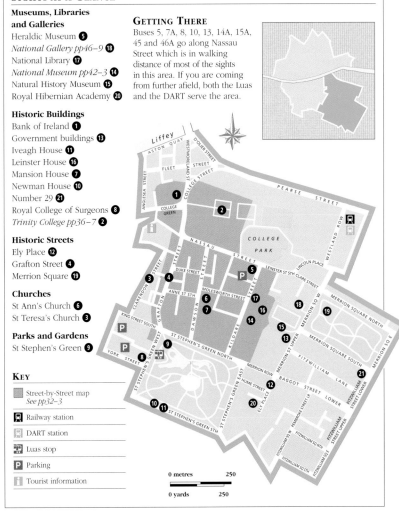

◁ **The lush gardens of Merrion Square**

Street-by-Street: Southeast Dublin

THE AREA AROUND COLLEGE GREEN, dominated by the façades of the Bank of Ireland and Trinity College, is very much the heart of Dublin. The alleys and malls cutting across busy pedestrianized Grafton Street boast many of Dublin's better shops, hotels and restaurants. Just off Kildare Street are the Irish Parliament, the National Library and the National Museum. To escape the city bustle many head for sanctuary in St Stephen's Green, which is overlooked by fine Georgian buildings.

← **Dublin Castle**

Bank of Ireland
This grand Georgian building was originally built as the Irish Parliament ❶

Statue of Molly Malone (1988)

Grafton Street
Brown Thomas department store is one of the main attractions on this pedestrianized street, alive with buskers and pavement artists ❹

St Ann's Church
The striking façade of the 18th-century church was added in 1868. The interior features lovely stained-glass windows ❻

Mansion House
This has been the official residence of Dublin's Lord Mayor since 1715 ❼

Fusiliers' Arch (1907)

★ **St Stephen's Green**
The relaxing city park is surrounded by many grand buildings. In summer, lunchtime concerts attract tourists and workers alike ❾

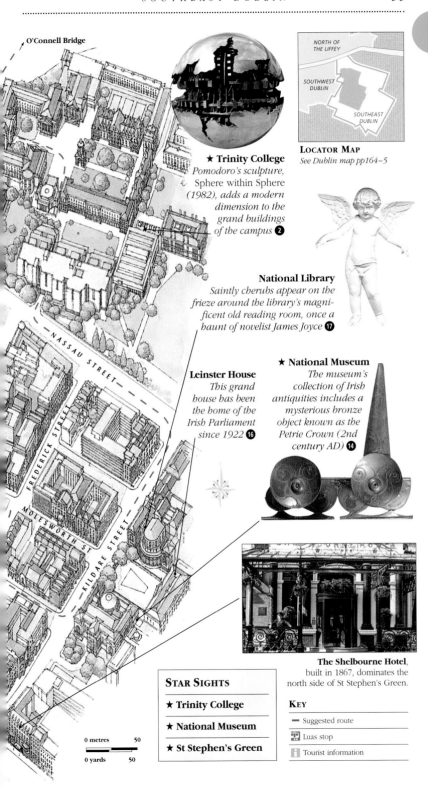

O'Connell Bridge

LOCATOR MAP
See Dublin map pp164–5

NORTH OF THE LIFFEY

SOUTHWEST DUBLIN

SOUTHEAST DUBLIN

★ **Trinity College**
Pomodoro's sculpture, Sphere within Sphere *(1982), adds a modern dimension to the grand buildings of the campus* ❷

National Library
Saintly cherubs appear on the frieze around the library's magnificent old reading room, once a haunt of novelist James Joyce ⓱

Leinster House
This grand house has been the home of the Irish Parliament since 1922 ⓰

★ **National Museum**
The museum's collection of Irish antiquities includes a mysterious bronze object known as the Petrie Crown (2nd century AD) ⓮

NASSAU STREET

FREDERICK STREET

MOLESWORTH ST

KILDARE STREET

The Shelbourne Hotel,
built in 1867, dominates the north side of St Stephen's Green.

STAR SIGHTS
★ Trinity College
★ National Museum
★ St Stephen's Green

KEY

━ Suggested route

Luas stop

Tourist information

0 metres   50

0 yards   50

Original Chamber of the Irish House of Lords at the Bank of Ireland

Bank of Ireland ❶

2 College Green. **Map** D3.
📞 671 2261. 🕐 9:30am–4pm Tue–
Sat. ⬤ public hols. **House of Lords**
📷 10:30am, 11:30am & 1:45pm Tue
or by appt. 🔲 www.boi.com/arts

THE PRESTIGIOUS offices of
the Bank of Ireland began
life as the first purpose-built
parliament house in Europe.
The original central section
was started by Irish architect
Edward Lovett Pearce and
completed in 1739 after his
death. Sadly, Pearce's master-
piece, the great octagonal
chamber of the House of
Commons, was removed by
order of the British government in 1802. The House of
Lords, however, remains intact.
Attendants lead tours that
point out the coffered ceiling
and oak panelling. There are
also huge tapestries of the
Battle of the Boyne and the
Siege of Londonderry, and
a 1,233-piece crystal
chandelier that dates
from 1788.

James Gandon
added the east
portico in 1785.
Further additions
were made
around 1797.
After the dissolu-
tion of the Irish
Parliament in
1800, the Bank of
Ireland bought
the building.
The present
structure was
completed in
1808 with the
transformation

**Statue of the Virgin and child
in St Teresa's Church**

of the former lobby of the
House of Commons into a
cash office and the addition of
a curving screen wall and the
Foster Place annexe, now the
Arts Centre. A statue by John
Foley of Henry Grattan *(see
p14)*, the most formidable
leader of the old parliament,
stands on College Green.

Trinity College ❷

See pp36–7.

St Teresa's Church ❸

Clarendon St or Johnson Court.
Map D4. 📞 671 8466. 🕐 6:45am–
6:30pm Mon–Fri, 6:45am–7:30pm Sat,
8:15am–7pm Sun.

THE FOUNDATION stone of
St Teresa's was laid in
1793, making it the first
post-Penal Law church to
be legally planned and
built in the city after
the passing of the
Catholic Relief
Act the same
year *(see p14)*.
The land was
leased by
a brewer named
John Sweetman
and was given to
the Discalced
Carmelite Fathers.
The church
did not in fact
open until
May 1797.
The eastern
transept was
added in 1863

and the western tran-
sept was completed in
1876, at which stage it
reached the form it
remains in today.

Located in the middle
of Dublin, St Teresa's is
a relatively busy place
of worship. Its T-shaped
interior means that, if
you enter through the
main door on Claren-
don Street and walk
through the church, you
will arrive in the tight
alleyway of Johnson
Court, a few yards from
the heart of bustling
Grafton Street. There
are seven stained-glass
windows in the church by
Phyllis Burke, which were
made in the 1990s, and a fine
sculpture of Christ by John
Hogan beneath the altar.

**Street musicians outside Brown
Thomas on Grafton Street**

Grafton Street ❹

Map D4.

THE SPINE OF DUBLIN'S most
popular and stylish shop-
ping district runs south from
Trinity College to the glass-
covered St Stephen's Green
Shopping Centre. At the north
end, at the junction with
Nassau Street, is a bronze
statue by Jean Rynhart of
Molly Malone (1988), the
celebrated "cockles and
mussels" street trader from
the traditional Irish folk song.

This busy pedestrianized
strip, characterized by numerous energetic buskers and
talented street theatre artists,
boasts many shops, including
many British chain stores.
Next, River Island, HMV and
Monsoon all contribute
toward making it Dublin's
fashion centre. Its most
exclusive store, however, is
Brown Thomas, one of

Monkeys playing billiards outside the Heraldic Museum

Dublin's most elegant department stores *(see p136),* selling designer clothes, exclusive perfumes and fabulous shoes by designers such as Patrick Cox. Dublin's largest and most exclusive jewellers, Weir's, is also here.

The shops here attract Dublin's most beautiful people, and Grafton Street itself can seem like one long fashion catwalk. But it's not all shopping, indeed No. 78 stands on the site of Samuel Whyte's school, whose illustrious roll included Robert Emmet *(see p14),* leader of the 1803 Rebellion, and the Duke of Wellington. At this time, Grafton Street was actually paved with pinewood blocks to deaden the area from the harsh sound of horses' hooves and carriage wheels.

On many of the sidestreets off Grafton Street there are numerous pubs providing welcome refreshment for the exhausted shopper, among them the famous Davy Byrne's *(see p132),* for years frequented by Dublin's literati.

Heraldic Museum and Genealogical Office ⑤

2 Kildare St. **Map** E4. **(** 603 0200.
National Library Reading Room
◯ 10am–9pm Mon–Wed, 10am–5pm
Thu–Fri, 10am–1pm Sat. **Heraldic Museum** ◯ 10am–12:30pm, 2–4pm
Mon–Fri. W www.nli.ie

THE GENEALOGICAL OFFICE is part of the National Library and offers a free advice service to anyone wishing to trace their Irish ancestry. Professional genealogists and library staff offer expert assistance together with access to reference material and finding aids.

The Heraldic Museum offers a small but interesting collection of seals, stamps, regimen-

tal colours, coins, porcelain, paintings, family crests and county shields.

The museum is housed in a red-brick building in the Venetian style, which is unusual for Dublin. The exterior features some fanciful decorative aspects such as three monkeys playing billiards and bears playing violins just to the right of the entrance.

Window depicting Faith, Hope and Charity in St Ann's Church

St Ann's Church ⑥

Dawson St. **Map** D2. **(** 676 7727.
◯ 10am–4pm Mon–Fri (also Sun
services 8am, 10:45am, 6:30pm).
W www.connect.ie/ccp

FOUNDED IN 1707, St Ann's striking Romanesque façade was added by the architects Deane and Woodward in 1868. The best view of the façade is from Grafton Street, looking down Anne Street South. Inside the church are many colourful stained-glass windows that date back to the mid-19th century. St Ann's has a long tradition of charity work: in 1723 Lord Newton left a bequest specifically to buy bread for the poor. The original shelf used for the bread still stands adjacent to the altar.

Famous past parishioners of St Ann's include the Irish patriot Wolfe Tone *(see p14),* who was married here in 1785, Douglas Hyde, the first president of Ireland, and Bram Stoker (1847–1912), the author of *Dracula (see p20).*

The milling crowds filling the pedestrianized Grafton Street

Trinity College ❷

Trinity College coat of arms

TRINITY COLLEGE was founded in 1592 by Queen Elizabeth I on the site of an Augustinian monastery. It was originally a Protestant college, and it was not until the 1970s that Catholics started entering the university. Among the many famous students to attend the college were playwrights Oliver Goldsmith and Samuel Beckett, and political writer Edmund Burke. Trinity's lawns and cobbled quads provide a pleasant haven in the heart of the city. The major attractions are the Old Library and the *Book of Kells*, housed in the Treasury.

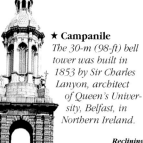

★ Campanile
The 30-m (98-ft) bell tower was built in 1853 by Sir Charles Lanyon, architect of Queen's University, Belfast, in Northern Ireland.

Reclining Connected Forms (1969) by Henry Moore

Dining Hall (1761)

Parliament Square

Chapel *(1798)*
This is the only chapel in the Republic to be shared by all denominations. The painted window above the altar dates from 1867.

Statue of Edmund Burke (1868) by John Foley

Main entrance

Statue of Oliver Goldsmith (1864) by John Foley

SAMUEL BECKETT (1906–89)

Nobel prizewinner Samuel Beckett was born at Foxrock, south of Dublin. In 1923 he entered Trinity, where he was placed first in his modern literature class. He was also a keen member of the college cricket team. Forsaking Ireland, Beckett moved to France in the early 1930s. Many of his works such as *Waiting for Godot* (1951) were written first in French, and then later translated, by Beckett, into English.

Provost's House (c. 1760)

Examination Hall
Completed in 1791 to a design by Sir William Chambers, the hall features a gilded oak chandelier and ornate ceilings by Michael Stapleton.

Library Square
The red-brick building (known as the Rubrics) on the east side of Library Square was built around 1700 and is the oldest surviving part of the college.

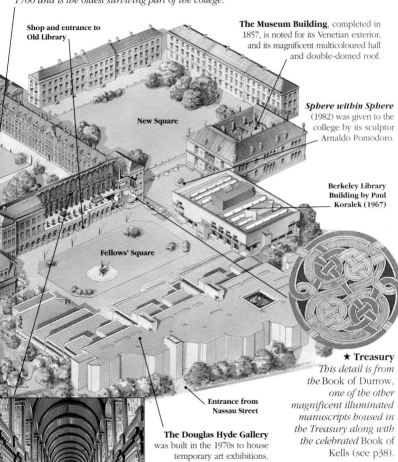

Shop and entrance to Old Library

The Museum Building, completed in 1857, is noted for its Venetian exterior, and its magnificent multicoloured hall and double-domed roof.

New Square

Sphere within Sphere
(1982) was given to the college by its sculptor Arnaldo Pomodoro.

Berkeley Library Building by Paul Koralek (1967)

Fellows' Square

Entrance from Nassau Street

★ Treasury
This detail is from the Book of Durrow, *one of the other magnificent illuminated manuscripts housed in the Treasury along with the celebrated* Book of Kells (see p38).

The Douglas Hyde Gallery was built in the 1970s to house temporary art exhibitions.

★ Old Library *(1732)*
The spectacular Long Room measures 64 m (210 ft) from end to end. It houses 200,000 antiquarian texts, marble busts of scholars and the oldest surviving harp in Ireland.

STAR FEATURES

★ Old Library

★ Treasury

★ Campanile

The Book of Kells

THE MOST RICHLY decorated of Ireland's illuminated manuscripts, the *Book of Kells*, may have been the work of monks from Iona, who fled to Kells, near Newgrange *(see pp112–13)*, in AD 806 after a Viking raid. The book, which was moved to Trinity College *(see*

pp36–7) in the 17th century, contains the four Gospels in Latin. The scribes who copied the texts embellished their calligraphy with intricate spirals as well as human figures and animals. Some of the dyes used were imported from as far as the Middle East.

Pair of moths

Stylized angel

The Greek letter "X"

The symbols of the four evangelists are used as decoration throughout the book. The figure of the man symbolizes St Matthew.

The letter that looks like a "P" is a Greek "R".

The letter "I"

Interlacing motifs

Cat watching rats

Rats eating bread could be a reference to sinners taking Holy Communion. The symbolism of the animals and people decorating the manuscript is often hard to interpret.

A full-page portrait of St Matthew, shown standing barefoot in front of a throne, precedes the opening words of his Gospel.

MONOGRAM PAGE

This, the most elaborate page of the book, contains the first three words of St Matthew's account of the birth of Christ. The first word "XRI" is an abbreviation of "Christi".

The text is in a beautifully rounded Celtic script with brightly ornamented initial letters. Animal and human forms are often used to decorate the end of a line.

Mansion House ❼

Dawson St. **Map** E4. ⬤ *to the public.*

SET BACK from Dawson Street with a neat cobbled fore-court, the Mansion House is an attractive Queen Anne-style building. It was built in 1710 for the aristocrat Joshua Dawson, after whom the street is named. The Dublin Corporation bought it from him in 1715 as the official residence of the city's Lord Mayor. A grey stucco façade was added in Victorian times.

The Dáil Éireann (*see p44*), which adopted the Declaration of Independence, first met here on 21 January 1919. The Fado Restaurant (*see p128*) in the old supper room is in period style.

Royal College of Surgeons ❽

123 St Stephen's Green. **Map** E4.
🄲 *402 2100.*

THE WEST SIDE of St Stephen's Green is home to one of the most striking buildings in the square, namely the squat granite-faced Royal College of Surgeons. The college opened in 1810 and 15 years later its façade was extended from three to seven bays when a central pediment was added. On top of this are three statues which from left to right are Hygieia, goddess of health, Asclepius, god of medicine and son of Apollo,

Royal College of Surgeons, which overlooks St Stephen's Green

and Athena, the goddess of wisdom and patron of the arts. Today, the main entrance is through the modern extension on York Street. The academy has almost 1,000 students.

The building itself played an important part in Irish history. During the 1916 Easter Rising (*see p15*), a section of the Irish Citizen Army under Michael Mallin and Countess Constance Markievicz were in control of the college. They were the last detachment of rebels to surrender and, although Mallin was execut-ed, Markievicz escaped sen-tence because of her gender and public status. She was later to become the first woman to be elected as an MP at Westminster in London, though she refused to take her seat in parliament. The front columns of the building still feature the old bullet holes, an ever-present reminder of its colourful past.

St Stephen's Green ❾

Map D5. ⬚ *daylight hours.*

ORIGINALLY ONE of three ancient commons in the old city, St Stephen's Green was enclosed in 1664. The 9-ha (22-acre) green was laid out in its present form in 1880, using a grant given by Lord Ardilaun, a member of the Guinness family. Landscaped with flowerbeds, trees, a fountain and a lake, the green is dotted with memorials to eminent Dubliners, including Ardilaun himself. There is a bust of James Joyce (*see p21*), and a memorial by Henry Moore (1967) dedicated to W B Yeats (*see p21*). At the Merrion Row corner stands a massive monument (1967) by Edward Delaney to 18th-century nationalist leader Wolfe Tone – it is known locally as "Tonehenge". The 1887 bandstand still has free daytime concerts in summer.

The busiest side of the Green is the north, known during the 19th century as the Beaux' Walk and still home to several gentlemen's clubs. The most prominent building is the venerable Shelbourne Hotel (*see p167*). Dating back to 1867, its entrance is adorn-ed by statues of Nubian prin-cesses and attendant slaves. It is well worth popping in for a look at the chandeliered foyer and for afternoon tea in the Lord Mayor's Lounge.

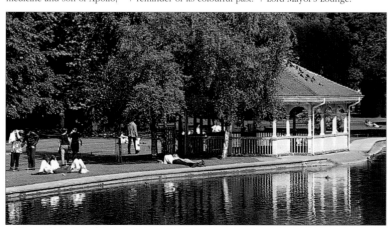

Dubliners relaxing by the lake in St Stephen's Green

Stucco work in the Apollo room of No. 85 in Newman House

Newman House

85 & 86 St Stephen's Green. **Map** D5.
716 7422. ☐ *Jun–Aug: Tue–Fri noon–4pm, Sat 2–5pm; Sep–May: by appt only.* 🅦 www.ucd.ie

NUMBERS 85 AND 86 on the south side of St Stephen's Green are collectively known as Newman House, named for John Henry Newman, later Cardinal Newman and the first rector of the Catholic University of Ireland.

Founded as an alternative to the Protestant Trinity College, it became part of University College Dublin in 1907 and is still owned by that institution.

During the 1990s it has seen one of the most painstaking and diligent restorations ever undertaken in the city. It is the much smaller No. 85, designed by Richard Castle in 1738, that contains the most beautiful rooms with plasterwork by the Franchini brothers. Of particular interest are the Apollo Room, with a figure of the god above the mantle, and the upstairs Saloon. In the late 1800s the Jesuits covered the naked plaster bodies on the ceiling of the Saloon with rudimentary plaster casts to conceal what they thought to be shameful nudity. One of the figures is still covered today. A classroom, decorated as it would have been in the days when James Joyce was a student

here, is open to the public, as is the study used by the poet Gerard Manley Hopkins, who was a professor here in the late 19th century. Other famous past pupils include the writer Flann O'Brien and former president Eamon De Valera.

Iveagh House and Iveagh Gardens ⓫

80 & 81 St Stephen's Green. **Map** D5.
● *to the public.* **Gardens** ☐ *daily.*

IVEAGH HOUSE, on the south side of St Stephen's Green, was originally two freestanding townhouses. No. 80 was designed in the 1730s by Richard Castle – his first commission in the city. The houses were combined in the 1860s when Sir Benjamin Guinness bought them. None of the original façade remains as Guinness linked the houses under a Portland stone façade and had the family arms engraved on the pediment. The Guinness family also carried out much interior reconstruction, including the addition of a large new ballroom, with a domed ceiling and liberal amounts of marble and onyx, to the rear of the house. Iveagh House was given to the state by Rupert Guinness, the second Earl of Iveagh, in 1939. It is now used by the Department of Foreign Affairs, both as the office of the minister and as a venue for state receptions. The rear

Enjoying the secluded peace of Iveagh Gardens

of Iveagh House faces on to Iveagh Gardens, an almost secret park that offers a quiet alternative to St Stephen's Green. It owes its tranquillity partly to the fact that its three entrances are discreet: one is behind the National Concert Hall on Earlsfort Terrace, another is off Clonmel Street and a new one, with disabled access, is off Hatch Street.

Ely Place ⓬

Map E5.

A CUL-DE-SAC with several well-preserved Georgian houses, Ely Place is at the end of Merrion Street Upper. Most of the houses along the street were built in the 1770s and Ely Place soon became one of the most desirable addresses in the city at this time. Behind its red brick façade, 8 Ely Place, known as Ely House, has elegant plasterwork by the stuccodore Michael Stapleton and an ornate staircase covered with engravings of characters from the tales of the Labours of Hercules below the banister rail.

Modern buildings seal the end of the street. The Royal Hibernian Academy Gallagher Gallery *(see p45)* was built in 1973 and may look somewhat out of place on this otherwise rather grand stretch, but it offers one of the best gallery spaces in the city, exhibiting mostly 20th-century Irish art.

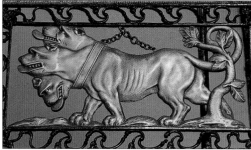

Detail of stucco from Ely House, featuring the mythical dog Cerberus

The elegant, Neo-Classical façade of the Government buildings

Government buildings ⓭

Upper Merrion St. **Map** E4. 📞 662 4888. ☐ Sat 10:30am– 12:30pm, 1:30–3:30pm (call to check). Tickets available from National Gallery. ✔ obligatory. ☒ www.gov.ie/taoiseach

ALONGSIDE THE Natural History Museum and the National Gallery on Upper Merrion Street, facing the Georgian town houses, stand the imposing Government buildings, built in a Neo-Georgian style.

The complex was opened in 1911 as the Royal College of Science (RCS) and it has the distinction of being the last major project planned by the British in Dublin. In 1922 the Irish government took over the north wing as offices and the RCS became part of University College Dublin. Academic pursuits continued here until 1989, when the government moved into the rest of the buildings and ordered a massive restoration of the façade. The city grime on the Portland stone was blasted away to restore it to its original near-white appearance.

The elegant domed buildings are set apart from the street by a cobbled courtyard and a large colonnade with columns that are strongly reminiscent of Gandon's Custom House (see p68). The tour takes in the office of the Taoiseach (pronounced Tee-Shuck) and the cabinet office. The interior is decorated with examples of works by contemporary Irish artists, most notably a huge stained-glass window, situated above the grand staircase, called *My Four Green Fields* by Dublin artist Evie Hone, which depicts the island's four provinces. This was designed for the 1939 World's Fair in New York. It was displayed in the Irish Pavilion there and afterwards returned to Dublin. For a number of years it lay packed away, until the 1960s, when it was put on display for a while in the Dublin Bus offices in O'Connell Street. It was finally moved to its present home in the Government buildings in 1991.

National Museum ⓮

See pp42–3.

Natural History Museum ⓯

Merrion St. **Map** E4. 📞 677 7444. ☐ 10am–5pm Tue–Sat, 2–5pm Sun. ⬤ public hols. 🚻 limited. ☒ www.museum.ie

KNOWN AFFECTIONATELY as the "Dead Zoo" by locals, this museum is crammed with antique glass cabinets housing stuffed animals from around the world. The museum was opened to the public in 1857 with an inaugural lecture by Dr David Livingstone. It remains virtually unchanged from Victorian times.

On the ground floor, the Irish room holds exhibits on local wildlife. Inside the front door are three skeletons of the extinct giant deer known as the "Irish elk". Also on this floor are shelves with jars of octopuses, leeches and worms, preserved in embalming fluid.

The upper gallery is home to the noted Blaschka Collection of glass models of marine life, and a display of buffalo and deer trophies. Hanging from the ceiling are the skeletons of a fin whale and a humpback whale, both found stranded on the Irish coast.

The advances made in taxidermy over the years are emphasized by a stuffed rhinoceros and an Indian elephant, both so heavily lacquered that they seem to be covered in tar.

Lawn and front entrance of the Natural History Museum on Merrion Street Upper

National Museum

THE NATIONAL MUSEUM OF IRELAND was built in the 1880s to the design of Sir Thomas Deane. Its splendid domed rotunda features marble pillars and a zodiac mosaic floor. The Treasury houses priceless items such as the Broighter gold boat, while an exhibition on Ireland's Bronze Age gold contains some beautiful jewellery. Many collections have now moved to the recently opened annexe of the museum at the impressive Collins Barracks (*see pp84–5*).

Egyptian Mummy
This mummy of the lady Tentdinebu is thought to date back to c.945–716 BC. Covered in brilliant colours, it is part of the stunning Egyptian collection.

★ Ór – Ireland's Gold
This is one of the most extensive collections of Bronze Age gold in Western Europe. This gold lunula (c.1800 BC), found in Athlone, is one of many pieces of ancient jewellery in this exhibition.

KEY TO FLOORPLAN

- ☐ The Road to Independence
- ☐ Ór – Ireland's Gold
- ☐ The Treasury
- ☐ Prehistoric Ireland
- ☐ Medieval Ireland
- ☐ Viking Ireland
- ☐ Ancient Egypt
- ☐ Temporary exhibition space
- ☐ Non-exhibition space

Flag from 1916 Rising
The Road to Independence *exhibition covers historical events between 1900 and 1921. This flag flew over Dublin's GPO during the Easter Rising (see p15).*

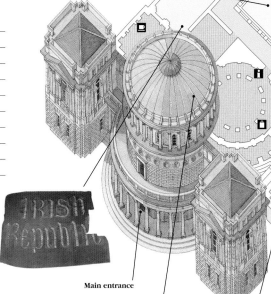

Main entrance

GALLERY GUIDE

The ground floor holds The Treasury, Ór – Ireland's Gold *exhibition,* The Road to Independence *and the* Prehistoric Ireland *display. On the first floor is the* Medieval Ireland *exhibition, which illustrates many aspects of life in later medieval Ireland. Also on the first floor are artifacts from Ancient Egypt and from the Viking settlement of Dublin.*

The domed rotunda, based on the design of the Altes Museum in Berlin, makes an impressive entrance hall.

The Treasury houses masterpieces of Irish crafts including the Ardagh Chalice.

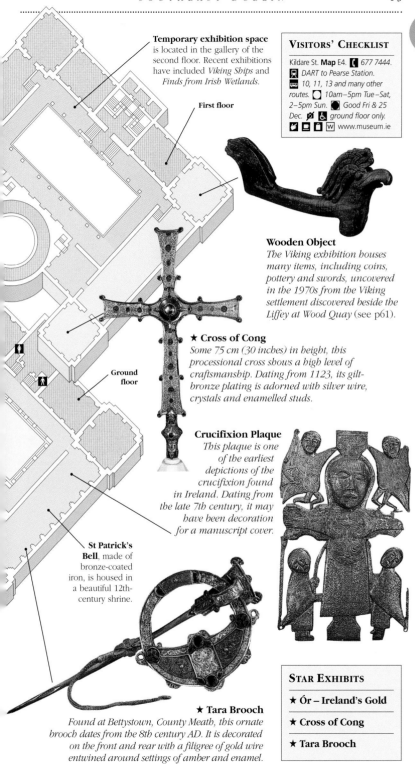

Temporary exhibition space is located in the gallery of the second floor. Recent exhibitions have included *Viking Ships* and *Finds from Irish Wetlands*.

First floor

VISITORS' CHECKLIST

Kildare St. **Map** E4. 677 7444.
DART to Pearse Station.
10, 11, 13 and many other routes. 10am–5pm Tue–Sat, 2–5pm Sun. Good Fri & 25 Dec. ground floor only.
www.museum.ie

Wooden Object
The Viking exhibition houses many items, including coins, pottery and swords, uncovered in the 1970s from the Viking settlement discovered beside the Liffey at Wood Quay (see p61).

★ **Cross of Cong**
Some 75 cm (30 inches) in height, this processional cross shows a high level of craftsmanship. Dating from 1123, its gilt-bronze plating is adorned with silver wire, crystals and enamelled studs.

Ground floor

Crucifixion Plaque
This plaque is one of the earliest depictions of the crucifixion found in Ireland. Dating from the late 7th century, it may have been decoration for a manuscript cover.

St Patrick's Bell, made of bronze-coated iron, is housed in a beautiful 12th-century shrine.

★ **Tara Brooch**
Found at Bettystown, County Meath, this ornate brooch dates from the 8th century AD. It is decorated on the front and rear with a filigree of gold wire entwined around settings of amber and enamel.

STAR EXHIBITS

★ **Ór – Ireland's Gold**

★ **Cross of Cong**

★ **Tara Brooch**

Domed reading room on the first floor of the National Library

Leinster House 🔟

Kildare St. **Map** E4. ☎ *618 3000.*
☐ *groups by appointment only
(foreign tourists must book through
their own embassy).* ☑ *phone for
details.* W *www.oireachtas.ie*

THIS STATELY MANSION houses
the Dáil and the Seanad –
the two chambers of the Irish
Parliament. It was originally
built for the Duke of Leinster
in 1745. Designed by Richard
Castle, the Kildare Street façade
resembles that of a large town
house. The rear, which looks
out on to Merrion Square, has
the air of a country estate. The
Royal Dublin Society bought
the building in 1815. The
government bought the entire
building in 1924.
   Visitors can arrange to tour
the main rooms, including the
Seanad chamber.

National Library 🔟

Kildare St. **Map** E4. ☎ *603 0200.*
☐ *10am–9pm Mon–Wed,
10am–5pm Thu & Fri, 10am–1pm
Sat.* ☐ *public hols.* W *www.nli.ie*

DESIGNED BY Sir Thomas
Deane, the National
Library was opened in 1890.
It was built to house the collection of the Royal Dublin
Society *(see p83).* The Library
contains first editions of every
major Irish writer and a copy
of almost every book ever
published in Ireland. There is

a huge collection of old maps,
papers, and a number of significant manuscripts. The first-
floor reading room has green-
shaded lamps and well-worn
desks. To go in, ask an attendant for a visitor's pass. A new
exhibition space, bookshop
and coffee shop are open to
both readers and non-readers.

National Gallery 🔟

See pp46–9.

Merrion Square 🔟

Map F4.

MERRION SQUARE is one of
Dublin's largest and
grandest Georgian squares.
Covering about 5 ha (12 acres),
the square was laid out
by John Ensor
around 1762.
   On the
west of the
square are

**Statue of Oscar Wilde by Danny
Osbourne in Merrion Square**

THE IRISH PARLIAMENT

The Irish Free State, the
forerunner of the
Republic of Ireland, was
inaugurated in 1922 *(see
p16),* although an
unofficial Irish parliament,
the Dáil, had already been
in existence since 1919.
Today, parliament is made
up of two houses: the
Dáil (House of Represen-
tatives) and Seanad
Éireann (Senate). The
prime minister is the
Taoiseach and the deputy,
the Tánaiste. The Dáil's
166 representatives –
Teachta Dála, commonly
known as TDs – are
elected by proportional
representation every five
years. The 60-strong
Seanad is appointed by
various individuals and
authorities, including the
Taoiseach and the
University of Dublin.

**The first parliament of the
Irish Free State in 1922**

---

the impressive façades of the
Natural History Museum, the
National Gallery and the front
garden of Leinster House.
However, this august trium-
virate does not compare with
the attractive Georgian townhouses on the other three
sides of the square. Many
have brightly painted doors
with original features such as
wrought-iron balconies, ornate
doorknockers and fanlights.
The oldest and finest houses
are on the north side.
   Many of the houses – now
predominantly used as office
space – have plaques detail-
ing the rich and famous who
once lived in them. These
include Catholic emancipation

leader Daniel O'Connell *(see p14)*, who lived at No. 58 and poet W B Yeats *(see p21)*, who lived at No. 82. Oscar Wilde *(see p21)* spent his childhood at No. 1.

The attractive central park features colourful flower and shrub beds. In the 1840s it served a grim function as an emergency soup kitchen, feeding the hungry during the Great Famine *(see p15)*. On the northwest side of the park stands the restored Rutland Fountain. It was originally erected in 1791 for the sole use of Dublin's poor.

Just off the square, at No. 24 Merrion Street Upper, is the birthplace of the Duke of Wellington, who, when he was teased about his Irish background, famously said, "Being born in a stable does not make one a horse."

Royal Hibernian Academy ⓴

15 Ely Place. **Map** E5. 661 2558.
11am–5pm Tue–Wed & Fri–Sat, 11am–8pm Thu, 2–5pm Sun.
public hols. limited access.
www.royalhibernianacademy.com

THE ACADEMY is one of the largest exhibition spaces in the city. It puts on exhibitions of Irish and international artists showing both traditional and innovative forms of visual art. This modern brick-and-

The recreated Georgian kitchen of Number 29, Fitzwilliam Street Lower

plate-glass building does, however, look out of place at the end of Ely Place, an attractive Georgian cul-de-sac.

Number 29 ㉑

29 Fitzwilliam St Lower. **Map** F5.
702 6165. 10am–5pm Tue–Sat, 2–5pm Sun. two weeks prior to Christmas.
www.esb.ie/education

NUMBER 29 IS A corner townhouse, built in 1794 for a Mrs Olivia Beattie whose late husband was a wine and paper merchant. While the period furniture comes from the collection of the National Museum, the main purpose of this exhibit is to give visitors a behind-the-scenes look at how middle-class

Georgians went about their daily business. Tours start with a short slide show and then work their way through the building from the cellar upwards. Along the way are mahogany tables, chandeliers, Turkish carpets and landscape paintings (by Thomas Roberts among others) but of most interest are some of the quirkier items. Guides point out rudimentary hostess trolleys, water filters and even a Georgian baby walker, as well as an early exercise machine, used to tone up the muscles for horse riding. A tea caddy takes pride of place in one of the reception rooms: at today's prices a kilo of tea would have cost €800 and hence the lady of the house kept the key to the caddy on her person at all times.

The elegant gardens in Merrion Square, a quiet backwater in the centre of Dublin

National Gallery ⑱

T HIS PURPOSE-BUILT gallery was opened to the public in 1864. It houses many excellent exhibits, largely due to generous bequests, such as the Milltown collection of works of art from Russborough House *(see p100)*. Playwright George Bernard Shaw was also a benefactor, leaving a third of his estate to the gallery. A new wing has been added to the gallery, which today has more than 500 works on display. Although the emphasis is on Irish art, the major schools of European painting are well represented.

The Houseless Wanderer by John Foley

GALLERY GUIDE
The main entrance to the gallery is through the lofty Millennium Wing on Clare Street. Irish and British collections are housed on level 1, with the National Portrait Gallery on the mezzanine level. The European schools are located on level 2, with changing special exhibitions installed in the adjacent Millennium Wing.

★ **Pierrot**
This Cubist-style work, by Spanish-born artist Juan Gris, is one of many variations he painted on the theme of Pierrot and Harlequin. This particular one dates from 1921.

National Portrait Gallery

Mezzanine level

★ **For the Road**
The Yeats Museum houses works by Jack B Yeats (1871–1957) and members of his family. This mysterious painting reflects the artist's obsession with the Sligo countryside.

Shaw Room

Merrion Square entrance

STAR PAINTINGS

★ **The Taking of Christ by Caravaggio**

★ **Pierrot by Juan Gris**

★ **For the Road by Jack Yeats**

★ **The Taking of Christ**
Rediscovered in the Dublin Jesuit House of Study in 1990, this 1602 composition by Caravaggio has enhanced the gallery's reputation.

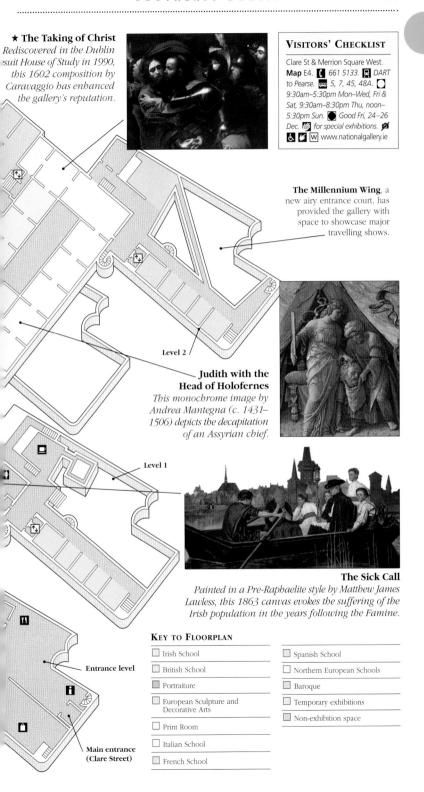

VISITORS' CHECKLIST

Clare St & Merrion Square West.
Map E4. ☎ 661 5133. 🚇 DART
to Pearse. 🚌 5, 7, 45, 48A. ◐
9:30am–5:30pm Mon–Wed, Fri &
Sat, 9:30am–8:30pm Thu, noon–
5:30pm Sun. ● Good Fri, 24–26
Dec. 🏛 for special exhibitions. Ⓟ
♿ 🖼 Ⓦ www.nationalgallery.ie

The Millennium Wing, a new airy entrance court, has provided the gallery with space to showcase major travelling shows.

Level 2

Judith with the Head of Holofernes
This monochrome image by Andrea Mantegna (c. 1431–1506) depicts the decapitation of an Assyrian chief.

Level 1

The Sick Call
Painted in a Pre-Raphaelite style by Matthew James Lawless, this 1863 canvas evokes the suffering of the Irish population in the years following the Famine.

Entrance level

Main entrance (Clare Street)

KEY TO FLOORPLAN

☐ Irish School	☐ Spanish School
☐ British School	☐ Northern European Schools
☐ Portraiture	☐ Baroque
☐ European Sculpture and Decorative Arts	☐ Temporary exhibitions
☐ Print Room	☐ Non-exhibition space
☐ Italian School	
☐ French School	

Exploring the National Gallery

EXHIBITIONS THROUGHOUT the gallery are laid out in an easy-to-follow manner. In addition to rooms dedicated to major Irish and European schools, there are displays illustrating such themes as art in the Dutch provinces, Caravaggio and his followers and Italian influences in the Northern countries. Major temporary exhibitions are held in the Millennium Wing, which also has a floor dedicated to the Irish schools of the 20th century.

IRISH SCHOOL

THIS IS THE largest collection on display and the richest part of the gallery. Stretching back to the late 17th century, works range from landscapes such as *A View of Powerscourt Waterfall* by George Barret to paintings by Nathaniel Hone the Elder, including *The Conjuror*. Portraiture includes work by James Barry and Hugh Douglas Hamilton.

The Romantic movement made a strong impression on artists in the early 19th century; Francis Danby's *The Opening of the Sixth Seal*, an apocalyptic interpretation from the Book of Revelations, is the best example of this genre. Other examples are the Irish landscapes of James Arthur O'Connor.

In the late 19th century many Irish artists lived in Breton colonies, absorbing Impressionist influences. Roderic O'Conor's *Farm at Lezaven, Finistère* and William Leech's *Convent Garden, Brittany*, with its

***Convent Garden, Brittany,* by William Leech (1881–1968)**

refreshing tones of green and white, are two of the best examples from this period.

Jack B Yeats is regarded as Ireland's first internationally known modern artist and the Yeats Museum is dedicated to him and his talented family. It includes works by Anne Yeats and his father John B Yeats, a famous portrait artist. Jack B Yeats' paintings portray life in the west of Ireland in the early 20th century. His later paintings, such as *Men of Destiny* and *Above the Fair*, are also national treasures.

BRITISH SCHOOL

WORKS DATING FROM the 18th century dominate in those rooms that are devoted to British artists. In particular William Hogarth, Thomas Gainsborough and Joshua Reynolds are well represented. Reynolds was one of the great portrait painters of his time and other portraits, by artists including Philip Reinagle, Francis Wheatley and Henry Raeburn, perfectly capture the family, military and aristocratic life of that period.

BAROQUE GALLERY

THIS LARGE ROOM accommodates 17th-century paintings, many by lesser-known artists. It also holds enormous canvases by more famous names such as Lanfranco, Jordaens and Castiglione, which are too big to fit into the spaces occupied by their respective schools. *The Annunciation* and *Peter Finding the Tribute Money* by Rubens are among the gallery's most eye-catching paintings.

FRENCH SCHOOL

THE PAINTINGS IN the galleries devoted to the French School are separated into the 17th and 18th centuries and the Barbizon, Impressionist, post-Impressionist and Cubist collections.

Among the earlier works are *The Annunciation*, a fine 15th-century panel by Jacques Yverni, and the *Lamentation over the Dead Christ* by Nicolas Poussin (1594–1665), one of the founders of European classicism.

The early 19th century saw the French colonization of North Africa. Many works were inspired by the colonization, including *Guards at the Door of a Tomb*, a painting by Jean-Léon Gérôme. Another fine 19th-century work is the painting known as *A Group of Cavalry in the Snow* by Jan Chelminski.

A View of Powerscourt Waterfall **by George Barret the Elder (c.1728–84)**

A Group of Cavalry in the Snow by Jan Chelminski (1851–1925)

The Impressionist paintings are among the most popular in the gallery and include Monet's *A River Scene, Autumn* from 1874. Works by Pissarro and Sisley are also displayed in this set of rooms.

Guards at the Door of a Tomb by Jean-Léon Gérôme (1824–1904)

SPANISH SCHOOL

WORKS FROM the Spanish school are rich and varied. One of the early pieces of note is El Greco's *St Francis Receiving the Stigmata*, a particularly dramatic work, dating from around 1595. Other notable acquisitions from this period are by Zurbarán, Velázquez and Murillo. There are four works on display by the controversial court painter Francisco de Goya (1746–1828) including a portrait of the actress Doña Antonia Zárata. Pablo Picasso's *Still Life With A Mandolin* and *Pierrot* by Juan Gris represent 20th-century Spanish art.

ITALIAN SCHOOL

AS A RESULT of a successful purchasing strategy at the time of the gallery's inauguration and various bequests, there is a strong collection of Italian art in the gallery.

Works of the Italian School spread over seven rooms. Andrea Mantegna's *Judith with the Head of Holofernes* is done in *grisaille*, a technique that creates a stone-like effect. Famous pieces by Uccello, Titian, Moroni and Fontana hang in this section, but it is Caravaggio's *The Taking of Christ* (1602) which is the most important item. It was discovered by chance in a Dublin Jesuit house where it had hung in obscurity for many years. It was first hung in the National Gallery in 1993.

Constantinople School icon

NORTHERN EUROPEAN SCHOOLS

THE EARLY Netherlandish School is comprised largely of paintings with a religious theme. One exception is Brueghel the Younger's lively *Peasant Wedding* (1620). In the Dutch collection there are many 17th-century works, including some by Rembrandt. Other highlights include *A Wooded Landscape* by Hobbema and *Lady Writing a Letter With Her Maid* by Vermeer. Rubens and van Dyck are two more famous names here, but there are also fine works by less well-known artists, such as van Uden's *Peasants Merry-making*. Portraits by artists such as Faber and Pencz from the 15th and 16th centuries dominate the German collection, though Emil Nolde's colourful *Two Women in the Garden* dates from 1915.

PORTRAITURE

THE IMPRESSIVE Shaw Room is lined with full-length historical portraits including one of Charles Coote, the first Earl of Bellamont, dressed in flamboyant pink ceremonial robes. In the National Portrait Gallery, portraits of those who have made a contribution to Ireland from the 16th century to the present are displayed.

Peasant Wedding by Pieter Brueghel the Younger (1564–1637)

SOUTHWEST DUBLIN

THE AREA around Dublin Castle was first settled in prehistoric times, and it was from here that the city grew. Dublin gets its name from the dark pool *(Dubb Linn)* which formed at the confluence of the Liffey and the Poddle, a river that originally ran through the site of Dublin Castle. It is now channelled underground. Archaeological excavations behind Wood Quay, on the banks of the river Liffey, reveal that the Vikings had a settlement here as early as AD 841.

Following Strongbow's invasion of 1170, a medieval city began to emerge; the Anglo-Normans built strong defensive walls around the castle.

Vibrant artwork typical of shops and galleries in Temple Bar

A small reconstructed section of these old city walls can be seen at St Audoen's Church. More conspicuous reminders of the Anglo-Normans appear in the medieval Christ Church Cathedral and St Patrick's Cathedral. When the city expanded during the Georgian era, the narrow cobbled streets of Temple Bar became a quarter inhabited by skilled craftsmen and merchants. Today this area is considered to be the trendiest part of town, and is home to a variety of alternative shops and cafés. The Powerscourt Townhouse is an elegant 18th-century mansion that has been converted into one of the city's best shopping centres.

SIGHTS AT A GLANCE

Museums and Libraries
Chester Beatty Library ❷
Dublin Civic Museum ❻
Dublinia ⓭
Marsh's Library ❽

Historic Buildings
City Hall ❸
Dublin Castle pp54–5 ❶
Powerscourt Townhouse ❺
Tailors' Hall ⓫

Historic Areas
Temple Bar pp56–7 ❹

Churches
Christ Church Cathedral pp62–3 ⓮
St Audoen's Church ⓬
St Patrick's Cathedral ❾
St Werburgh's Church ❿
Whitefriar Street Carmelite Church ❼

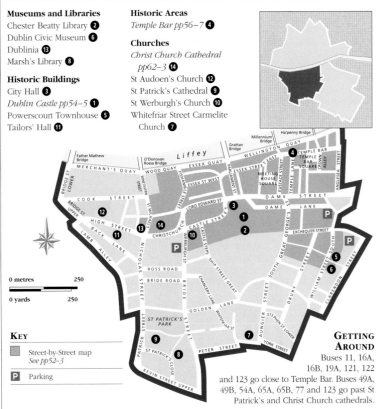

KEY

Street-by-Street map
See pp52–3

P Parking

0 metres 250
0 yards 250

GETTING AROUND
Buses 11, 16A, 16B, 19A, 121, 122 and 123 go close to Temple Bar. Buses 49A, 49B, 54A, 65A, 65B, 77 and 123 go past St Patrick's and Christ Church cathedrals.

◁ **Colourful street in bustling Temple Bar**

Street-by-Street: Southwest Dublin

DESPITE ITS WEALTH of ancient buildings, such as Dublin Castle and Christ Church Cathedral, this part of Dublin lacks the sleek appeal of the neighbouring streets around Grafton Street. In recent years, however, redevelopment has rejuvenated the area, especially around Temple Bar, where the attractive cobbled streets are lined with shops, futuristic arts centres, galleries, bars and cafés.

Sunlight Chambers were built in 1900 for the Lever Brothers company. The delightful terracotta decoration on the façade advertises their main business of soap manufacturing.

Wood Quay is where the Vikings established their first permanent settlement in Ireland around 841.

Dublin Viking Adventure

★ Christ Church Cathedral
Huge family monuments, including that of the 19th Earl of Kildare, can be found in Ireland's oldest cathedral, which also has a fascinating crypt **⑭**

St Werburgh's Church
An ornate interior hides behind the somewhat drab exterior of this 18th-century church **⑩**

Dublinia
Medieval Dublin is the subject of this interactive museum, located in the former Synod Hall of the Church of Ireland. It is linked to Christ Church by a bridge **⑬**

City Hall
Originally built as the Royal Exchange in 1779, the city's municipal headquarters is fronted by a huge Corinthian portico **③**

★ Dublin Castle
The Drawing Room, with its Waterford crystal chandelier, is part of a suite of luxurious rooms built in the 18th century for the Viceroys of Ireland **①**

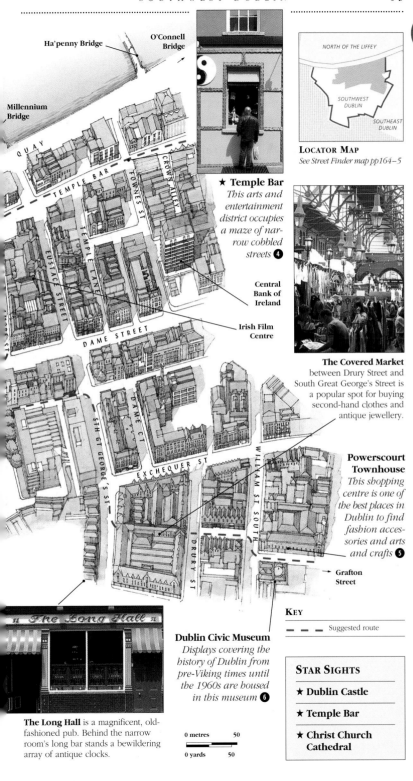

Ha'penny Bridge

O'Connell Bridge

Millennium Bridge

QUAY

TEMPLE BAR

FOWNES ST

CROWN ALLEY

TEMPLE LANE

EUSTACE STREET

DAME STREET

DAME ST

DAME CT

STH GT GEORGE'S ST

EXCHEQUER ST

WILLIAM ST SOUTH

DRURY ST

★ **Temple Bar**
*This arts and
entertainment
district occupies
a maze of nar-
row cobbled
streets* ❹

Central Bank of Ireland

Irish Film Centre

LOCATOR MAP
See Street Finder map pp164–5

NORTH OF THE LIFFEY

SOUTHWEST DUBLIN

SOUTHEAST DUBLIN

The Covered Market
between Drury Street and
South Great George's Street is
a popular spot for buying
second-hand clothes and
antique jewellery.

Powerscourt Townhouse
*This shopping
centre is one of
the best places in
Dublin to find
fashion acces-
sories and arts
and crafts* ❺

→ **Grafton Street**

KEY

▬ ▬ ▬   Suggested route

Dublin Civic Museum
*Displays covering the
history of Dublin from
pre-Viking times until
the 1960s are housed
in this museum* ❻

The Long Hall is a magnificent, old-
fashioned pub. Behind the narrow
room's long bar stands a bewildering
array of antique clocks.

0 metres   50

0 yards   50

STAR SIGHTS

★ **Dublin Castle**

★ **Temple Bar**

★ **Christ Church Cathedral**

Dublin Castle ❶

FOR SEVEN CENTURIES Dublin Castle was a symbol of English rule, ever since the Anglo-Normans built a fortress here in the 13th century. Nothing remains of the original structure except the much modified Record Tower. Following a fire in 1684, the Surveyor-General, Sir William Robinson, laid down the plans for the Upper and Lower Castle Yards in their present form. On the first floor of the south side of the Upper Yard are the luxury State Apartments, including St Patrick's Hall. These rooms, with Killybegs carpets and chandeliers of Waterford glass, served as home to the British-appointed Viceroys of Ireland.

St Patrick by Edward Smyth

Figure of Justice
Facing the Upper Yard above the main entrance from Cork Hill, this statue aroused much cynicism among Dubliners, who felt she was turning her back on the city.

★ Throne Room
Built in 1740, this room contains a throne said to have been presented by William of Orange after his victory at the Battle of the Boyne (see p13).

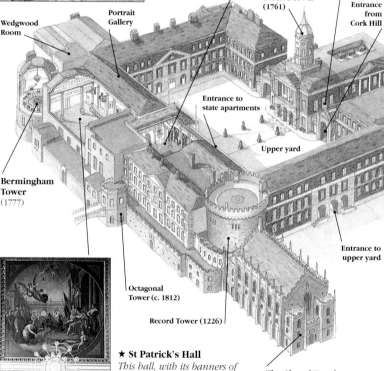

Wedgwood Room

Portrait Gallery

Bedford Tower (1761)

Entrance from Cork Hill

Entrance to state apartments

Upper yard

Bermingham Tower (1777)

Entrance to upper yard

Octagonal Tower (c. 1812)

Record Tower (1226)

★ St Patrick's Hall
This hall, with its banners of the now defunct Knights of St Patrick, has ceiling paintings by Vincenzo Valdré (1778), symbolizing the relationship between Britain and Ireland.

The Chapel Royal was completed in 1814 by Francis Johnston. The 100 heads on the exterior of this Neo-Gothic church were carved by Edward Smyth.

ROBERT EMMET

Robert Emmet (1778–1803),
leader of the abortive 1803
rebellion, is remembered
as a heroic champion of
Irish liberty. His plan was
to capture Dublin Castle
as a signal for the country
to rise up against the Act
of Union *(see p14)*. Emmet
was caught and publicly
hanged, but the defiant,
patriotic speech he made
from the dock helped to
inspire future generations
of Irish freedom fighters.

Government
offices

ower yard

Dame Street

STAR FEATURES

★ **St Patrick's Hall**

★ **Throne Room**

Manuscript (1874) from the Holy Koran written by calligrapher Ahmad Shaikh in Kashmir, Chester Beatty Library

Chester Beatty Library ❷

Clock Tower Building, Dubh Linn
Gardens, Dublin Castle. **Map** C4.
407 0750. May–Sep: 10am–
5pm Mon– Fri; Oct–Apr: 10am–5pm
Tue–Fri; 11am–5pm Sat, 1pm–5pm
Sun all year. public hols.
www.cbl.ie

THIS WORLD-RENOWNED
collection of Oriental manuscripts and art was named
European Museum of the Year
in 2002. It was bequeathed to
Ireland by American mining
magnate Sir Alfred Chester
Beatty, who died in 1968.
This generous act no doubt
led to his selection as Ireland's
first honorary citizen in 1957.

During his lifetime Beatty
accumulated almost 300 copies
of the Koran, representing the
works of master calligraphers
from Iran, Turkey and the
Arab world. Other exhibits
include some 6,000-year-old
Babylonian stone tablets,
Greek papyri dating from the
2nd century AD and biblical
material written in Coptic, the
original language of Egypt.

In the Far Eastern collection
is a display of Chinese jade
books – each leaf is made from
thinly cut jade. Burmese and
Siamese art is represented in
the fine collection of 18th- and
19th-century Parabaiks, books
of illustrated folk tales. The
Japanese collection also
includes many books as well
as paintings from the 16th to
the 18th centuries.

Turkish and Persian
miniatures, striking Buddhist
paintings and Chinese dragon
robes are among many other
fascinating exhibits in this
unusual museum.

City Hall ❸

Cork Hill, Dame St. **Map** C3. 222
2204. 10am–5:15pm Mon–Sat,
2–5pm Sun, public hols. Good Fri,
24th–26th Dec.
www.dublincity.ie/cityhall

DESIGNED BY Thomas Cooley,
this imposing building
was built between 1769 and
1779 as the Royal Exchange.
It was taken over by Dublin
Corporation in 1852 as a meeting place for the city council,
a role it keeps to this day.

Tours are available of the
building, recently restored to
its original condition.
*Dublin City Hall – The Story
of the Capital*, is a permanent
exhibition housed in the
lower ground floor covering
1,000 years of history.

Façade of City Hall

Temple Bar ❹

THE COBBLED streets between Dame Street and the Liffey are named after Sir William Temple who acquired the land in the early 1600s. The term "bar" meant a riverside path. In the 1800s it was home to small businesses but over the years went into decline. In the early 1960s the land was bought

Palm tree seat

up with plans to build a new bus station. Artists and retailers took short-term leases but stayed on when the redevelopment plans were scrapped. Temple Bar prospered and today it is an exciting place, with bars, restaurants, shops and galleries. Stylish and eco-friendly architectural development is contributing further to the area's appeal.

Modern, floor-lit entrance hall of the Irish Film Institute

Exploring Temple Bar
The most dramatic way to enter Temple Bar is through the **Merchants' Arch** opposite Ha'penny Bridge *(see p75).* Underneath the arch is a short, dark alley lined with bazaar-like retail outlets. The alley opens out into the modern airy space of **Temple Bar Square**, a popular lunchtime hangout, where there is a small but eclectic **book market** at weekends. Along the east side is **Crown Alley** with its brightly painted shops and cafés.

Galleries and gallery shops abound. In the northwest corner of the square is the **Temple Bar Gallery and Studios**, a renovated factory that combines exhibition and studio spaces. The **Original Print Gallery** on Temple Bar street and the **Graphic Studio Gallery** off Cope Street sell handmade prints.

The **Contemporary Music Centre**, on Fishamble Street, is Ireland's national archive and resource centre for new music, supporting the work of composers throughout Ireland. The **Temple Bar Information Centre**, on East Essex Street, provides details of arts, culture and entertainment in the area.

Near Christ Church Cathedral in the Old City district, is **Cow's Lane**, a new pedestrian street complete with designer shops and its own fashion and design market every Saturday.

In the evening, there are a huge number of restaurants, bars and pubs to choose from, many with live jazz, rock, and traditional Irish music. The **Temple Bar Music Centre** offers an exciting mix of mainly homegrown talent, playing everything from alternative to R&B and garage. They also have a weekly salsa night. For international names, try the

TEMPLE BAR

The Temple Bar logo

Olympia Theatre, where the world's biggest bands have played. This Victorian theatre also stages comedy, musicals and, occasionally, drama.

Meeting House Square
Named after a Quaker place of worship which once stood here, this outdoor performance space is a wonderful asset to the city. It is one of the main venues for Diversions, a free outdoor cultural programme that runs from May to September, featuring lunchtime and evening concerts, and open-air theatre. Screenings of films and numerous family events also take place in the square. Every Saturday, an excellent gourmet food market is held here.

Project
39 East Essex Street. 📞 679 6622. ⏰ 11am–7pm Mon–Sat; shows nightly. 🚻 🅿 📶 🅆 www.project.ie
Begun in 1966, Project has developed from a voluntary, artist-led co-operative to a modern arts centre, with an international reputation for avant garde theatre, dance, music, film and visual art. Project has launched the careers of actors Gabriel Byrne and Liam Neeson, and even U2 cut their teeth here. It also runs a weekly clubnight. Perfomance and exhibition space in the custom-designed building is flexible and fluid, allowing room for artistic invention.

Shoppers in the streets of Temple Bar

Gallery of Photography

Meeting House Square. **C** 671 4654.
◷ 11am–6pm Tue–Sat, 2–6pm Sun.
▮ **w** www.irish-photography.com

This bright, contemporary space runs exhibitions of high quality Irish and international photography, some of which feature talks by the artist exhibiting. The shop has an extensive selection of photos, postcards and specialist titles.

National Photographic Archive

Meeting House Square. **C** 603 0374.
◷ 10am–5pm Mon–Fri, 10am–2pm Sat. **w** www.nli.ie

The National Library's collection of around 300,000 photographs is housed here.

The Archive has rolling exhibitions, mainly featuring items from the collections. Subject matter ranges from social and political history to early tourist postcards and dramatic landscape shots, offering a window into a time when Ireland really was a land of thatched cottages and donkey carts.

Irish Film Institute

6 Eustace Street. **C** 679 5744.
◷ daily. **▮▮** **▮** **w** www.irishfilm.ie

Opened in November 1992, in the wake of international hits such as *The Commitments* (1991), this was the first major

Cheese stall at the weekly gourmet market in Meeting House Square

cultural project completed in Temple Bar. A neon sign indicates the main entrance, which runs through a floor-lit corridor before opening into an airy atrium where visitors can browse in the bookshop or have a snack, meal or drink in the bar and restaurant. The IFI's two screens focus on cult, arthouse and independent films as well as showing archive screenings and documentaries. There are also seminars, workshops, seasons on various themes, nations or directors, and the Jameson International Film Festival each year. A small temporary membership fee is payable on top of the ticket price.

Cultivate Sustainable Living Centre

15–19 Essex Street West. **C** 674 6396.
◷ 11am–6:30pm Mon–Sat (7:30pm Thurs). **●** public hols. **▮**
w www.sustainable.ie

Learn about the green development of Temple Bar at this ecological centre with exhibitions, screenings of cutting-edge films and a demonstration garden. Interactive maps show sites of environmental interest, from bicycle routes to eco-cultural tourist sites.

Four times a year, Cultivate hosts the four-day Convergence Festival, highlighting key ecological issues through drama, film, live music, art, workshops and presentations.

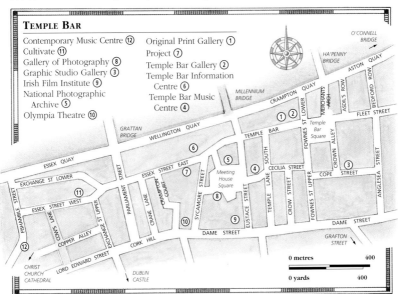

TEMPLE BAR

Contemporary Music Centre ⑫
Cultivate ⑪
Gallery of Photography ⑧
Graphic Studio Gallery ③
Irish Film Institute ⑨
National Photographic Archive ⑤
Olympia Theatre ⑩

Original Print Gallery ①
Project ⑦
Temple Bar Gallery ②
Temple Bar Information Centre ⑥
Temple Bar Music Centre ④

The light and airy interior of Powerscourt Townhouse shopping centre

Powerscourt Townhouse **5**

South William St. **Map** D4. 679
4144. 10am–6pm Mon–Fri (8pm
Thurs), 9am–6pm Sat, noon–6pm Sun.
See also **Shopping in Dublin**
pp134–9.
W www.powerscourtcentre.com

COMPLETED IN 1774 by
Robert Mack, this grand
mansion was originally built
as the city home of Viscount
Powerscourt, who also had a
country estate at
Enniskerry just south
of Dublin.
Granite from the
Powerscourt
estate was used in
its construction.
Today the build-
ing houses one
of Dublin's best
shopping centres. Inside it still
features the original grand
mahogany staircase, and finely
detailed plasterwork by
stuccodore Michael Stapleton.
The building became a dra-
pery warehouse in the 1830s,
and major restoration in the
late 1970s turned it into a
centre of galleries, antique
shops, jewellery stalls, cafés
and other shop units. The
central courtyard café, topped
by a glass dome, is a popular

**Shoes of an Irish Giant in
Dublin Civic Museum**

meeting place with many
Dubliners. Another entrance is
via the narrow Johnson Court
alley, just off Grafton Street.

Dublin Civic Museum **6**

58 South William St. **Map** D4. 679
4260. Temporarily closed for
refurbishment so visitors should call in
advance to check if it has re-opened.

THIS SMALL MUSEUM, housed
in the former Georgian
City Assembly House,
depicts Dublin's
history from
Viking times
through to the
20th century by
means of photo-
graphs, paintings,
old newspaper
cuttings and an
assortment of very unusual
objects, including the old
shoes of an Irish giant. One
of the star exhibits is the head
from the 40-m (134-ft) high
Nelson Pillar. This massive
monument was erected in
1808, and predated Nelson's
Column in London's Trafalgar
Square by several decades. It
loomed high over O'Connell
Street until it was destroyed by
an explosion by anti-British
protestors on 8 March 1966.

Whitefriar Street Carmelite Church **7**

56 Aungier St. **Map** C4. 475 8821.
8am–6:30pm Mon & Wed–Fri,
8am–9pm Tue, 8am–7pm Sat, 8am–
7:30pm Sun, 9.30am–1pm public hols.
W www.carmelites.ie

DESIGNED BY George
Papworth, this Catholic
church was built in 1827. It
stands alongside the site of a
medieval Carmelite foundation.
In contrast to the two
Church of Ireland cathedrals,
St Patrick's and Christ Church,
which are usually full of
tourists, this church is frequented by worshippers from all
over Dublin. Every day they
come to light candles to
various saints, including St
Valentine – the patron saint of
lovers. His remains, previously
buried in the cemetery of St
Hippolytus in Rome, were
offered to the church as a gift
from Pope Gregory XVI in
1836. Today they rest beneath
the commemorative statue to
the saint, which stands in the
northeast corner of the
church beside the high altar.
Nearby is the figure of Our
Lady of Dublin, a Flemish oak
statue dating from the late 15th
or early 16th century. It may
have belonged to St Mary's
Abbey (see p74) and is thought
to be the only wooden statue
of its kind to have escaped
destruction when Ireland's
monasteries were sacked
during the time of the
Reformation (see p12).

Statue of Our Lady of Dublin in
Whitefriar Street Carmelite Church

The entrance to Marsh's Library, adjacent to St Patrick's Cathedral

Marsh's Library ❽

St Patrick's Close. **Map** B4. ◾ *454 3511.* ⬜ *10am–1pm, 2–5pm Mon, Wed–Fri, 10:30am–1pm Sat.* ◗ *24 Dec–2 Jan, public hols.* 🅦 *www.marshlibrary.ie*

BUILT IN 1701 for Archbishop Narcissus Marsh, this is the oldest public library in Ireland. It was designed by Sir William Robinson, architect of the Royal Hospital Kilmainham *(see p82).*

To the rear of the library are wired alcoves where readers were locked in with rare books. The collection of books from the 16th–18th centuries includes a volume of Clarendon's *History of the Rebellion*, with margin notes by Jonathan Swift.

St Patrick's Cathedral ❾

St Patrick's Close. **Map** B4. ◾ *475 4817.* ⬜ *Mar–Oct: 9am–5pm Mon–Sat, 9am–5pm Sun; Nov–Feb: 9am–5pm Mon–Sat, 9am–3pm Sun. Sun services: 11am–3:15pm. Tours are not admitted during services.* 🅦 *www.stpatrickscathedral.ie*

IRELAND'S LARGEST CHURCH was founded beside a sacred well where St Patrick is said to have baptized converts around AD 450. The original building was just a wooden chapel and remained so until 1192 when Archbishop John Comyn rebuilt it in stone.

In the mid-17th century, Huguenot refugees from France arrived in Dublin, and were given the Lady Chapel

JONATHAN SWIFT (1667–1745)

Jonathan Swift was born in Dublin and educated at Trinity College *(see pp36–7).* He left for England in 1689, but returned in 1694 when his political career failed. He began a life in the church, becoming Dean of St Patrick's in 1713. In addition, he was a prolific political commentator – his best-known work, *Gulliver's Travels*, contains a bitter satire on Anglo-Irish relations. Swift's personal life, particularly his friendship with two younger women, Ester Johnson, better known as Stella, and Hester Vanhomrigh, attracted criticism. In later life, he suffered from Menière's disease (an illness of the ear), which led many to believe he was insane.

by the Dean and Chapter as their place of worship. The chapel was separated from the rest of the cathedral and used by the Huguenots until the late 18th century. Today St Patrick's is the Protestant Church of Ireland's national cathedral.

Much of the present building dates back to work completed between 1254 and 1270. The cathedral suffered over the centuries from desecration, fire and neglect but, thanks to Sir Benjamin Guinness, it underwent extensive restoration during the 1860s. The building is 91 m (300 ft) long; at the western end is a 43-m (141-ft) tower, restored by Archbishop Minot in 1370 and now known as Minot's Tower. The spire was added in the 18th century.

The interior is dotted with memorial busts, brasses and monuments. A leaflet available at the front desk helps identify and locate them. Famous citizens remembered in the church include the harpist Turlough O'Carolan (1670–1738), Douglas Hyde (1860–1949), the first President of Ireland and of course Jonathan Swift and his beloved Stella.

At the west end of the nave is an old door with a hole in it – a relic from a feud between the Lords Kildare and Ormonde in 1492. The latter took refuge in the Chapter House, but a truce was soon made and a hole was cut in the door by Lord Kildare so that the two could shake hands in friendship.

St Patrick's Cathedral with Minot's Tower and spire

Nave of St Werburgh's Church, showing gallery and organ case

St Werburgh's Church ⑩

Entrance through 7–8 Castle St. **Map** C4. **[** 478 3710. **◯** 10am–4pm Mon–Fri, ring bell if doors locked.

BUILT ON LATE 12th-century foundations, St Werburgh's was designed by Thomas Burgh in 1715, after an act of parliament which appointed commissioners to build a new church. Around 85 people made donations. By 1719 the church was complete but had an unfinished tower. Then in 1728 James Southwell bequeathed money for a clock and bells for the church on condition that the tower was completed within three years of his death. It was finally finished in 1732. After a fire in 1754 it was rebuilt with the financial help of George II. It served as the parish church of Dublin Castle, hosting many state ceremonies, including the swearing-in of viceroys. However, this role was later taken over by the Church of the Most Holy Trinity within the castle walls.

Beyond the shabby pallor of its exterior walls lies some fine decorative work. There are massive memorials to members of the Guinness family, and a finely carved Gothic pulpit by Richard Stewart. Also worth seeing are the 1767 organ case and the beautiful stuccowork in the chancel.

Beneath the church lie 27 vaults including that of Lord Edward Fitzgerald, who died during the 1798 Rebellion (see p14), and also Sir James Ware. The body of Fitzgerald's captor, Major Henry Sirr, is in the graveyard. John Field, the creator of the nocturne, was baptized here in 1782.

Tailors' Hall ⑪

Back Lane. **Map** B4. **[** 454 1786. **●** to the public. **[W]** www.antaisce.org

DUBLIN'S ONLY surviving guildhall preserves a delightful corner of old Dublin in an otherwise busy redevelopment zone. Built in 1706, it stands behind a limestone arch in a quiet cobbled yard. The building is the oldest guildhall in Ireland and was used by various trade groups including hosiers, saddlers and barber-surgeons as well as tailors. It was regarded as the most fashionable venue in Dublin for social occasions such as balls and concerts for many years until the New Music Hall in Fishamble Street opened and the social scene transferred to there. It also hosted many political meetings – the Protestant leader of the United Irishmen, Wolfe Tone, famously made a speech at the convention of the Catholic Committee on 2nd December 1792 before the 1798 rebellion (see p14).

The building closed in the early 1960s due to neglect, but an appeal by Desmond Guinness saw the hall totally refurbished. Since 1985 is has been the home of An Taisce (the Irish National Trust).

Façade of Tailors' Hall, today the home of the Irish National Trust

St Audoen's Church ⑫

High St, Cornmarket. **Map** B3. **[** 677 0088 **◯** Jun–Sep: 9:30am–5:30pm, last adm 4:45pm. **[ ]** **[ ]** **[W]** www.heritageireland.ie

SITED IN THE heart of the walled Medieval City, and designated a National Monument, St Audoen's Church is Dublin's earliest surviving medieval church. It is dedicated to Saint Ouen, the 7th century Bishop of

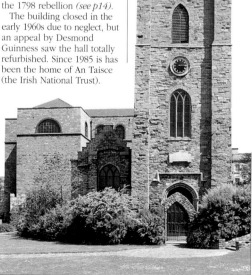

The 12th-century tower of St Audoen's Church, the oldest in Ireland

Rouen and Patron Saint of Normandy. The 15th-century nave remains intact and the three bells date from 1423. The Guild Chapel of St Anne houses an exhibition on the importance of this church in the life of the medieval city. To the rear, steps lead down to St Audoen's Arch, the last remaining gateway of the old city. Flanking the gate are restored sections of the 13th-century city walls.

Next door stands St Audoen's Roman Catholic Church, which was begun in 1841 and completed in 1847. It was built by Patrick Byrne, of Talbot Street, who studied at the Dublin Society School. The parish priest, Patrick Mooney, completed the plasterwork and also installed the organ. In 1884 the dome of the church collapsed and was replaced with a plaster circle. The portico was added to the building in 1899. The Great Bell, dedicated on All Saints Day in 1848 and known as The Liberator after Daniel O'Connell, rang to announce his release from prison and also tolled on the day of his funeral. The two Pacific clam shells by the front of the church hold holy water.

Medieval key in the Dublinia exhibition

Dublinia ⓭

St Michael's Hill. **Map** B3. 📞 679 4611. ◻ Apr–Sep: 10am–5pm daily; Oct–Mar: 11am–4pm Tue–Sat, 10am–4:30pm Sun, Mon & public hols. ● 17 Mar, 23–26 Dec. ◪ minimum charge to enter Christ Church Cathedral via bridge. ♿ Ⓦ www.dublinia.ie

Mᴀɴᴀɢᴇᴅ ʙʏ the non-profit-making Medieval Trust, the Dublinia exhibition covers the formative period of Dublin's history from the arrival of the Anglo-Normans in 1170 to the closure of the monasteries in the 1540s. The exhibition is housed in the Neo-Gothic Synod Hall, which, up until 1983, was home to the ruling body of the Church of Ireland. The building and the bridge linking it to Christ Church Cathedral date from the

Former Synod Hall, now home to the Dublinia Exhibition

1870s. Before Dublinia was established in 1993, the Synod Hall was briefly used as a nightclub.

The exhibition is entered via the basement where visitors walk through life-sized reconstructions of the Medieval City complete with realistic sounds and smells. These depict major events in Dublin's history, such as the Black Death and the rebellion of Silken Thomas (see p12). The ground floor houses a large-scale model of Dublin as it was around 1500, and reconstructions including the inside of a late medieval merchant's kitchen. There is also a display of artifacts from the Wood Quay excavation. This was the site of the first Viking settlement in Ireland. Excavations in the 1970s revealed remains of Norse and Norman villages, and artifacts includ-

ing pottery, swords, coins and leatherwork. Many of these finds are also on display at the National Museum (see pp42–3). However, the city chose not to develop the Wood Quay site, but instead built two large civic offices there. If you go to Wood Quay today all you will find is a plaque and an unusual picnic site by the Liffey in the shape of a Viking longboat.

Also in the exhibition are information panels on the themes of trade, merchants and religion. On the first floor is the wood-panelled Great Hall, one of the finest examples of Victorian Gothic style in Dublin. From Easter 2005 the Great Hall will house *The Viking World*, an exhibition exploring the impact the Vikings had on those they encountered and the legacy they left behind. This exhibition will complement the one on medieval Dublin, providing an overview of the city during the Viking and medieval period.

Mid 13th-century jug in Dublinia

Reconstruction of a Viking street in Dublinia

Christic Church Cathedral ⑭

C HRIST CHURCH CATHEDRAL was established by the Hiberno-Norse king of Dublin, Sitric "Silkbeard", and the first bishop of Dublin, Dunan. It was rebuilt by the Anglo-Norman archbishop, John Cumin from 1186. It is the cathedral for the Church of Ireland

Arms on Lord Mayor's pew

(Anglican) diocese of Dublin and Glendalough. By the 19th century it was in a bad state of repair, but was completely remodelled by architect George Street in the 1870s. The vast 12th-century crypt was restored in 2000.

★ **Medieval Lectern**
This beautiful brass lectern was hand-made during the Middle Ages. It stands on the north side of the nave, in front of the pulpit. The matching lectern on the south side is Victorian.

Nave
The 25-m (68-ft) high nave has some fine early Gothic arches. On the north side, the 13th-century wall leans out by as much as 50 cm (18 in) due to the weight of the original roof.

The Lord Mayor's pew is usually kept in the north aisle, but is moved to the front of the nave when used by Dublin's civic dignitaries. It features a carving of the city arms and a stand for the civic mace.

Entrance

The bridge to the Synod Hall was added when the cathedral was being rebuilt in the 1870s.

★ **Strongbow Monument**
The large effigy in chain armour is probably not Strongbow (see p12). However, his remains are buried in the cathedral and the curious half-figure may be part of his original tomb.

STAR FEATURES

★ **Strongbow Monument**

★ **Crypt**

★ **Medieval Lectern**

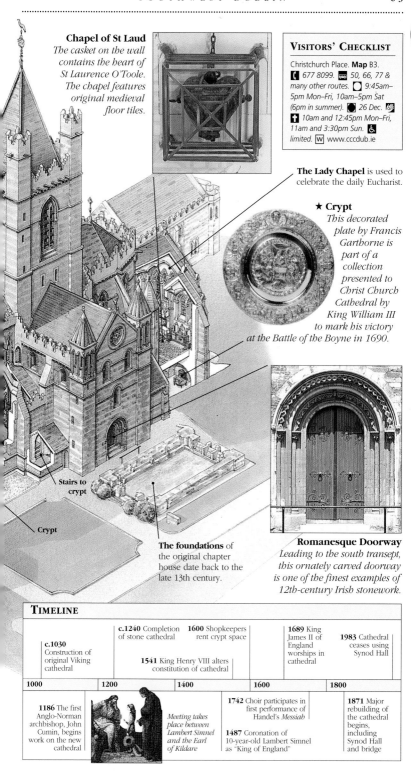

Chapel of St Laud
The casket on the wall contains the heart of St Laurence O'Toole. The chapel features original medieval floor tiles.

VISITORS' CHECKLIST

Christchurch Place. **Map** B3.
677 8099. 50, 66, 77 & many other routes. 9:45am–5pm Mon–Fri, 10am–5pm Sat (6pm in summer). 26 Dec. 10am and 12:45pm Mon–Fri, 11am and 3:30pm Sun. limited. www.cccdub.ie

The Lady Chapel is used to celebrate the daily Eucharist.

★ **Crypt**
This decorated plate by Francis Garthorne is part of a collection presented to Christ Church Cathedral by King William III to mark his victory at the Battle of the Boyne in 1690.

Stairs to crypt

Crypt

The foundations of the original chapter house date back to the late 13th century.

Romanesque Doorway
Leading to the south transept, this ornately carved doorway is one of the finest examples of 12th-century Irish stonework.

TIMELINE

1000	1200	1400	1600	1800
c.1030 Construction of original Viking cathedral	**c.1240** Completion of stone cathedral	**1600** Shopkeepers rent crypt space	**1689** King James II of England worships in cathedral	**1983** Cathedral ceases using Synod Hall
		1541 King Henry VIII alters constitution of cathedral		
1186 The first Anglo-Norman archbishop, John Cumin, begins work on the new cathedral	*Meeting takes place between Lambert Simnel and the Earl of Kildare*	**1487** Coronation of 10-year-old Lambert Simnel as "King of England"	**1742** Choir participates in first performance of Handel's *Messiah*	**1871** Major rebuilding of the cathedral begins, including Synod Hall and bridge

NORTH OF THE LIFFEY

UBLIN'S NORTH SIDE was the last part of the city to be developed during the 18th century. The city authorities envisioned an elegant area of leafy avenues, but the reality of today's traffic has rather spoiled their original plans. Nonetheless, O'Connell Street is an impressive thoroughfare, lined with department stores, monuments and historic public buildings.

Bookshop sign on Ormond Quay Lower

There are many notable buildings in the area, such as James Gandon's

glorious Custom House and majestic Four Courts, together with the famous General Post Office, or GPO *(see p69)*.

The Rotunda Hospital, Europe's first purpose-built maternity hospital, is another fine building. Dublin's two most celebrated theatres, the Abbey and the Gate, act as cultural magnets, as do the Dublin Writers' Museum and the James Joyce Cultural Centre, two museums that are dedicated to writers who spent most of their lives in the city.

SIGHTS AT A GLANCE

Historic Buildings
Custom House ❶
Four Courts ⓬
King's Inns ❾
Tyrone House ❹

Historic Streets and Bridges
Ha'penny Bridge ⓰
O'Connell Street ❸
Parnell Square ❼
Smithfield ❿

Theatres
Abbey Theatre ❷

Churches
St Mary's Church ⓯
St Mary's Pro-Cathedral ❺
St Michan's Church ⓭

Museums and Galleries
Old Jameson Distillery ⓫
James Joyce Cultural Centre ❻
National Wax Museum ❽
St Mary's Abbey Exhibition ⓮

GETTING AROUND
Numerous buses, including the 3, 10, 11, 13, 16 and 16A, go along O'Connell Street and round Parnell Square. To get to Smithfield, take a 67A, 68, 69, 79 or 90. The Tallaght to Connolly Station Luas line runs through the area.

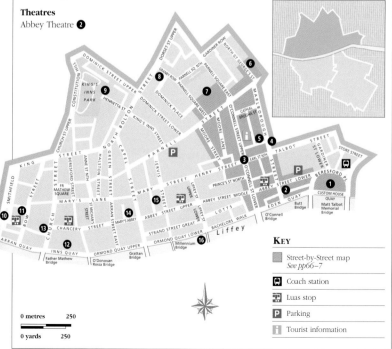

KEY

▨	Street-by-Street map *See pp66–7*
🚌	Coach station
🚏	Luas stop
🅿	Parking
ℹ	Tourist information

0 metres 250
0 yards 250

◁ **The impressive columns of the General Post Office on O'Connell Street**

Street-by-Street: Around O'Connell Street

THROUGHOUT THE Georgian era, O'Connell Street was the fashionable part of Dublin in which to live. However, the 1916 Easter Rising destroyed many of its fine buildings, including much of the General Post Office – only its original façade remains. Today, this main thoroughfare is lined with shops and businesses. Other nearby attractions include St Mary's Pro-Cathedral and James Gandon's Custom House, overlooking the Liffey.

Pavement mosaic, Moore Street

James Joyce Cultural Centre
This well-restored Georgian town house contains a small Joyce museum ❻

Parnell Monument (1911)

The Gate Theatre was founded in 1928 and is renowned for its productions of contemporary drama.

The Rotunda Hospital houses a chapel built in the 1750s to the design of German architect Richard Castle. It features lovely stained-glass windows, fluted columns, panelling and intricate iron balustrades.

Moore Street Market is the busiest of the streets off O'Connell. Be prepared for the shrill cries of the stall holders offering an enormous variety of fresh fruit, vegetables and cut flowers.

The Monument of Light, an elegant stainless steel spire, rises to 120 m (394 ft).

The General Post Office, the grandest building on O'Connell Street, was the centre of the 1916 Rising.

James Larkin Statue (1981)

KEY

— Suggested route

▯ Luas stop

ℹ Tourist information

0 metres   50

0 yards   50

STAR SIGHTS

★ **Custom House**

★ **O'Connell Street**

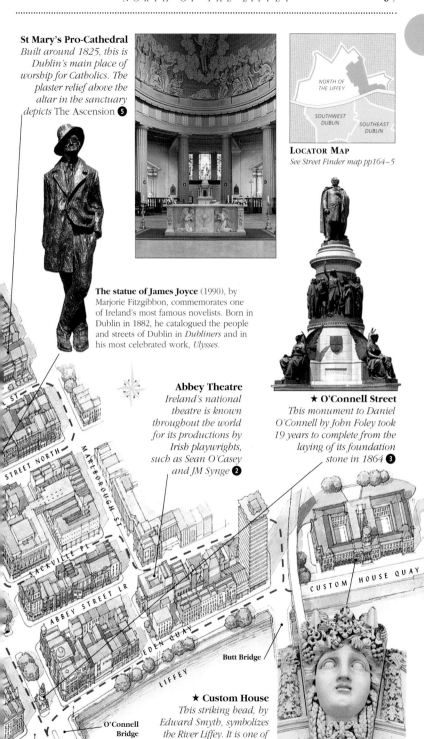

St Mary's Pro-Cathedral
Built around 1825, this is Dublin's main place of worship for Catholics. The plaster relief above the altar in the sanctuary depicts The Ascension ❺

LOCATOR MAP
See Street Finder map pp164–5

The statue of James Joyce (1990), by Marjorie Fitzgibbon, commemorates one of Ireland's most famous novelists. Born in Dublin in 1882, he catalogued the people and streets of Dublin in *Dubliners* and in his most celebrated work, *Ulysses.*

Abbey Theatre
Ireland's national theatre is known throughout the world for its productions by Irish playwrights, such as Sean O'Casey and JM Synge ❷

★ O'Connell Street
This monument to Daniel O'Connell by John Foley took 19 years to complete from the laying of its foundation stone in 1864 ❸

Butt Bridge

★ Custom House
This striking head, by Edward Smyth, symbolizes the River Liffey. It is one of 14 carved keystones that adorn the building ❶

O'Connell
Bridge

Trinity
College

Illuminated façade of the Custom House reflected in the Liffey

Custom House ❶

Custom House Quay. **Map** E2.
☎ 888 2538. **◯** 10am–12:30pm
Mon–Fri (Nov–Mar: Wed–Fri),
2–5pm Sat, Sun. **▨** **♿** weekdays.
Ⓦ www.visitdublin.com

THIS MAJESTIC BUILDING was designed as the Custom House by the English architect James Gandon. However, the 1800 Act of Union *(see p14)* transferred the custom and excise business to London, rendering the building practically obsolete. In 1921, Sinn Féin voters celebrated their election victory by setting light to what they saw as a symbol of British imperialism. The fire blazed for five days causing extensive damage. Reconstruction took place in 1926, but the building was not completely restored until 1991, when it reopened as government offices.

The main façade is made up of pavilions at each end with a Doric portico in its centre. The arms of Ireland crown the two pavilions, and a series of 14 allegorical heads by Dublin sculptor Edward Smyth form the keystones of arches and entrances. These

heads depict Ireland's main rivers and the Atlantic Ocean. A statue of Commerce tops the central copper dome.

The best view of the building is from the south of the Liffey beyond Matt Talbot Bridge.

Logo of the Abbey Theatre

Abbey Theatre ❷

26 Lower Abbey St. **Map** E2. **☎** 878
7222 Box office. **◯** for performances,
some tours. See also **Entertainment**
pp140–45. **Ⓦ** www.abbeytheatre.ie

FOUNDED in 1898 with W B Yeats and Lady Gregory as co-directors, the Abbey staged its first play in 1904. The early years of this much lauded national theatre saw works by W B Yeats, J M Synge and Sean O'Casey. Many were controversial: nationalist sensitivities were severely tested in 1926 at the premiere of O'Casey's *The Plough and the Stars*, when the flag of the Irish Free State appeared in a scene featuring a pub frequented by prostitutes.

While presenting the work of eminent foreign authors from time to time, the prime objective of the Abbey, and the smaller Peacock Theatre downstairs, is to provide a performance space for Irish dramatic writing. Some of the most acclaimed performances have been Brian Friel's *Dancing At Lughnasa*, Patrick Kavanagh's *Tarry Flynn*, *The Colleen Bawn* by Dion Boucicault and Hugh Leonard's *Love in the Title*.

O'Connell Street ❸

Map D1–D2.

O'CONNELL STREET is very different from the original plans of Irish aristocrat Luke Gardiner. When he bought the land in the 18th century, Gardiner envisioned a grand residential parade with an elegant mall running along its centre. Such plans were short-lived. The

O'Connell Bridge spanning the Liffey, viewed from the Butt Bridge

construction of Carlisle (now O'Connell) Bridge in 1790 transformed the street into the city's main north-south route. Also, several buildings were destroyed during the 1916 Easter Rising and the Irish Civil War. Since the 1960s many of the old buildings have been replaced by the plate glass and neon of fast food joints and amusement arcades.

A few venerable buildings remain, such as the General Post Office (1818), Gresham Hotel (1817), Clery's department store (1822) and the Royal Dublin Hotel, part of which occupies the street's only original townhouse.

A walk down the central mall is the most enjoyable way to see the street's mix of architectural styles. At the south end stands a huge monument to Daniel O'Connell *(see p14)*, unveiled in 1882. The street, which throughout the 19th century had been called Sackville Street, was renamed for O'Connell in 1922. Higher up, almost facing the General Post Office, is an expressive statue of James Larkin (1867–1943),

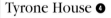

Clock outside Clery's department store

leader of the Dublin general strike in 1913. The next statue is of Father Theobald Mathew (1790–1856), founder of the Pioneer Total Abstinence Movement. At the north end of the street is the obelisk-shaped monument to Charles Stewart Parnell (1846–91), who was leader of the Home Rule Party and known as the "uncrowned King of Ireland" *(see p15)*. A new addition to O'Connell Street is the Monument of Light, erected on the site where Nelson's column used to be. The monument is a stainless steel, conical spire which tapers from a three-metre diameter base to a 10-centimetre pointed tip of optical glass at a height of 120 metres.

Tyrone House ❹

Marlborough St. **Map** D2.
❶ *to the public.*

Considered to be the most important Dublin building by German-born Richard Castle (also known as Cassels)

after Leinster House, this Palladian-style structure was completed around 1740 as a townhouse for Sir Marcus Beresford, later Earl of Tyrone. Its interior features elaborate plasterwork by the Swiss Francini brothers, as well as a grand mahogany staircase. The premises were bought by the government in the 1830s and today house a section of the Department of Education; the minister has one of the most ornate state offices in what used to be a reception room.

Austere Neo-Classical interior of St Mary's Pro-Cathedral

St Mary's Pro-Cathedral ❺

Marlborough St. **Map** D2. 874 5441. ◯ *7:30am–6:45pm Mon–Fri (7:15pm Sat), 9am–1:45pm & 5:30–7:45pm Sun.* W www.procathedral.ie

Dedicated in 1825 before Catholic emancipation *(see p14)*, St Mary's backstreet site was the best the city's Anglo-Irish leaders would allow a Catholic cathedral.

The façade is based on the Temple of Theseus in Athens. Its six Doric columns support a pediment with statues of St Laurence O'Toole, 12th-century Archbishop of Dublin and patron saint of the city, St Mary and St Patrick. The most striking feature of the interior is the intricately carved high altar.

St Mary's is home to the famous Palestrina Choir. In 1904 the great Irish tenor, John McCormack, began his career with the choir, which sings at the 11am Sunday service.

The General Post Office (GPO)

Built in 1818 halfway along O'Connell Street, the GPO became a symbol of the 1916 Irish Rising. Members of the Irish Volunteers and Irish Citizen Army seized the building on Easter Monday, and Patrick Pearse *(see p15)* read out the Proclamation of the Irish Republic from its steps. Shelling from the British finally forced the rebels out after a week. At first, many Irish people viewed the Rising unfavourably. However, as WB Yeats wrote, matters "changed utterly" and a "terrible beauty was born" when, during the

***Irish Life* magazine cover showing the 1916 Easter Rising**

following weeks, 14 of the leaders were shot at Kilmainham Gaol *(see p79)*. Inside the GPO is a sculpture of the Irish mythical warrior Cúchulainn, dedicated to those who died.

James Joyce Cultural Centre ❻

35 North Great George's St. **Map** D1.
(878 8547. **◗** 9:30am–5pm Mon–
Sat, 12:30–5pm Sun. **●** Good Fri,
23–27 Dec. 🅰 **✔**
w www.jamesjoyce.ie

A LTHOUGH BORN IN Dublin, Joyce spent most of his adult life in Europe. He used Dublin as the setting for his major works, including *Ulysses*, *A Portrait of the Artist as a Young Man* and *Dubliners*.

This centre is located in a 1784 townhouse which was built for the Earl of Kenmare. Michael Stapleton, one of the greatest stuccodores of his time, contributed to the plaster-work with noteworthy friezes.

The main literary display is an absorbing set of biographies of around 50 characters from *Ulysses*, who were based on real Dublin people. Professor Dennis J Maginni, a peripheral character in *Ulysses*, ran a dancing school from this town-house. Leopold and Molly Bloom, the central characters of *Ulysses*, lived a short walk away at No. 7 Eccles Street. The centre also organizes walking tours of Joyce's Dublin, so a visit is a must for all Joycean zealots.

At the top of the road, on Great Denmark Street, is the Jesuit-run Belvedere College attended by Joyce between 1893 and 1898. He recalls his unhappy schooldays there in *A Portrait of the Artist as a Young Man*. The college's interior contains some of Stapleton's best and most colourful plasterwork (1785).

Portrait of James Joyce (1882–1941) by Jacques Emile Blanche

Parnell Square ❼

O NCE AS AFFLUENT as the now-restored squares to the south of the Liffey, Parnell Square is today sadly neglected. However, it still holds many points of interest, including the historic Gate Theatre and the peaceful Garden of Remembrance. There are hopes that this once-elegant part of the city will one day be renovated and restored to its original splendour.

Stained-glass window (c. 1863) in the Rotunda Hospital's chapel

Gate Theatre

1 Cavendish Row. **Map** D1. **◗** *for performances only.* **Box Office (**
874 4045. **◗** 10am–7pm Mon–Sat.
See also **Entertainment in Dublin**
pp140–45. **w** www.gate-theatre.ie
Originally the grand supper room in the Rotunda, today the Gate Theatre is renowned for its staging of contemporary international drama in Dublin. It was founded in 1928 by Hilton Edwards and Mícheál Mac Liammóir. The latter is now best remembered for *The Importance of Being Oscar*, his long-running one-man show about the writer Oscar Wilde *(see p21)*. An early success was Denis Johnston's

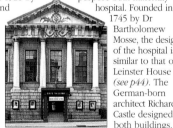

Entrance to the Gate Theatre

The Old Lady Says No, so-called because of the margin notes made on one of his scripts by Lady Gregory, founding director of the Abbey Theatre *(see p68)*. Although still noted for stag-ing productions of new plays, the Gate's current output often includes classic Irish plays including Sean O'Casey's *Juno and the Paycock*.

Many famous names in the acting world got their first break at the Gate Theatre, including James Mason and a teenage Orson Welles.

Rotunda Hospital

Parnell Square West. **Map** D1.
(873 0700.
Standing in the middle of Parnell Square is Europe's first purpose-built maternity hospital. Founded in 1745 by Dr Bartholomew Mosse, the design of the hospital is similar to that of Leinster House *(see p44)*. The German-born architect Richard Castle designed both buildings. At the east end of the hospital is the Rotunda, after which the hospital is named. It was built in 1764 by John Ensor as Assembly Rooms to host fund-raising functions and concerts. Franz Liszt gave a concert here in 1843.

On the first floor is a chapel featuring striking stained-glass windows and Rococo plaster-work and ceiling (1755) by the stuccodore Bartholomew

Cramillion. On the other side of the road from the hospital is Conway's Pub. Opened in 1745, it has been popular with expectant fathers for years.

Garden of Remembrance

Parnell Square. **Map** C1.
⬜ *dawn–dusk daily.*
At the northern end of Parnell Square is a small, peaceful park, dedicated to the men and women who have died in the pursuit of Irish freedom. The Garden of Remembrance marks the spot where several leaders of the Easter Rising were held overnight before being taken to Kilmainham Gaol *(see p79)*, and is also where the Irish Volunteers movement was formed in 1913.

Designed by Daithí Hanly, the garden was opened by President Eamon de Valera *(see p16)* in 1966, to mark the 50th anniversary of the Easter Rising. In the centre is a cruciform pool with a mosaic depicting broken swords, shields and spears, symbolizing peace. At one end of the garden is a large bronze sculpture by Oisín Kelly (1971) of the legendary *Children of Lir*, the children of King Lir who were changed into swans by their jealous stepmother.

Gallery of Writers at Dublin Writers' Museum

Dublin Writers' Museum

18 Parnell Square North. **Map** C1.
⬛ *872 2077.* ⬜ *10am–5pm, Mon–Sat, 11am–5pm Sun & public hols (last adm: 4:15pm); Jun–Aug: 10am–6pm Mon–Fri (last adm: 5:15pm).* ⬤ *25–26 Dec.* 🅿 🅦 *www.writersmuseum.com*
Opened in 1991, the museum occupies an 18th-century townhouse. There are displays relating to Irish literature over the last thousand years, although there is little about writers in the latter part of the 20th century. The exhibits include paintings, manuscripts, letters, rare editions and mementoes of Ireland's finest

Children of Lir **in the Garden of Remembrance**

authors. There are many temporary exhibits and a lavishly decorated Gallery of Writers. The museum also hosts poetry readings and lectures.

There is also a pleasant café and a specialist bookstore, which provides a useful out-of-print search service.

Hugh Lane Municipal Gallery of Modern Art

Charlemont House, Parnell Square North. **Map** C1. ⬛ *222 5565.* ⬜ *9:30am–6pm Tue–Thu, 9:30am–5pm Fri, Sat, 11am–5pm Sun.* ⬤ *24–25 Dec, public hols.* 🅿 🅦 *www.hughlane.ie*
Noted art collector Sir Hugh Lane donated his valuable collection of Impressionist paintings to Dublin Corporation in 1905. However, the failure to find a suitable location for them prompted Lane to consider transferring his gift to the National Gallery in London. The Corporation then proposed Charlemont House, the townhouse of Lord Charlemont, who built Marino Casino *(see p86)* and Lane relented. However, in 1915, before Lane's revised will could be witnessed, he died on board the torpedoed liner *Lusitania*. This led to a 50-year dispute which has been resolved by Dublin Corporation and the National Gallery swapping the collection every five years. As well as the Lane bequest the gallery also has a sculpture hall with work by Rodin and others. There is also a collection of modern Irish paintings.

An exciting new addition is the contents of Francis Bacon's studio at 7 Reece Mews, London, donated by Bacon's sole heir, John Edwards and reconstructed in the Gallery in its entirety.

By early 2006 an extension to the side of the Gallery will double the exhibition space.

Sur la Plage (c. 1876) by Edgar Degas, Hugh Lane Municipal Gallery

The impressive façade of the King's Inns, on Constitution Hill

National Wax Museum **8**

Granby Row, Parnell Square. **Map** C1.
(872 6340. **◯** Mon–Sat 10am–
5:30pm, Sun noon–5:30pm. 🎫

JUST OFF THE northwest edge of Parnell Square, this museum firmly sets its sights on attracting children. Significant space is given over to fairytale and cartoon characters such as the Flintstones, Ninja Turtles and the Simpsons. Further amusement comes in the form of a hall of mirrors while the dimly-lit Chamber of Horrors is good fun. The largest area traces Ireland's history and culture with characters from the past almost to the present day. The wax dummies of all the figures, from Wolfe Tone to President Mary McAleese, make the subjects look incredibly young – including the Reverend Ian Paisley and Pope John Paul II (who appears with the original Popemobile).

Many of the displays, encased behind glass screens, offer an audio definition of their cultural or historical importance; a useful feature as some of the subjects are not particularly well known outside Ireland. The final sec-

tion groups together several leading lights in the entertainment world, including U2, Garth Brooks and Madonna. The latest and much praised addition is a spectacular Star Wars exhibit.

King's Inns **9**

Henrietta St/Constitution Hill.
Map B1. **◯** *to the public.*

Statue at the entrance to King's Inns

THIS CLASSICALLY proportioned public building was founded in 1795 as a place of both residence and study for barristers in Dublin. The King's Inns was the name taken by the Irish lawyers' society upon Henry VIII declaring himself King of Ireland. To build it, James Gandon, famous as the architect of the Custom House *(see p68)*, chose to seal off the end of Henrietta Street, which was Dublin's first Georgian street and, at the time, one of the city's most fashionable addresses. Francis Johnston added the graceful cupola in 1816, and the building was finally completed in 1817. Inside there is a fine dining hall, and the Registry of Deeds (formerly the Prerogative Court). The west

façade has two doorways flanked by elegant Classical caryatids (statues used in place of pillars) carved by sculptor Edward Smyth. The male figure, holding book and quill, is representative of the law.

Sadly, much of the area around Constitution Hill today is less attractive than it was in Georgian times. However, the King's Inns' gardens, which are open to the public, are still pleasant to stroll around.

Smithfield **10**

Map A2.

LAID OUT in the mid-17th century as a marketplace, Smithfield used to be one of Dublin's oldest trading and residential areas hosting people coming to the cattle and horsefairs for which the area was famous. The Horsefair is still held here on the first Sunday of every month even though the two and a half acre area has received a

Children riding saddle-free through the cobbled streets of Smithfield market

£3.5 million makeover and is subject to extensive property development. The transformation of this square beside the famous fruit and fish markets is part of Dublin Council's Historical Area Regeneration Programme. The well-designed cobbled pedestrian plaza is lit by 12 gas lighting masts, each 26-m (85-ft) high, and provides Dublin with its first dedicated venue for outdoor civic events. The Chimney Viewing Tower offers 360-degree panoramic views of the city.

Old Jameson Distillery ⓫

Bow St. **Map** A2. 807 2355.
daily 9am–6pm (last tour at 5:30pm). Good Fri, 25–26 Dec.
www.irishwhiskey.ie

Proof of significant investment in the emerging Smithfield area of Dublin's northside is evident in this large exhibition, set in a restored building that formed part of John Jameson's distillery. Whiskey was produced here from 1780 until 1971. While the place is run by Irish Distillers Limited, who are obviously keen to talk up their products (the four main names are Jameson, Paddy, Bushmills and John Power), it is an impressive, entertaining and educational experience. Visits start with a video, *Uisce Beatha* (the Water of Life; *uisce* meaning "water"

Sampling different whiskeys at the Old Jameson Distillery

and the origin of the word "whiskey"). Further whiskey-related facts are then explained to visitors in the 40-minute tour. This moves around displays set out as a working distillery with different rooms devoted to the various stages of whiskey production, from grain storage right through to bottling. The tour guides are keen to point how the barley drying process differs from that used in the production of Scotch whisky: in Ireland the grain is dried through clean dry air while in Scotland it is smoked over peat. They claim that this results in a smoother Irish tipple compared to its more smoky Scottish counterpart. At the end of the tour, visitors can test this claim in the nicely appointed bar.

Horses tethered at the Sunday Horsefair

IRISH WHISKEY

It is widely claimed that the Irish were the first to produce whiskey. This is quite possibly the case, since the monks spreading Christianity across Europe supposedly learnt the skills of distillation in the East where perfume was made. Some even believe that it was St Patrick who introduced the art. In the late 1800s and early 1900s Irish whiskey was superseded somewhat by the lighter blended Scotch. In addition, sales suffered in the United States as a result of the Prohibition. Today however, Irish whiskeys are enjoying a comeback and provide fierce competition for Scotch whiskies.

Jameson 1780, at 12 years old, has a classic smooth Jameson character. It is a hearty taste of Dublin's distilling heritage.

Old Bushmills is a blended whiskey made from just one malt and a single grain. The end result is a pleasant blend of malty sweetness and aromatic dryness.

PADDY *is the classic whiskey of Cork, Ireland's second city. It is firm-bodied, with the crisp finish typical of native Cork whiskeys.*

Power and Son's Gold Label Irish, sometimes known as "Three Swallows", is a well-balanced and malty whiskey. Originally from Dublin, today it is very much a national brand.

James Gandon's Four Courts overlooking the River Liffey

Four Courts ⓬

Inns Quay. **Map** B3. **☎** 872 5555.
○ 9:30am–12:30pm, 2–4:30pm
Mon–Fri (when courts in session).

COMPLETED IN 1796 by James Gandon, this majestic building was virtually gutted 120 years later during the Irish Civil War *(see p15)* when government forces bombarded anti-Treaty rebels into submission. The adjacent Public Records Office, with documents dating back to the 12th century, was destroyed by fire. In 1932, the main buildings were restored using Gandon's original design. A copper-covered lantern dome rises above the six-columned Corinthian portico, which is crowned with the figures of Moses, Justice, Mercy, Wisdom and Authority. This central section is flanked by two wings holding the four original courts: Common Pleas, Chancery,

Exchequer and King's Bench. It is possible to walk in to the central waiting hall under the grand dome. An information panel to the right of the entrance details the building's history and functions.

St Michan's Church ⓭

Church St. **Map** B3. **☎** 872 4154.
○ mid-Mar–Oct: 10am–12:45pm,
2–4:45pm Mon–Fri, 10am–12:45pm
Sat; Nov–mid-Mar: 12:30–3:30pm
Mon–Fri; 10am–12:45pm Sat. **◫ ☑**
◫ ☒ limited.

LARGELY REBUILT in 1686 on the site of an 11th-century Hiberno-Viking church, the dull façade of St Michan's hides a more exciting interior. Deep in its vaults lie several bodies that have barely decomposed due to the dry atmosphere created by the church's magnesian limestone walls. Their

wooden caskets have cracked open, revealing the preserved bodies, complete with skin and hair. Among those thought to have been mummified in this way are the brothers John and Henry Sheares, leaders of the 1798 rebellion *(see p14)*, who were executed that year.

Other, less gory, attractions include the magnificent wood-carving of fruits and violins and other instruments above the choir. There is also an organ (1724) on which Handel is said to have played.

St Mary's Abbey Exhibition ⓮

Meetinghouse Lane. **Map** C2.
☎ 872 1490. **○** mid-Jun–mid-Sep:
10am–5pm Wed, Sun. **◫**
W www.heritageireland.ie

FOUNDED BY Benedictine monks in 1139, but then transferred to the Cistercian order eight years later, this was one of the largest and most important monasteries in medieval Ireland. When it was built, the surrounding land was peaceful countryside; to-day, what is left of this historically important abbey is hidden away in

Detail of woodcarving (c. 1724) at St Michan's Church

the sprawling backstreets that are found on the north side of the river Liffey.

As well as having control over extensive estates, including whole villages, mills and fisheries, the abbey acted as state treasury and meeting place for the Council of Ireland. It was during a council meeting in St Mary's that "Silken Thomas" Fitzgerald *(see p12)* renounced his allegiance to Henry VIII and marched out to raise the short-lived rebellion of 1534. The monastery was dissolved a few years later in 1539 and, during the 17th century, the site served as a quarry. Stone from St Mary's was pillaged and used in the construction of Essex Bridge (which was later replaced by Grattan Bridge in 1874), just to the south of the abbey.

Sadly, all that remains of the abbey today is the vaulted chamber of the old Chapter House. This houses a display on the history of the abbey and a model of how it would have looked 800 years ago.

Impressive organ in St Mary's Church

gallery. Famous past parishioners here include Arthur Guinness, who got married here in 1793, and Wolfe Tone, the leader of the United Irishmen, who was born within a stone's throw of the church and baptized here in the 1760s. The cross street and the small park to the rear of the church are named in his honour today. The playwright Sean O'Casey was also baptized at St Mary's in 1880. Church services finally ceased in the mid-1980s and, since then St Mary's has been through numerous incarnations. Now owned privately, all the listed features were restored by specialist craftsmen and it opened as a bar and restaurant in 2003. Look out for the organ and impressive stained-glass windows.

Detail of carving in St Mary's Church

The old vaulted Chapter House in St Mary's Abbey

St Mary's Church ⓯

Mary St (at Wolfe Tone St).
Map C2. 📞 *872 4088.*

IN AMONG THE produce stalls and family-run stores in the warren of streets to the west of O'Connell Street stands what was once one of the most important society churches in 18th- and 19th-century Dublin. Dating back to 1627, its design is usually credited to Sir William Robinson, the Surveyor General who also built the beautiful Royal Hospital Kilmainham *(see p82)*, and it is reckoned to be the first church in the city with a

Ha'penny Bridge ⓰

Map D3.

LINKING Temple Bar and Liffey Street on the north bank of the river, this attractive high-arched footbridge is made of cast iron and is used by thousands of people every day to cross Dublin's river. It was built by John Windsor, an ironworker from Shropshire, England. One of Dublin's most popular and most photographed sights, it was originally named the Wellington Bridge, after the Duke of Wellington. Its official name today is in fact the Liffey Bridge, but it is also known simply as the Metal Bridge. Originally opened in 1816, the bridge got its better-known nickname from the halfpenny toll that was first levied on it. The toll was scrapped in 1919 but the nickname stuck and is still used with some fondness by Dubliners and visitors alike.

A recent restoration job on the bridge, which included the installation of original period lanterns, has made it even more attractive. This is particularly true at night when it is lit up as people cross over it to go through Merchant's Arch and into the bustling nightlife of the Temple Bar area *(see pp56–7)* with all its pubs, clubs and restaurants.

The Ha'penny Bridge looking from Temple Bar to Liffey Street

FURTHER AFIELD

THERE ARE many interesting sights just outside Dublin. In the western suburbs is the Museum of Modern Art, housed in the splendid setting of the Royal Hospital Kilmainham. Phoenix Park, Europe's largest city park, offers the opportunity for a stroll in a leafy setting. Further north are the National Botanic Gardens, home to over 20,000 plant species from around the world. Nearby, Marino Casino is a fine example of Palladian architecture. The magnificent coastline is easily admired by taking the DART railway. The highlight of the riviera-like southern stretch is around Dalkey village, especially lovely Killiney Bay. One of the many Martello towers built as defences now houses a museum to James Joyce. To the northeast, slightly further from the centre, is Malahide Castle, once home of the Talbot family.

Michael Collins' gravestone

SIGHTS AT A GLANCE

Museums and Galleries
Collins Barracks **6**
Fry Model Railway Museum **14**
Guinness Storehouse **4**
James Joyce Tower **17**
Kilmainham Gaol **3**
Irish Museum of Modern Art/
    Royal Hospital Kilmainham **5**

Shaw's Birthplace **7**
Waterways Visitors' Centre **9**

Parks and Gardens
Dublin Zoo **2**
Glasnevin Cemetery **12**
National Botanic Gardens **11**
Phoenix Park **1**

Historic Buildings
Malahide Castle **13**
Marino Casino **10**

Towns and Villages
Ballsbridge **8**
Dalkey **18**
Dun Laoghaire **16**
Howth **15**
Killiney **19**

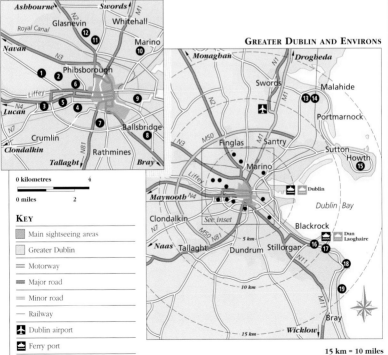

CENTRAL DUBLIN

GREATER DUBLIN AND ENVIRONS

0 kilometres   4

0 miles   2

KEY

	Main sightseeing areas
	Greater Dublin

Motorway

Major road

Minor road

Railway

Dublin airport

Ferry port

Fast ferry port

15 km = 10 miles

◁ **Boat moored in Dun Laoghaire harbour at dusk**

Phoenix Park ❶

Park Gate, Conyngham Rd, Dublin 8.
🚌 *10, 25, 26, 37, 38, 39.* 🕐 *7am–
11pm daily.* **Phoenix Park Visitor
Centre** 🔲 *677 0095.* 🕐 *Nov–mid
Mar: 9:30am–4:30pm Sat & Sun;
Apr–May: 9:30am–5:30pm daily (late
Mar & Oct to 5pm); Jun–Sep: 10am–
6pm daily.* 🔳 🔳 🔳 **President's
House** 🔳 *Oct–mid-Apr: 10:30am–
3:30pm Sat; mid-Apr–Sep: 10:30am–
4:30pm Sat.* 🆆 www.heritageireland.ie

The Phoenix Column topped by a
statue of the mythical bird

A LITTLE TO the west of the
city centre, ringed by a
wall 11 km (7 miles) long, is
Europe's largest enclosed city
park. Phoenix Park is over
700 ha (1700 acres) in size.
The name "Phoenix" is said to
be a corruption of the Gaelic
Fionn Uisce, meaning "clear
water". The **Phoenix
Column** is crowned by a
statue of the mythical bird.

Phoenix Park originated in
1662, when the Duke of
Ormonde turned the land into
a deer park. Deer still roam in
the park today. In 1745 it was
landscaped and opened to the
public by Lord Chesterfield.

Near Park Gate is the lakeside **People's Garden** – the
only part of the park which
has been cultivated. A little
further on is the
famous **Dublin Zoo**.

In addition to the
Phoenix Column, the
park has two other
striking monuments.
The **Wellington

Testimonial, a 63-m (204-ft)
obelisk, was begun in 1817
and completed in 1861. It
allegedly took so long to be
built because of the Duke of
Wellington's fall from public
favour. Its bronze bas-reliefs
were made from captured
French cannons. The 27-m
(90-ft) steel **Papal Cross**
marks the spot where Pope
John Paul II celebrated Mass
in front of more than one
million people in 1979.

Every Saturday 525 tickets
are issued to the public for a
free guided tour of **Áras an
Uachtaráin**, the Irish
President's official residence,
which was built within the
park in 1751. It was home to
various British viceroys before
becoming the residence of
the president in 1937.
Deerfield, also dating to the
18th century, is the residence
of the US Ambassador and
was once the home of Lord
Cavendish, the British Chief
Secretary for Ireland who was
murdered in 1882 by an Irish
nationalist. **Ashtown Castle**,
a restored 17th-century tower

Jogging in Phoenix Park

PHOENIX PARK

Áras An Uachtaráin ⑤
Ashtown Castle ①
Deerfield ②
Dublin Zoo ⑥
Papal Cross ③
People's Garden ⑧
Phoenix Column ④
Wellington Testimonial ⑦

KEY

🚌 Bus stop

🅿 Parking

ℹ️ Tourist information

▦▦▦ Park wall

0 metres   500

0 yards   500

Orang-utan mother and baby at Dublin Zoo

house, is adjacent to the Phoenix Park Visitor Centre.

Five times the size of Hyde Park in London and over double the size of New York's Central Park, Phoenix Park can fit playing fields for Gaelic football, hurling and polo, plus running, cycling and horseriding trails.

Visitors watching giraffe at Dublin Zoo

Dublin Zoo ❷

Phoenix Park, Dublin 8. 🎬 474 8900. 🚌 10, 10A, 25, 25A, 26, 66, 66A, 66B, 67, 67A, 68, 69, 90. ◐ Mar–Sep: 9:30am–6pm Mon–Sat, 10:30am–6pm Sun; Oct–Feb: 9:30am–dusk Mon–Sat, 10:30am–dusk Sun . 🎬 🕭 🍴 🛗 W www.dublinzoo.ie

Opened in 1830 with one wild boar and an admission price of 6d (2.5 pence), Dublin Zoo was one of the world's first zoos. In its long history, there have been many changes, and today's facility would be unrecognizable to its first visitors.

A recent development is the impressive African Plains sector. This 13-ha (32-acre) savannah, with a large lake and mature woodland, has doubled the size of the zoo and is home to giraffe, rhino, lion, zebra, hippo and cheetah.

Other sectors include the World of Primates, World of Cats, and Fringes of the Arctic, with highlights such as the orang-utan, Sumatran tiger, snow leopard and grey wolf.

Dublin Zoo has always prided itself on its breeding programme and cooperates with zoos worldwide in the conservation of endangered species. Lion breeding began in 1857, and 670 lions have been born here, including the lion that roars at the start of MGM movies.

Education is another aspect of the zoo's work: visitors will find skulls, skins, eggs and other objects at the Discovery Centre. Kids also enjoy the City Farm and the Nakuru Safari Train that runs daily in summer and at weekends in winter from the African Plains.

Kilmainham Gaol ❸

Inchicore Rd, Kilmainham, Dublin 8. 🎬 453 5984. 🚌 51B, 78A, 79. ◐ Apr–Sep: 9:30am–5pm daily; Oct–Mar: 9:30am–4pm Mon–Sat, 10am–5pm Sun; (last adm 1hr before closing). ◑ 25–26 Dec. 🎬 🛗 🛗 💻

A long tree-lined avenue runs from the Royal Hospital Kilmainham to the grim, grey bulk of Kilmainham Gaol.

The building dates from 1796, but was restored in the 1960s. From the 1790s to the mid-19th century, Kilmainham was used as a transportation depot for prisoners bound for Australia.

During its 130 years as a prison, Kilmainham housed many of those involved in the fight for Irish independence, including Robert Emmet *(see p14)* and Charles Stewart Parnell *(p15)*. The last prisoner held during the Civil War was Eamon de Valera *(p16)*, the future President of Ireland, who was released on 16 July 1924, just prior to the gaol's closure.

The tour of the Gaol starts in the chapel, where Joseph Plunkett married Grace Gifford just a few hours before he faced the firing squad for his part in the 1916 Rising *(see p15)*. The tour ends in the prison yard where Plunkett's badly wounded colleague James Connolly, unable to stand up, was strapped into a chair before being shot. It also passes the dank cells of those involved in the 1798, 1803, 1848 and 1867 uprisings, as well as the punishment cells and hanging room. Of the 16 executions that took place in the few days following the Easter Rising, 14 were carried out here. There is a video presentation, and in the exhibition space are pieces depicting various events which took place in the gaol until it finally closed in 1924. There are also personal mementoes of some of the former inmates.

Doorway and gates of the historic Kilmainham Gaol

Tasting Guinness at a local pub

Guinness Storehouse ❹

St James's Gate, Dublin 8. **C** 408 4800. ▦ 51B, 78A, 123. 🕓 9:30am–5pm daily (8pm Jul–Aug). ● Good Fri, 24–26 Dec & 1 Jan. ⬚ ♿ ⬚ 🖵 W www.guinness-storehouse.com

THE GUINNESS STOREHOUSE is a new development based in St James's Gate Brewery, the original house of Guinness, now completely remodelled. This 1904 listed building covers nearly four acres of floor space over six floors built around a huge pint glass atrium. The first impression the visitor has is of walking into a large glass pint with light spilling down from above and a copy of the original lease signed by Arthur Guinness enshrined on the floor. The Ingredients section is next where visitors can touch, smell and feel the ingredients through interactive displays. The tour continues into an authentic Georgian anteroom to 'meet' Arthur Guinness and see him at work. The Brewing Process is a noisy, steamy and 'hoppy' area giving the impression of brewing all around with full explanation of the process. The historical development of Guinness cooperage is accompanied by video footage of the craft. Models and displays tell the story of Guinness's transportation, the appeal of Guinness worldwide, and their popular advertising campaigns. The tour ends with a generous tasting of draught Guinness, either in the traditional Brewery Bar or the rooftop Gravity Bar with 360 degree views across Dublin.

The Brewing of Guinness

Label from a Guinness bottle

GUINNESS IS A BLACK BEER, known as "stout", renowned for its distinctive malty flavour and smooth, creamy head. From its humble beginnings over 200 years ago, the Guinness brewery site at St James's Gate now covers 26 ha (65 acres) and has its own water and electricity supply. It is the largest brewery in Europe and exports beers to more than 120 countries. Other brands owned by Guinness include Harp Lager and Smithwick's Ale.

HOW GUINNESS IS MADE

The four main ingredients used to brew Guinness are barley, hops, yeast and water which, contrary to popular belief, comes from the Wicklow Mountains rather than the River Liffey.

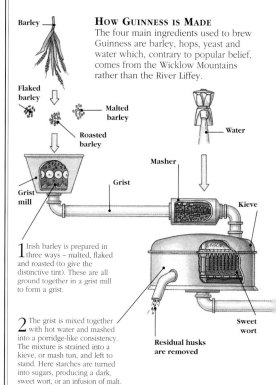

Barley

Flaked barley

Malted barley

Roasted barley

Grist mill

Grist

Water

Masher

Kieve

Sweet wort

Residual husks are removed

1 Irish barley is prepared in three ways – malted, flaked and roasted (to give the distinctive tint). These are all ground together in a grist mill to form a grist.

2 The grist is mixed together with hot water and mashed into a porridge-like consistency. The mixture is strained into a kieve, or mash tun, and left to stand. Here starches are turned into sugars, producing a dark, sweet wort, or an infusion of malt.

Guinness advertising has become almost as famous as the product itself. Since 1929, when the first advertisement announced that "Guinness is Good for You", poster and television advertising campaigns have employed many amusing images of both animals and people.

ARTHUR GUINNESS

Arthur Guinness

In December 1759, 34-year-old Arthur Guinness signed a 9,000-year lease at an annual rent of £45 to take over St James's Gate Brewery, which had lain vacant for almost ten years. At the time the brewing industry in Dublin was at a low ebb – the standard of ale was much criticized and in rural Ireland beer was virtually unknown, as whiskey, gin and poteen were the more favoured drinks. Furthermore, Irish beer was under threat from imports. Guinness started brewing ale, but was also aware of a black ale called porter, produced in London. This new beer was so called because of its popularity with porters at Billingsgate and Covent Garden markets. Guinness decided to stop making ales and develop his own recipe for porter (the word "stout" was not used until the 1920s). So successful was the switch that he made his first export shipment in 1769.

Engraving (c. 1794) of a satisfied customer

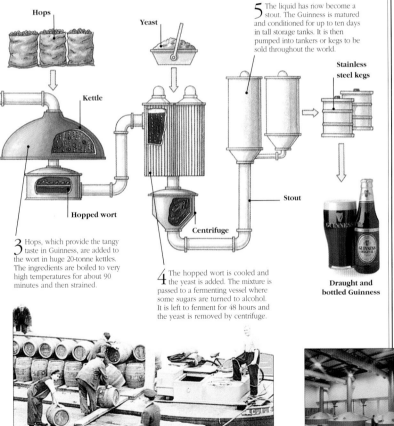

Hops

Yeast

Kettle

Hopped wort

Centrifuge

5 The liquid has now become a stout. The Guinness is matured and conditioned for up to ten days in tall storage tanks. It is then pumped into tankers or kegs to be sold throughout the world.

Stainless steel kegs

Stout

3 Hops, which provide the tangy taste in Guinness, are added to the wort in huge 20-tonne kettles. The ingredients are boiled to very high temperatures for about 90 minutes and then strained.

4 The hopped wort is cooled and the yeast is added. The mixture is passed to a fermenting vessel where some sugars are turned to alcohol. It is left to ferment for 48 hours and the yeast is removed by centrifuge.

Draught and bottled Guinness

The Guinness brewery *has relied heavily on water transport since its first export was shipped to England in 1769. The barges which, up until 1961, made the short trip with their cargo down the Liffey to Dublin Port, were a familiar sight on the river. Once at port, the stout would be loaded on to huge tanker ships for worldwide distribution.*

Steel kettles used in modern-day brewing

The elegant façade of the Royal Hospital Kilmainham

Irish Museum of Modern Art – Royal Hospital Kilmainham ❺

Kilmainham, Dublin 8. 📞 612 9900.
🚉 Heuston Station. 🚌 26, 51, 51B,
78A, 79, 90, 123. **Irish Museum of
Modern Art** 🕐 10am–5:30pm
Tue–Sat, noon–5:30pm Sun & public
hols (last adm: 5:15pm). ⚫ Good Fri,
24–26, 30 Dec. 🔒 📷 📷
♿ limited. 🌐 www.imma.ie

IRELAND'S FINEST surviving 17th-century building was laid out in 1680, and styled on Les Invalides in Paris. It was built by Sir William Robinson, who also built Marsh's Library (*see p59*), as a home for 300 wounded soldiers, rather than as a hospital as its name suggests. It retained this role until 1927 and was the first such institution in the British Isles, erected even before the Chelsea Hospital in London. When it was completed, people were so impressed by its elegant Classical symmetry that it was suggested it would be better used as the main campus of Trinity College. The building's design is functional, but the Baroque chapel has fine wood carvings and intricate heraldic stained glass. The plaster ceiling is a replica of the original, which fell down in 1902.

In 1991, the hospital's former residential quarters were imaginatively converted to house the **Irish Museum of Modern Art**. The collection includes a cross-section of Irish and international modern and contemporary art. Works are displayed on a rotating basis and include group and solo shows, retrospectives and special visiting exhibitions.

National Museum at Collins Barracks ❻

See pp84–5.

Shaw's Birthplace ❼

33 Synge St, Dublin 8. 📞 475 0854.
🚌 16, 19, 22. 🕐 May–Sep: 10am–1pm
& 2–5pm Mon–Fri, 2–5pm Sat, Sun &
public hols (groups by arrangement). ⚫
Wed. 📷 📷 🌐 www.visitdublinia.com

PLAYWRIGHT and Nobel prize-winner George Bernard Shaw was born in this Victorian house on 26 July 1856. In 1876 he followed his mother to London. She had left four years earlier with her

The recreated Victorian kitchen in Shaw's Birthplace

daughters, fed up with her husband's drinking habits. In London Shaw met his wife-to-be Charlotte Payne-Townsend. He never returned to his home in Dublin, remaining in England until his death.

Inside the house, visitors can see the young Shaw's bedroom and the kitchen where the author drank "much tea out of brown delft left to 'draw' on the hob until it was pure tannin". Also on view are the nursery, the maid's room and the drawing room, all furnished in period style.

Although there is little in the museum on Shaw's productive years, the house does give an interesting insight into the lives of a typical middle-class

GEORGE BERNARD SHAW

Born in Dublin in 1856, Shaw moved to England at the age of 20 where he began his literary career somewhat unsuccessfully as a critic and novelist. It was not until his first play was produced in 1892 that his career finally took off. One of the most prolific writers of his time, Shaw's many works include *Heartbreak House, Man and Superman*, and, perhaps most famously, *Pygmalion*, which was later adapted into the successful musical *My Fair Lady*. He often attacked conventional thinking and was a supporter of many causes, including vegetarianism and feminism. He lived an abstemious life and died in 1950 at the age of 94.

Ballsbridge ❽

Co Dublin. 🚌 5,7, 7A, 8, 18, 45.

LAID OUT mostly between 1830 and 1860, the suburb of Ballsbridge is a very exclusive part of Dublin, attracting many wealthy residents. Many of the streets are named after military heroes. Running off Pembroke Road the elegant tree-lined streets such as Raglan Road and Wellington Road are lined with prestigious red-brick houses. The area is also home to several foreign embassies – look for the striking cylindrical US Embassy building at the junction of Northumberland and Eglin roads – as well as a number of upmarket hotels and guesthouses.

Close to Baggot Street Bridge is a statue of the poet Patrick Kavanagh, depicted reclining on a bench. This attractive stretch of the Grand Canal at Lower Baggot Street was one of the poet's favourite parts of Dublin.

The southeast sector of Ballsbridge, just across the River Dodder, is dominated by the Royal Dublin Society Showgrounds (often simply abbreviated to RDS). Founded in 1731 to promote science, the arts and agriculture, the Royal Dublin Society was an instrumental mover behind the creation of most of Ireland's national museums

Late 18th-century engraving of a passenger ferry passing Harcourt Lock on the Grand Canal, taken from a painting by James Barralet

DUBLIN'S CANALS

The affluent Georgian era witnessed the building of the Grand and Royal canals linking Dublin with the River Shannon and the west coast. These two canals became the main arteries of trade and public transport in Ireland from the 1760s until the coming of the railways, which took much of the passenger business, almost a century later. However, the canals continued to carry freight until after World War II, finally closing to commercial traffic in 1960. Today the canals are well maintained and used mainly for pleasure-boating, cruising and fishing.

and galleries. The two major events at the sprawling yet graceful showgrounds are the Spring Show in May and the Horse Show in August (see p25). Throughout the rest of the year the showground plays host to various conventions, exhibitions and concerts.

The Lansdowne Road stadium, the home of the Irish national rugby and soccer teams, is another Ballsbridge landmark. Supporters in the teams' orange, green and white colours can often be seen in the area.

Stretch of the Grand Canal near the Waterways Visitors' Centre

Waterways Visitors' Centre ❾

Grand Canal Quay, Dublin 2. 📞 677 7510. 🚆 DART to Grand Canal Dock. 🚌 2, 3. 🕐 Jun–Sep: 9:30am–5:30pm daily; Oct–May: 12:30–5pm Wed–Sun. ⬤ 25 Dec. 🏷 📷 on request.

FIFTEEN MINUTES' walk from Trinity College along Pearse Street, the Waterways Visitors' Centre overlooks the Grand Canal Basin. Audiovisual displays and models illustrate the history of Ireland's inland waterways. One of the most interesting focuses on their construction: in the 18th century, canals were often called "navigations" and the men who built them were "navigators", a term shortened to "navvies". There are also exhibits on the wildlife found in the canals and surrounding marshlands.

The Royal Dublin Showground at Ballsbridge

The National Museum at Collins Barracks ❻

COMMISSIONED BY William III in 1700, this was the largest barracks in his domain, with living accommodation for over 5,000 soldiers. Originally known as Dublin Barracks it was renamed Collins Barracks after Michael Collins *(see p16)* following Irish independence. This refurbished annex of the National Museum *(see pp42–3)* displays the fine exhibits, from furniture to silver, by making full use of up-to-date technology including a multimedia catalogue and clever lighting. Currently occupying only two blocks, the museum is planned to extend eventually to fill all four wings.

Silver coffee pot

Scientific Instruments
The fascinating display of surveying and navigation instruments includes this astrolabe (c.1580–90), which was made in Prague by Erasmus Habermel.

★ Irish Silver
This silver-gilt bowl by Thomas Bolton dates from 1703. Also known as a monteith, it was used for cooling wine glasses.

Ground floor

So bl

Entran

STAR EXHIBITS

★ **William Smith O'Brien Gold Cup**

★ **Irish Silver**

★ **The Fonthill Vase**

Skinners Alley Chair
Dating back to c.1730, this gilt chair is part of the furniture collection and was made for the Protestant aldermen of Skinners Alley who were removed from the Dublin Assembly by James II.

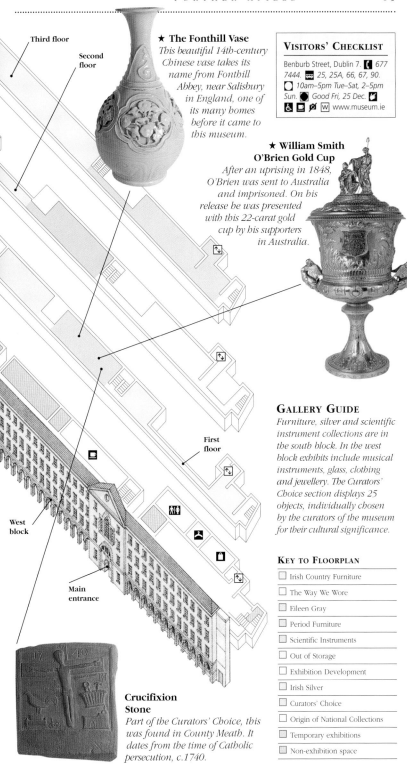

Third floor

Second floor

★ **The Fonthill Vase**
This beautiful 14th-century Chinese vase takes its name from Fonthill Abbey, near Salisbury in England, one of its many homes before it came to this museum.

VISITORS' CHECKLIST

Benburb Street, Dublin 7. (677 7444. 25, 25A, 66, 67, 90. 10am–5pm Tue–Sat, 2–5pm Sun. Good Fri, 25 Dec. & W www.museum.ie

★ **William Smith O'Brien Gold Cup**
After an uprising in 1848, O'Brien was sent to Australia and imprisoned. On his release he was presented with this 22-carat gold cup by his supporters in Australia.

First floor

GALLERY GUIDE
Furniture, silver and scientific instrument collections are in the south block. In the west block exhibits include musical instruments, glass, clothing and jewellery. The Curators' Choice section displays 25 objects, individually chosen by the curators of the museum for their cultural significance.

West block

Main entrance

KEY TO FLOORPLAN

☐ Irish Country Furniture
☐ The Way We Wore
☐ Eileen Gray
☐ Period Furniture
☐ Scientific Instruments
☐ Out of Storage
☐ Exhibition Development
☐ Irish Silver
☐ Curators' Choice
☐ Origin of National Collections
☐ Temporary exhibitions
☐ Non-exhibition space

Crucifixion Stone
Part of the Curators' Choice, this was found in County Meath. It dates from the time of Catholic persecution, c.1740.

Marino Casino ⑩

Cherrymount Crescent, off Malahide
Rd. 833 1618. DART to
Clontarf. 20A, 20B, 27A, 27B, 42,
42C, 123 IMP. Apr: noon–5pm Sat
& Sun; May: 10am–5pm daily; Jun–Oct
10am–6pm daily (Oct: 5pm); Nov–Mar
10am–4pm Sat & Sun. obligatory (last tour: 45 min before
closing). www.heritageireland.ie

THIS DELIGHTFUL little villa,
designed by Sir William
Chambers in the 1760s for
Lord Charlemont, now sits
next to a busy road. Originally built as a summer house
for the Marino
Estate, the villa
survives today
although the
main house was
pulled down in
1921. The Casino is
acknowledged to be one
of the finest examples of Neo-
Classical architecture in
Ireland. Some innovative
features were used in its construction, including chimneys
disguised as urns and hollow
columns that accommodate
drains. Outside, four fine

carved stone lions stand guard
at each of the corners. The
building's squat, compact exterior conceals 16 rooms ar-
ranged on three floors around
a central staircase. The ground
floor comprises a spacious hall
and a saloon, with beautiful
silk hangings. On the first floor
is the state bedroom.

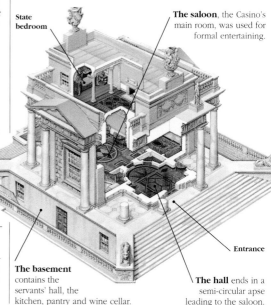

State bedroom

The saloon, the Casino's
main room, was used for
formal entertaining.

The basement
contains the
servants' hall, the
kitchen, pantry and wine cellar.

Entrance

The hall ends in a
semi-circular apse
leading to the saloon.

**Spectacular giant water lilies in the Lily
House, National Botanic Gardens**

National Botanic Gardens ⑪

Botanic Ave, Glasnevin, Dublin 9.
857 0909. 13, 19, 19A, 83, 134.
Apr–Oct: 9am–6pm Mon–Sat,
10am–6pm Sun; Nov–Mar: 10am–
4:30pm daily. 25 Dec.
free Sun at 2:30pm.

OPENED IN 1795, these
gardens are home to
Ireland's foremost centre of
botany and horticulture. They

still possess an old-
world feel, thanks to
the beautiful cast-iron
Palm House and
other curvilinear
glasshouses. These
were built between
1843 and 1869 by
Richard Turner, who
was also responsible
for the Palm House at
Kew Gardens, Lon-
don, and the glass-
houses in Belfast's
Botanic Gardens.
The 20-ha (48-acre)
park contains over
16,000 different plant species.
A particularly attractive feature is the colourful display of
Victorian carpet bedding.
Other highlights include a
renowned rose garden and
rich collections of cacti and
orchids. Pampas grass and the
giant lily were first grown in
Europe here.
  One path, known as Yew
Walk, has trees that date back
to the early 18th century and
there is also a giant redwood
that towers to 30 m (100 ft).

Glasnevin Cemetery ⑫

Finglas Rd, Glasnevin. 830 1133.
40, 40A, 40B from Parnell St, 40C.
8am–4:30pm daily.

ORIGINALLY KNOWN as
Prospect Cemetery, this
is Ireland's largest graveyard,

**Impressive gravestones in
Glasnevin Cemetery**

with approximately 1.2 million people buried here. It was established by Daniel O'Connell in 1832 and was viewed as a great achievement on his part, since Catholics were previously unable to conduct graveside ceremonies because of the Penal Laws.

O'Connell's endeavours have been rewarded with the most conspicuous monument – a 51-m (167-ft) tall round-tower in the early Irish Christian style stands over his crypt.

While the maze of head-stones exhibits a tremendous variety of designs, none, apart from O'Connell's, has been allowed by the cemetery's committee to be too resplendent. However the graves conjure up a very Irish feel with high crosses and insignia such as shamrocks, harps and Irish wolfhounds.

The most interesting sector is the oldest part by Prospect Square, on the far right-hand side. Look for the two watch-towers built into the medieval-looking walls. These were erected as lookouts for the bodysnatchers hired by 19th-century surgeons. Before the Anatomy Act permitted corpses to be donated to science, this was the only way medical students could learn. Staff at the cemetery office will gladly give directions to graves of famous people such as Charles Stewart Parnell, Eamon De Valera, Michael Collins and Brendan Behan. A small Republican plot holds the remains of Countess Constance Markievicz and Maud Gonne MacBride, while the body of poet Gerard Manley Hopkins lies in the Jesuit Plot.

Glasnevin also reveals some interesting landscaping; the paths that run between the plots follow the same routes as the original woodland trails. Copses of mature syca-more and oak have been maintained while some of the more interesting imports among the thousand trees to be found here include a Californian Giant Sequoia and a Cedar of Lebanon.

Candelabra at Malahide Castle

The oak-beamed Great Hall at Malahide Castle

Malahide Castle ⓭

Malahide, Co Dublin. 🚃 🚌 42.
📞 846 2184. 🕐 Apr–Sep:
10am–5pm Mon–Sat, 10am–6pm
Sun, public hols; Oct–Mar: 10am–5pm
Mon–Sat, 11am–5pm Sun, public hols.
♿ 📷 🎫 last tours 4:30pm.
🌐 www.visitdublin.com

NEAR THE SEASIDE dormitory town of Malahide stands a huge castle set in 100 ha (250 acres) of grounds. The castle's core dates from the 14th century but later additions, such as its rounded towers, have given it a classic fairy-tale appearance. Originally a fortress, the building served as a stately home for the Talbot family until 1973. They were staunch supporters of James II: the story goes that, on the day of the Battle of the Boyne in 1690 (see p13), 14 members of the family breakfasted here; none came back for supper. Guided tours take in the impressive oak-beamed Great Hall, the Oak Room with its carved panelling, and the castle's collection of 18th-century Irish furniture. Part of the Portrait Collection, on loan from the National Gallery (see pp46–9), can be seen here. It includes portraits of the Talbot family, and other figures such as Wolfe Tone (see p14).

Fry Model Railway Museum ⓮

Malahide Castle grounds, Malahide,
Co Dublin. 📞 846 3779. 🚌 42
from Beresford Place, near Busáras.
🚃 and DART to Malahide. 🕐 Apr–
Sep: 10am–1pm, 2–5pm Sat–Thu,
2–6pm Sun, public hols. ● Fri &
Oct–Mar. ♿ ♿
🌐 www.visitdublin.com

SET IN THE grounds of Mala-hide Castle, this collection of handmade models of Irish trains and trams was started by Cyril Fry, a railway engin-eer and draughtsman, in the 1920s. It is one of the largest such displays in the world. Running on a 32-mm wide (0-gauge) track, each detailed piece is made to scale and journeys through a landscape featuring the major Dublin landmarks, including the River Liffey complete with model barges. As well as historic trains, there are also models of the DART line, trains, buses and ferries.

A smaller room exhibits static displays of memorabilia and larger-scale models.

Howth ⓯

Co Dublin. 🚉 *DART*. **Howth Castle grounds** ◯ *8am–sunset daily.*

T HE COMMERCIAL fishing town
of Howth marks the north-
ern limit of Dublin Bay.
Before Dun Laoghaire, or
Kingstown as it was known
then, took over, Howth was
the main harbour for Dublin.
Howth Head, a huge rocky
mass, has lovely views of the
bay. A footpath runs around
the tip of Howth Head, which
is known locally as the "Nose".
Nearby is Baily Lighthouse
(1814). Sadly, much of this
area – some of Ireland's prime
real estate – has suffered from
building development.

To the west of the town is
Howth Castle, which dates
back to Norman times. Its
grounds are particularly
beautiful in May and June
when the rhododendrons and
azaleas are in full bloom. The
National Transport Museum in
the grounds is worth a visit.

Ireland's Eye, an islet and
bird sanctuary where puffins
nest, can be reached by a
short boat trip from Howth.

Yachts anchored in Dun Laoghaire harbour

Dun Laoghaire ⓰

Co Dublin. 🚉 *DART*. **National
Maritime Museum** 📞 *280 0969.*
Comhaltas Ceoltóirí Éireann 📞 *280
0295.* ◯ *music Tue, Wed, Fri & Sat
nights, céilís Fri.* 📷 🍴 🎭 **Lambert
Puppet Theatre** 📞 *280 0974.* ◯
for performances Sat & Sun 3:30pm.
📷

D UBLIN'S SOUTHERN ferry port
and yachting centre, with
its bright villas, parks and
palm trees, makes a surprising
introduction to Ireland, usually

known for its grey dampness.
On a sunny day it exudes a
decidedly Continental feel.
For a time Dun Laoghaire
(pronounced Dunleary) was
called Kingstown, after a visit
by King George IV of England
in 1821. Its original name was
restored under the Free State
in 1921, though the building
of a rail line to Dublin in 1834
resulted in the demolition of
the original *dún* or fort after
which it is named.

Many visitors arriving on the
ferry head straight for Dublin
or the countryside. However,
the town offers some magnificent walks around the harbour
and to the lighthouse along
the east pier. The pretty
People's Park at the end of
George's Street has a coffee
shop and hosts a flower show
on the second weekend in
August, while the outlying
villages of Sandycove and
Dalkey can be reached via
"The Metals"; a footpath that
runs alongside the railway line.

In the Mariners' Church is the
National Maritime Museum,
now under renovation. Exhibits
include a longboat used by
French officers during Wolfe
Tone's unsuccessful invasion
at Bantry in 1796.

Just up the road (or DART
line) in Monkstown's Belgrave
Square, is the **Comhaltas
Ceoltóirí Éireann**, Ireland's
main centre for traditional
music and dancing, with
regular music sessions and
céilís (dances). Nearby, the
Lambert Puppet Theatre on
Clifton Lane offers classic
pantomime fun for kids by the
creators of beloved children's

Martello Tower at Howth Head just north of Dublin

James Joyce Tower ⑰

Sandycove, Co Dublin. ☎ 280 9265.
🚆 DART to Sandycove. ⭘ Apr–Oct:
10am–5pm Mon–Sat, 2–6pm Sun,
public hols. ⬤ 1–2pm weekdays. 📷

STANDING ON A rocky promontory above the village of Sandycove is this Martello tower. It is one of 15 defensive towers which were erected between Dublin and Bray in 1804 to withstand a threatened invasion by Napoleon. They were named after a tower on Cape Mortella in Corsica. One hundred years later James Joyce (see p21) stayed in this tower for a week as the guest of Oliver St John Gogarty, poet and model for the Ulysses character Buck Mulligan. Gogarty rented the tower for a mere £8 per year. Today, inside the squat 12-m (40-ft) tower's granite walls is a small museum with some of Joyce's correspondence, personal belongings, such as his guitar, cigar case and walking stick, and his death mask. There are also photographs and several first editions of his works, including a deluxe edition (1935) of Ulysses illustrated by Henri Matisse. The roof, originally a gun platform but later used as a sunbathing deck by Gogarty, affords marvellous views across Dublin Bay. Directly below the tower is the Forty Foot Pool, which was traditionally an all-male nude bathing spot, but is now open to both sexes.

Guitar at the museum, James Joyce Tower

Dalkey ⑱

Co Dublin. 🚆 DART.

DALKEY WAS ONCE known as the "Town of Seven Castles", but only two of these fortified mansions, dating from the 15th and 16th centuries, now remain. They are both on the main street of this attractive village whose tight, winding roads and charming villas give it a Mediterranean feel. A little way offshore is tiny Dalkey Island, a rocky bird sanctuary with a Martello tower and a medieval Benedictine church, both now in a poor state of repair. In summer the island can be reached by a boat ride from the town's Coliemore Harbour. The island was, at one time, held by Danish pirates. In the 18th century, a Dublin club used to gather on the island to crown a mock "King of Dalkey" and his officers of state. Originally done simply for fun, the ceremony was stopped in 1797 by Lord Clare when it became a political issue. It began again in the late 1970s.

Shopfronts lining the main street of Dalkey village

Killiney ⑲

Co Dublin. 🚆 DART to Dalkey or Killiney.

SOUTH OF DALKEY, the coastal road climbs uphill before tumbling down into the winding leafy lanes around Killiney village. The route offers one of the most scenic vistas on this stretch of the east coast, with views that are often compared to those across the Bay of Naples in Italy. Howth Head is clearly visible to the north, with Bray Head (see p108) and the foothills of the Wicklow Mountains (see p105) to the south. There is another exhilarating view from the top of windswept Killiney Hill Park, off Victoria Road. It is well worth tackling the steep trail up from the village to see it. Down below is the popular pebbly beach, Killiney Strand.

View southwards from Killiney Hill over Killiney Bay towards the Wicklow Mountains

BEYOND DUBLIN

BEYOND DUBLIN

A SHORT WAY *out of central Dublin, the beautiful Irish countryside offers a wealth of pretty villages, dramatic mountains and elegant stately homes to visit. South of Dublin, the coastline down to Dun Laoghaire and beyond, with its dramatic backdrop of the Wicklow Mountains, is stunning. To the north can be found traces of some of the earliest residents in the area – the Celts.*

North of Dublin, the fertile Boyne Valley in County Meath was settled during the Stone Age. The remains of ancient sites from this early civilization fill the area and include Newgrange, the finest Neolithic tomb in Ireland. In Celtic times, the focus shifted south to the Hill of Tara, the seat of the High Kings of Ireland and the Celts' spiritual and political capital. Tara's heyday was in the 3rd century AD, but it retained its importance until the Norman invasion in the 1100s.

Norman castles, such as the immense fortress at Trim in County Meath, attest to the shifting frontiers around the region of English influence known as the Pale *(see p100)*. By the end of the 16th century, this area

Coracle from the Millmount Museum in Drogheda

incorporated nearly all the counties in the Midlands. The Boyne Valley returned to prominence in 1690, when the Battle of the Boyne ended in a landmark Protestant victory over the Catholics *(see p13)*.

The area to the south of Dublin had the strongest English influence in all of Ireland. From the 18th century onwards, wealthy Anglo-Irish families were drawn to what they saw as a stable zone, and felt confident enough to build fine mansions like the Palladian masterpieces of Russborough, Newbridge and Castletown.

For a refreshing breath of fresh air, stroll along the cliffs at Bray Head, or follow one of the invigorating walking routes in the Wicklow Mountains.

Traditional kitchen in Newbridge House

◁ **View towards the sea beyond Ardgillan Castle**

Exploring Beyond Dublin

THE COUNTRYSIDE AROUND Dublin is stunning and offers everything from stately homes to ancient burial sites and dramatic mountains to seaside villages. The Wicklow Mountains have excellent walking territory and are also home to some of the best sights, such as the elegant gardens of Powerscourt House and the monastic complex at Glendalough. The coastal stretch to the south of Dublin towards Bray is particularly scenic.

The lush gardens at Ardgillan Demesne, situated on the coast north of Dublin

SIGHTS AT A GLANCE

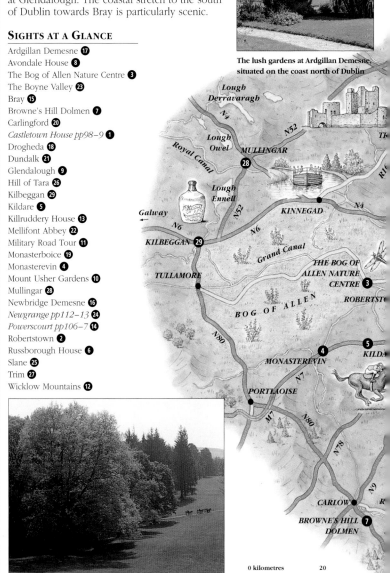

Lough Derravaragh

Lough Owel

Royal Canal

MULLINGAR 28

Lough Ennell

Galway

N6

N52

N4

N52

KINNEGAD

N4

KILBEGGAN 29

Grand Canal

THE BOG OF ALLEN NATURE CENTRE 3

TULLAMORE

BOG OF ALLEN

ROBERTST

N80

MONASTEREVIN 4

KILDA 5

PORTLAOISE

N7

M7

N80

N78

N9

CARLOW

R

BROWNE'S HILL DOLMEN 7

0 kilometres   20

0 miles   10

The extensive gardens at Avondale House

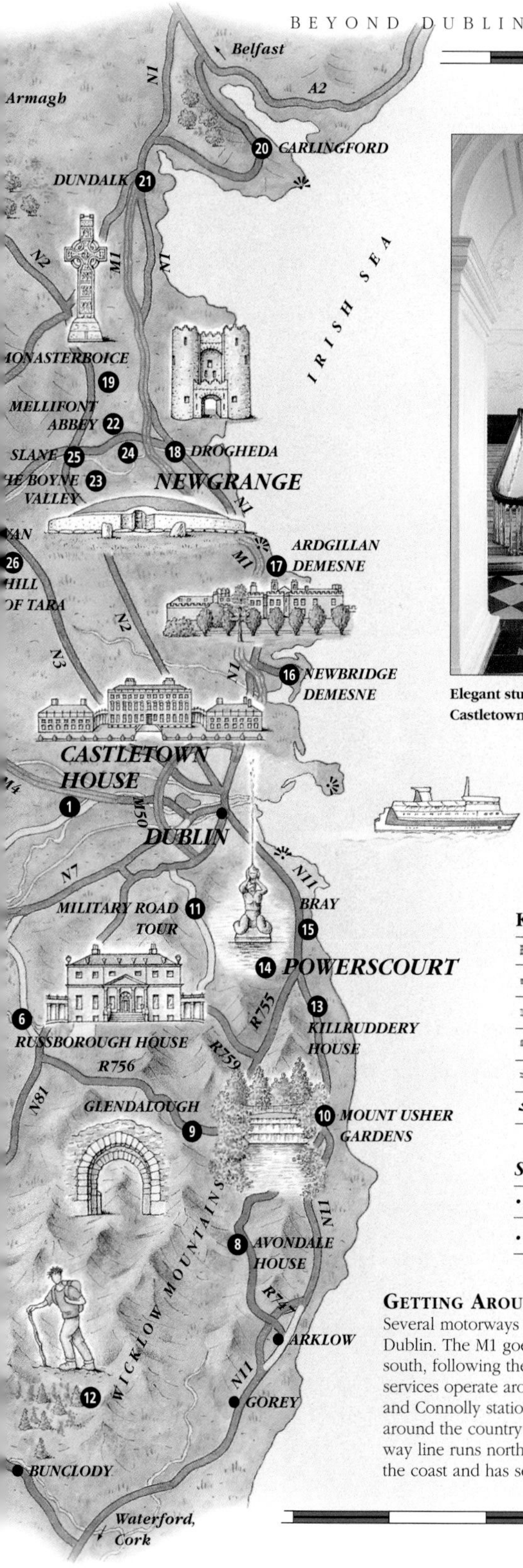

Belfast

A2

Armagh

N1

20 CARLINGFORD

DUNDALK 21

N2

I R I S H   S E A

MONASTERBOICE

19

MELLIFONT
ABBEY 22

SLANE 25   24   18 DROGHEDA

THE BOYNE 23
VALLEY   NEWGRANGE

26
HILL
OF TARA   ARDGILLAN
17 DEMESNE

N2

N3

16 NEWBRIDGE
DEMESNE

CASTLETOWN
HOUSE

M50

1

DUBLIN

N7

MILITARY ROAD 11
TOUR   BRAY

15

14 POWERSCOURT

R755

6   13 KILLRUDDERY
RUSSBOROUGH HOUSE   HOUSE
R756   R759

N81

GLENDALOUGH

9   10 MOUNT USHER
GARDENS

W I C K L O W   M O U N T A I N S

8 AVONDALE
HOUSE

R74

12   ● ARKLOW

N11

● GOREY

● BUNCLODY

Waterford,
Cork

Elegant stuccoed hall and staircase in
Castletown House

KEY

▬▬	Motorway
▬▬	Major road
▬▬	Minor road
≈	Scenic route
≋	River
✼	Viewpoint

SEE ALSO

- **Where to Stay** pp118–23

- **Where to Eat** pp124–31

GETTING AROUND

Several motorways and main roads fan out from
Dublin. The M1 goes north to Dundalk, the N11
south, following the scenic coastline. Regular train
services operate around the country from Heuston
and Connolly stations. Coach services also run all
around the country from Dublin. The DART railway line runs north and south from the city along
the coast and has several stops in central Dublin.

Castletown House **①**

See pp98–9.

Robertstown **②**

Co Kildare. 🚶 *240.* 🚌

TEN LOCKS WEST along the Grand Canal from Dublin, Robertstown is a characteristic 19th-century canalside village, with warehouses and cottages flanking the waterfront. Freight barges plied the route until about 1960, but pleasure boats have since replaced them. Visitors can take barge cruises from the quay and the Grand Canal Company's Hotel, built in 1801 for canal passengers, is now used for banquets.

Near Sallins, about 8 km (5 miles) east of Robertstown, the canal is carried over the River Liffey along the **Leinster Aqueduct**, an impressive structure built in 1783.

Bog of Allen Nature Centre **③**

Lullymore, Co Kildare. 📞 *045 860133.* 🚌 *to Newbridge & Kildare.* 🚌 *to Allenwood.* 🕐 *all year: 9:30am–5:30pm Mon–Fri.* 🏷️ 🚻 *limited.* 🌐 *www.ipcc.ie*

ANYONE INTERESTED in the natural history of Irish bogs should visit the Nature Centre, an exhibition housed in an old farm at Lullymore, 9 km (6 miles) northeast of Rathangan. It lies at the heart of the Bog of Allen, a vast expanse of raised bog that extends across the counties of Offaly, Laois and Kildare.

Japanese Gardens at Tully near Kildare

The exhibition explains the history and ecology of the bog, and features displays of flora and fauna as well as archaeological finds from the surrounding area. Guided walks are also organized to introduce visitors to the bog's delicate ecosystem and the careful conservation work that is being done.

Stacking peat for use as fuel

Monasterevin **④**

Co Kildare. 🚶 *2,200.* 🚌

THIS GEORGIAN market town lies west of Kildare, where the Grand Canal crosses the River Barrow. Waterborne trade brought prosperity to Monasterevin in the 18th century, but the locks now see little traffic. However, you can still admire the aqueduct, which is a superb example of canal engineering.

Moore Abbey, next to the church, was built in the 18th century on the site of a Cistercian monastery which was founded by St Evin, but the grand Gothic mansion owes a great deal to Victorian remodelling. Originally the ancestral seat of the earls of Drogheda, in the 1920s Moore Abbey became the home of the internationally celebrated Irish tenor, John McCormack. It has now been turned into a hospital.

Kildare **⑤**

Co Kildare. 🚶 *4,200.* 🚌 🚌
ℹ️ *Market House, May–Sep: 045 522696.* 🚌 *Thu.*

THE CHARMING and tidy town of Kildare is dominated by **St Brigid's Cathedral**, which commemorates the saint who founded a religious community on this site in AD 480. Unusually, monks and nuns lived

The Grand Canal Company's Hotel in Robertstown

here under the same roof, but this was not the only unorthodox practice associated with the community. Curious pagan rituals, including the burning of a perpetual fire, continued until the 16th century. The fire pit is visible in the grounds today. So too is a round tower, which was probably built in the 12th century and has a Romanesque doorway. The cathedral was rebuilt in the Victorian era, but the restorers largely adhered to the original 13th-century design.

🔓 **St Brigid's Cathedral**
Market Square. ○ May–Sep: daily. 🖾 donation. ♿

ENVIRONS: Kildare lies at the heart of racing country: the Curragh racecourse is nearby, stables are scattered all around and bloodstock sales take place at Kill, northeast of town.

The **National Stud** is a semi state-run bloodstock farm at Tully, just south of Kildare. It was founded in 1900 by an eccentric Anglo-Irish colonel called William Hall-Walker. He sold his foals on the basis of their astrological charts, and put skylights in the stables to allow the horses to be "touched" by sunlight or moonbeams. Hall-Walker received the title Lord Wavertree in reward for bequeathing the farm to the British Crown in 1915.

Visitors can explore the 400-ha (1,000-acre) grounds and watch the horses being exercised. Mares and stallions are generally kept in separate paddocks. The breeding stallions are expected to cover more than 100

mares per season. There is a special foaling unit where the mare and foal can rest for a few days after the birth.

The farm has its own forge and saddlery, and also a Horse Museum. Housed in old stable block, this illustrates the importance of horses in Irish life. Exhibits include the frail skeleton of Arkle, the champion steeplechaser who raced to fame in the 1960s.

Sharing the same estate as the National Stud are the **Japanese Gardens**, created by Lord Wavertree at the height of the Edwardian penchant for Orientalism. The gardens were laid out in 1906–10 by a Japanese landscape gardener called Tassa Eida, with the help of his son Minoru and 40 assistants. The impres-

HORSE RACING IN IRELAND

Ireland has a strong racing culture and, thanks to its non-elitist image, the sport is enjoyed by all. Much of the thoroughbred industry centres around the Curragh, a grassy plain in County Kildare stretching unfenced for more than 2,000 ha (5,000 acres). This area is home to many of the country's studs and training yards, and every morning horses are put through their paces on the gallops. Most of the major flat races, including the Irish Derby, take place at the Curragh racecourse just east of Kildare. Other popular fixtures are held at nearby Punchestown – most famously the steeplechase festival in April – and at Leopardstown, which also hosts major National Hunt races (*see p27*).

Finishing straight at the Curragh racecourse

sive array of trees and shrubs includes maples, mulberries, bonsai, magnolias, cherry trees and sacred bamboos.

The gardens take the form of an allegorical journey from the cradle to the grave, beginning with life emerging from the Gate of Oblivion (a cave) and leading to the Gateway of Eternity, a Zen rock garden.

St Fiachra's Garden was a millennium project completed in 1999. It was designed by Professor Martin Hallinan and commemorates St Fiachra, the Patron Saint of Gardeners.

🌺 **National Stud, Japanese & St Fiachra Gardens**
Tully. 🎫 045 521617. ○ mid-Feb–mid-Nov: 9:30am–6pm daily. 🖾♿🅿 Stud only. 🅿 🛍 W www.irish-national-stud.ie

St Brigid's Cathedral and roofless round tower in Kildare town

Castletown House ●

BUILT IN 1722–32 for William Conolly, the Speaker of the Irish Parliament, the façade of Castletown was the work of Florentine architect Alessandro Galilei and gave Ireland its first taste of Palladianism. The magnificent interiors date from the second half of the 18th century. They were commissioned by Lady Louisa Lennox, wife of William Conolly's great-nephew, Tom, who lived here from 1759. Castletown remained in the family until 1965, when it was taken over by the Irish Georgian Society. The state now owns the house and it is open to the public.

Conolly crest on an armchair

★ **Long Gallery**
The heavy ceiling sections and friezes date from the 1720s and the walls were decorated in the Pompeian manner in the 1770s.

Green drawing room

Red drawing room
The red damask covering the walls of this room is probably French and dates from the 19th century. This exquisite mahogany bureau was made for Lady Louisa in the 1760s.

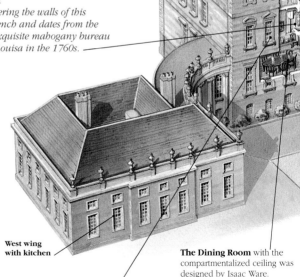

West wing with kitchen

Boudoir wall paintings
The boudoir's decorative panels, moved here from the Long Gallery, were inspired by the Raphael Loggia in the Vatican.

The Dining Room with the compartmentalized ceiling was designed by Isaac Ware.

★ Print room
In this, the only intact 18th-century print room in Ireland, Lady Louisa indulged her taste for Italian engravings. It was fashionable at the time for ladies to paste prints directly on to the wall and frame them with elaborate festoons.

VISITORS' CHECKLIST

Celbridge, Co Kildare.
628 8252. 67, 67A from Dublin. Easter Day–Sep: 10am–6pm Mon–Fri, 1–6pm Sat, Sun, public hols; Oct: 10am–5pm Mon–Fri, 1–5pm Sun, public hols. obligatory.
Summer concerts.

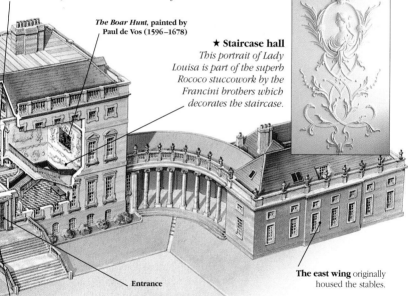

The Boar Hunt, painted by
Paul de Vos (1596–1678)

★ Staircase hall
This portrait of Lady Louisa is part of the superb Rococo stuccowork by the Francini brothers which decorates the staircase.

The east wing originally housed the stables.

Entrance

The entrance hall is an austere Neo-Classical room. Its most decorative feature is the delicate carving on the pilasters of the upper gallery.

STAR FEATURES

★ **Long Gallery**

★ **Print room**

★ **Staircase hall**

CONOLLY'S FOLLY

This folly, which lies just beyond the grounds of Castletown House, provides the focus of the view from the Long Gallery. Speaker Conolly's widow, Katherine, commissioned it in 1740 as a memorial to her late husband, and to provide employment after a harsh winter. The unusual structure of superimposed arches crowned by an obelisk was designed by Richard Castle, architect of Russborough House (*see p100*).

Saloon in Russborough House with original fireplace and stuccowork

Russborough House ❻

Blessington, Co Wicklow. ☎ 045
865239. 🚌 65 from Dublin (check
times). 🕐 May–Sep: 10am–5pm daily;
Apr & Oct: 10am–5pm Sun & public
hols only. 📷 🎫 obligatory. 🖥 🎁

T HIS PALLADIAN MANSION, built
in the 1740s for Joseph
Leeson, later Earl of Milltown,
is one of Ireland's finest
houses. Its architect, a
German called Richard Castle,
also designed Powerscourt
House *(see pp106–7)* and is
credited with introducing the
Palladian style to Ireland.

Unlike many grand estates in
the Pale, Russborough has
survived magnificently, both
inside and out. The
house claims the
longest frontage in
Ireland, with a
façade adorned
by heraldic lions
and curved
colonnades. The
interior is even
more impressive.
Many rooms feature
superb stucco dec-
oration, which was
done largely by the Italian
Francini brothers, who also
worked on Castletown House
(see pp98–9). The best

**Vernet seascape in
the drawing room**

examples are found in the
music room, saloon and
library, which are embellished
with exuberant foliage and
cherubs. Around the main
staircase, a riot of Rococo
plasterwork depicts a hunt,
with hounds clasping gar-
lands of flowers. The stucco
mouldings in the drawing
room were designed espe-
cially to enclose marine
scenes by the French artist,
Joseph Vernet (1714–89). The
paintings were sold in 1926,
but were tracked down more
than 40 years afterwards and
returned to the house.

Russborough House has
many other treasures to be
seen, including finely worked
fireplaces made of Italian
marble, imposing mahogany
doorways and priceless collections of silver, porcelain
and Gobelins tapestries.

Such riches aside, one of the
principal reasons to
visit Russborough is
to see the **Beit
Art Collection**,
famous for its
Flemish, Dutch
and Spanish Old
Master paintings.
Sir Alfred Beit,
who bought the
house in 1952,
inherited the
pictures from his
uncle – also named Alfred
Beit. The family's wealth had
come from gold mines and
diamond dealing in

**An 18th-century family enjoying the privileged lifestyle
that was typical within the Pale**

THE HISTORY OF THE PALE

The term "Pale" refers to an area around
Dublin which marked the limits of
English influence from Norman to Tudor
times. The frontier fluctuated but, at its
largest, the Pale stretched from Dundalk
in County Louth to Waterford town.
Gaelic chieftains outside the area could
keep their lands provided they agreed to
raise their heirs within the Pale.

The Palesmen supported their rulers'
interests and considered themselves the
upholders of English values. This widened
the gap between the Gaelic majority and
the Anglo-Irish, foretelling England's
doomed involvement in the country. Long
after its fortifications were dismantled,
the idea of the Pale lived on as a state of
mind. The expression "beyond the pale"
survives as a definition of those outside
the bounds of civilized society.

Kimberley, South Africa. The Beit family donated Russborough to the Beit Foundation, opening the house to the public while living in one of the wings of the house.

In 1974, 1986, 2000 and 2001, several masterpieces were stolen from the house, but all were later retrieved. Only a selection of paintings is on view at any one time, while others are on permanent loan to the National Gallery in the centre of Dublin (see pp46–9). Other paintings from the National Gallery are also on view in the house from time to time.

Russborough enjoys a fine position near the village of **Blessington**, which has a good view of the Wicklow Mountains. The house lies in the midst of wooded parkland rather than elaborate gardens. As Alfred Beit said of Irish Palladianism, "Fine architecture standing in a green sward was considered enough".

ENVIRONS: The **Poulaphouca Reservoir**, which was formed by the damming of the River Liffey, extends south from Blessington. The placid lake is popular with watersports enthusiasts, especially during the summer months, while others come simply to enjoy the lovely views of the nearby Wicklow Mountains.

Avondale House, with its colourful gardens in the foreground

Browne's Hill Dolmen ❼

Co Carlow. 🚌 🚍 to Carlow. 🅿 daily.

IN A FIELD 3 km (2 miles) east of Carlow, along the R726, stands a huge dolmen boasting the biggest capstone in Ireland. It stands in the area of Browne's Hill, where there is a stone house dating from 1763. Weighing a reputed 100 tonnes, this massive stone is embedded in the earth at one end and supported at the other by three much smaller stones. Dating back to 2000 BC, the Dolmen is thought to mark the tomb of a local chieftain. A path from the road skirts the field before reaching it.

Parnell's chair in Avondale House

Browne's Hill Dolmen, famous for its enormous capstone

Avondale House ❽

Co Wicklow. 📞 0404 46111. 🚌 🚍 to Rathdrum. **House and grounds** 🕐 mid-Mar–Oct: 11am–6pm daily (last adm to house: 5pm). 🔴 Mar–Apr, Sep–Oct: Mon, Good Fri. 🏷 🍴 🅿

LYING JUST south of Rathdrum, Avondale House was the birthplace of the 19th-century politician and patriot, Charles Stewart Parnell (see p15). Built in 1779, it passed into the hands of the Parnell family in 1795 and Charles Stewart was born here on 27 June 1846. The Georgian mansion now houses a museum dedicated to Parnell and the fight for Home Rule. The birthplace of Irish Forestry, Avondale is managed by the Irish Forestry Board but the public is free to explore the 200 ha (512 acres) of grounds, complete with picnic and children's play areas. Known as **Avondale Forest Park**, the former estate includes an impressive arboretum which was first planted in the 18th century and has had many additions made to it since 1900.

There are some lovely walks through the woods, including the magnificent Great Ride, which is one of the best, with pleasant views along the River Avonmore. There is also much wildlife in the area, including hares, rabbits and otters.

Glendalough 9

Co Wicklow. 🚌 *St Kevin's bus from Dublin.* **Ruins** ☐ *daily.* 🎫 *in summer.* **Visitors' centre** 📞 *0404 45325/ 45352.* ☐ *daily* ● *24–27 Dec.* 🎫 ♿ 🎫 *on request.*

THE STEEP, WOODED slopes of Glendalough, the "valley of the two lakes", harbour one of Ireland's most atmospheric monastic sites. Established by St Kevin in the 6th century, the settlement was sacked time and again by the Vikings but nevertheless flourished for over 600 years. Decline set in only after English forces partially razed the site in 1398, though it functioned as a monastic centre until the Dissolution of the Monasteries in 1539 (*see p12*). Pilgrims kept on coming to Glendalough even after that, particularly on St Kevin's feast day, 3 June, which was often a riotous event.

The age of the buildings is uncertain, but most date from the 8th to 12th centuries. Many were restored during the 1870s.

View along the Upper Lake at Glendalough

The main group of ruins lies east of the Lower Lake, but other buildings associated with St Kevin are found by the Upper Lake. Here, where the scenery is much wilder, it is possible to enjoy more the tranquillity of Glendalough and to escape the crowds which inevitably descend on the site. Try to arrive as early as possible in the day, particularly during the peak tourist season. Enter the monastery through the double stone arch of the **Gatehouse**, the only surviving example in Ireland of a gateway into a monastic enclosure.

St Kevin's Kitchen

A short walk leads to a graveyard with a **Round tower** in one corner. Reaching 30 m (100 ft) in height, this is one of the finest of its kind in the country. Its cap was rebuilt in the 1870s using stones found inside the tower. The roofless **Cathedral** nearby dates mainly from the 12th century and is

Remains of the Gatehouse, the original entrance to Glendalough

the valley's largest ruin. At the centre of the churchyard stands the tiny **Priests' House**, whose name derives from the fact that it was a burial place for local clergy. The worn carving of a robed figure above the door is thought possibly to be St Kevin, flanked by two disciples. East of here, **St Kevin's Cross** dates from the 8th century and is one of the best preserved of Glendalough's various High Crosses. Made of granite, the cross may once have marked the boundary of the monastic cemetery. Below, nestled in the lush valley, a minuscule oratory with a steeply pitched stone roof is a charming sight. Erected in the 11th century or even earlier, it is popularly known as **St Kevin's Kitchen**; this is perhaps because its belfry, which is thought to be a later addition, resembles a chimney. One of the earliest churches at Glendalough, **St Mary's**, lies across a field to

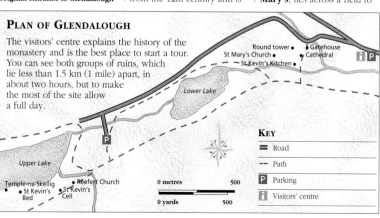

PLAN OF GLENDALOUGH

The visitors' centre explains the history of the monastery and is the best place to start a tour. You can see both groups of ruins, which lie less than 1.5 km (1 mile) apart, in about two hours, but to make the most of the site allow a full day.

Round tower •　　• Gatehouse
St Mary's Church •　　• Cathedral
　　• St Kevin's Kitchen •
　　　　Lower Lake

ℹ️ P

Upper Lake

Temple-na-Skellig •　• Reefert Church
• St Kevin's　• St Kevin's
　Bed　　Cell

P

KEY

🟦	Road
--	Path
P	Parking
ℹ️	Visitors' centre

0 metres　　　　　500

0 yards　　　　　500

ST KEVIN AT GLENDALOUGH

St Kevin was born in 498, a descendant of the royal house of Leinster. He rejected his life of privilege, however, choosing to live instead as a hermit in a cave at Glendalough. He later founded a monastery here, and went on to establish a notable centre of learning devoted to the care of the sick and the copying and illumination of manuscripts. St Kevin attracted many disciples to Glendalough during his lifetime, but the monastery became more celebrated as a place of pilgrimage after his death in around 618.

Colourful legends about the saint make up for the dearth of facts about him. That he lived to the age of 120 is just one of the many stories told about him. Another tale claims that one day, when St Kevin was at prayer, a blackbird laid an egg in one of his outstretched hands. According to legend the saint remained in the same position until the bird was hatched.

Round tower at Glendalough

the west. Some traces of hood moulding (intended to throw off water) are visible outside the east window. The path along the south bank of the river leads visitors to the Upper Lake. This is the site of more monastic ruins and is also the chief starting point for walks through the valley and to a number of abandoned lead and zinc mines.

Situated in a grove not far from the Poulanass waterfall are the ruins of the **Reefert Church**, a simple building. Its unusual name is a corruption of *Righ Fearta*, meaning "burial place of the kings"; the church may mark the site of an ancient cemetery. Near

here, on a rocky spur overlooking the Upper Lake, stands **St Kevin's Cell**, the foundation of a beehive-shaped structure which is thought to have once been the home of the hermit.

There are two sites on the south side of the lake which cannot be reached on foot but are visible from the shore on the other side. **Temple-na-Skellig**, or the "church on the rock", was supposedly built on the site of the first church that was founded by St Kevin at Glendalough. To the east of it, carved into the cliff, is **St Kevin's Bed**. This small cave, in fact little more than a rocky ledge, is thought possibly to

have been used as a tomb in the Bronze Age, but it is more famous as St Kevin's favourite retreat. It was from this point that the saint allegedly rejected the advances of a naked woman by picking her up and throwing her into the lake.

Mount Usher Gardens ⑩

Ashford, Co Wicklow. ☏ 0404 40116. 🚌 to Ashford. ☐ 4 Mar–31 Oct: 10:30am–6pm daily (last adm: 5:20pm). 🅿 🚻 🛍 🛍 limited. 🎫 call to book. 🖥 www.mount-usher-gardens.com

SET ON THE BANKS of the River Vartry just east of Ashford are the Mount Usher Gardens. They were designed in 1868 by a Dubliner, Edward Walpole, who imbued them with his strong sense of romanticism.

The 8 ha (20 acres) are laid out in a wild, informal style and contain around 4,000 different species of plants including rare shrubs and trees, from Chinese conifers and bamboos to Mexican pines and pampas grass. The Maple Walk is particularly glorious in the autumn, and in spring the rhododendron collection is brilliant with reds and pinks.

The river provides the main focus of the Mount Usher Gardens and, amid the exotic and lush vegetation, the visitor can usually catch a glimpse of herons standing on the many weirs and little bridges that cross the river.

Mount Usher Gardens, on the banks of the River Vartry

A Tour of the Military Road ⑪

Rare red squirrel

THE BRITISH BUILT the Military Road through the heart of the Wicklow Mountains during a campaign to flush out Irish rebels after an uprising in 1798 *(see p14)*. Now known as the R115, this winding road takes you through the emptiest and most rugged landscapes of County Wicklow. Beautiful countryside, in which deer and other wildlife flourish, is characteristic of the whole of this tour.

Powerscourt Waterfall ⑨
The River Dargle cascades 130 m (425 ft) over a granite escarpment to form Ireland's highest waterfall.

Glencree ①
The former British barracks in Glencree are among several found along the Military Road.

Great Sugar Loaf ⑧
The granite cone of Great Sugar Loaf Mountain can be climbed in under an hour from the car park on its southern side.

Sally Gap ②
This remote pass is surrounded by a vast expanse of blanket bog dotted with pools and streams.

Lough Tay ⑦
Stark, rocky slopes plunge down to the dark waters of Lough Tay. Though it lies within a Guinness-owned estate, the lake is accessible to walkers.

Glenmacnass ③
After Sally Gap, the road drops into a deep glen where a waterfall spills dramatically over rocks.

Roundwood ⑥
The highest village in Ireland at 238 m (780 ft) above sea level, Roundwood enjoys a fine setting. Its main street is lined with pubs, cafés and craft shops.

Glendalough ④
This ancient lakeside monastery *(see pp102–3)*, enclosed by wooded slopes, is the prime historical sight in the Wicklow Mountains.

TIPS FOR DRIVERS

Length: 96 km (60 miles).
Stopping-off points: There are several pubs and cafés in Enniskerry (including Poppies, an old-fashioned tearoom), and also in Roundwood, but this area is better suited for picnics. There are numerous marked picnic spots south of Enniskerry.

0 kilometres   5

0 miles   3

KEY

▬▬▬ Tour route

═ ═ ═ Other roads

🌾 Viewpoint

Vale of Clara ⑤
This picturesque wooded valley follows the River Avonmore. It contains the tiny village of Clara, which consists of two houses, a church and a school.

Wicklow Mountains ⑫

Co Wicklow. 🚆 to Rathdrum & Wicklow. 🚌 to Enniskerry, Wicklow, Glendalough, Rathdrum & Avoca. 🛈 Rialto House, Fitzwilliam Square, Wicklow, 0404 69117. 🌐 www.eastcoastmidlands.ie

THE INACCESSIBILITY of the rugged Wicklow Mountains meant that they once provided a safe hideout for opponents of English rule. Rebels who took part in the 1798 uprising sought refuge here. The building of the **Military Road**, started in 1800, made the area slightly more accessible, but the mountains are still thinly populated. There is little traffic to disturb enjoyment of the exhilarating scenery of rock-strewn glens, lush forest and bogland where heather gives a purple sheen to the land. Turf-cutting is still a thriving cottage industry, and you can often see peat stacked up by the road. Numerous walking trails weave through these landscapes. Among them is the **Wicklow Way**, which extends 132 km (82 miles) from Marlay Park in Dublin to Clonegal in County Carlow. It is marked but not always easy to follow, so do not set out without a good map. Although no peak exceeds 915 m (3,000 ft), the Wicklow Mountains can be dangerous in bad weather.

A good starting point for exploring the northern area is the picture-postcard estate village of **Enniskerry**, close

View across the Long Ponds to Killruddery House

to Powerscourt *(see pp106–7)*. To the south, you can reach Glendalough *(see pp102–3)* and the **Vale of Avoca**. The beauty of this gentle valley was captured in the poetry of Thomas Moore (1779–1852): "There is not in the wide world a valley so sweet as that vale in whose bosom the bright waters meet" – a reference to the confluence of the Avonbeg and Avonmore rivers, the so-called **Meeting of the Waters** *(see p101)*. Nestled among wooded hills at the heart of the valley is the hamlet of Avoca, where the **Avoca Handweavers** produce colourful tweeds in the oldest hand-weaving mill in Ireland, in operation since 1723.

Further north, towards the coast near Ashford, the River Vartry rushes through the deep chasm of the **Devil's Glen**. On entering the valley, the river falls 30 m (100 ft) into a pool known as the Devil's Punchbowl. There are good walks around here, with fine views of the coast.

🏛 Avoca Handweavers
Avoca. 📞 0402 35105. ◷ 9:30am–5:30pm daily. ⬤ 25–26 Dec. **Weaving shed** ◷ 8am–4:30pm Mon–Fri, 10am–5pm Sat & Sun. 🍴 🏛 ♿

Killruddery House and Gardens ⑬

Bray, Co Wicklow. 📞 0404 46024. ◷ Apr–Sep (House: May–Sep): 1pm–5pm daily. 🎫 ♿ limited. 🌐 www.killruddery.com

KILLRUDDERY HOUSE lies just to the south of Bray, in the shadow of Little Sugar Loaf Mountain. Built in 1651, it has been the family seat of the Earls of Meath ever since, although it was remodelled in the 19th century.

The house contains some good carving and stuccowork, but it is a rather faded stately home. The real charm stems from its formal gardens. Laid out in the 1680s by a French gardener named Bonet, who also worked at Versailles, they feature romantic parterres and an array of hedges, trees and shrubs. The sylvan theatre, a small enclosure surrounded by a bay hedge, is the only known example in Ireland.

The garden centres on the Long Ponds, a pair of canals which extend 165 m (550 ft) and were once used to stock fish. Beyond, an enclosed pool leads to a Victorian arrangement of paths flanked by statues and hedges of yew, beech, lime and hornbeam.

Colourful moorland around Sally Gap in the Wicklow Mountains

Powerscourt ⑭

Laocöon statue on upper terrace

THE GARDENS AT POWERSCOURT are probably the finest in Ireland, both for their design and their dramatic setting at the foot of Great Sugar Loaf Mountain. The house and grounds were commissioned in the 1730s by Richard Wingfield, the first Viscount Powerscourt. The gardens fell into decline but, in 1840, the original scheme was revived. New ornamental gardens were completed in 1858–75 by the seventh Viscount, who added gates, urns and statues collected during his travels on the Continent. Gutted by an accidental fire in 1974, the ground floor and the ballroom on the first floor have been renovated.

Bamberg Gate
Made in Vienna in the 1770s, this gilded wrought-iron gate was brought to Powerscourt by the seventh Viscount from Bamberg Cathedral in Bavaria.

The walled gardens include a formal arrangement of clipped laurel trees but are also used for growing plants for Powerscourt's gardens.

Entrance

Statue of Laocöon

The pets' cemetery contains the graves of Wingfield family dogs, cats and even horses and cattle.

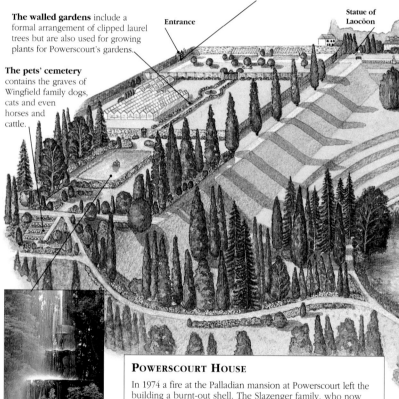

Dolphin pond
This pool, designed as a fish pond in the 18th century, is enclosed by exotic conifers in a lovely secluded garden.

POWERSCOURT HOUSE

In 1974 a fire at the Palladian mansion at Powerscourt left the building a burnt-out shell. The Slazenger family, who now own the estate, have restored part of the house; the ground floor now incorporates a terrace café, speciality shops and house exhibition describing the history of the estate. Originally built in 1731 on the site of a Norman castle, the house was designed by Richard Castle, also the architect of Russborough House (*see p100*).

Powerscourt ablaze in 1974

★ The Perron
This superb Italianate stairway, added in 1874, leads down to the Triton Lake, which is guarded by two statues of the winged horse Pegasus and the emblem of the Wingfield family.

VISITORS' CHECKLIST

Enniskerry, Co Wicklow. 📞 204 6000. 🚌 Alpine Coach from Bray DART station. ⬤ 9:30am–5:30pm daily (gardens open until dusk). 🅿 ♿ 🍴 🛍 garden centre. 🌐 www.powerscourt.ie.

Pebble mosaic
Many tonnes of pebbles were gathered from nearby Bray beach to build the Perron and to make this mosaic on the terrace.

The Italian garden is laid out on terraces which were first cut into the steep hillside in the 1730s.

The Pepper Pot Tower was built in 1911.

★ Triton Lake
Made for the first garden, the lake takes its name from its central fountain, which is modelled on a 17th-century work by Bernini in Rome.

★ Japanese gardens
These enchanting Edwardian gardens, created out of bogland, contain Chinese conifers and bamboo trees.

STAR FEATURES

★ The Perron

★ Japanese gardens

★ Triton Lake

Bray ⑮

Co Wicklow. 🚶 33,000. 🚇 DART.
🅿 ℹ Old Court House, Main St,
286 7128/286 6796. 🆆 www.bray.ie

ONCE A REFINED Victorian
resort, Bray is nowadays
a brash holiday town, with
amusement arcades and fish-
and-chip shops lining the
seafront. Its beach attracts huge
crowds in summer, including
many young families. Anyone
in search of peace and quiet
can escape to nearby Bray
Head, where there is scope for
bracing cliffside walks. Bray
also makes a good base from
which to explore the Wicklow
Mountains (see p105), the
delightful coastal villages of
Killiney and Dalkey (see p89)
and Powerscourt House and
Gardens (see pp106–7).

**Tourist road train on the seafront
esplanade at Bray**

Newbridge
Demesne ⑯

Donabate, Co Dublin. 📞 843 6534.
🚇 to Donabate. 🚌 33B from
Swords. **House and Courtyard**
⭕ Apr–Sep: Tue–Sun, public hols;
Oct–Mar: Sat, Sun, public hols (pm
only). ⚫ 25–26 Dec. 📷 house
only (obligatory). ♿ courtyard only.
Park ⭕ daily. 🆆 www.fingal-
dublin.com

NEWBRIDGE IS ON the edge
of the seaside village of
Donabate, 19 km (12 miles)
north of Dublin. The house
itself is a delight for enthusiasts
of Georgian architecture and
decor. The house was designed
by George Semple in 1737 for
Archbishop Charles Cobbe,
and it remained the family

Connemara Pony stabled at Newbridge House

home until 1986, when it was
bought by the local council.
The Cobbe family retains the
use of the upstairs quarters.

The highlight of the house
tour is the red drawing room,
one of the best-preserved
Georgian rooms in the country.
Its rich red decor is comple-
mented by fine plasterwork
by Richard Williams and by
some impressive portrait and
landscape paintings. Its contents have remained unaltered
since at least the 1820s.

Also on view are the size-
able, airy dining room, a large
kitchen with an enormous
stock of utensils, and the
Museum of Curiosities –
a small room filled to the
rafters with artifacts collected
from 1790 onwards by Cobbe
family members on their
foreign travels. Housed in
cabinets, some of which date
back to the late 1700s, are
unusual and bizarre items
such as delicately carved
ostrich eggs, snakeskins and
stuffed animals.

The cobbled courtyard has
been restored and now has
displays of aspects of late

18th-century
life, including
dairy production,
carpentry and
forging. This
and the new
playground make
it a popular spot
with families.
It also houses
rare goat and
pony breeds,
including the
native Conne-
mara pony, as well as a
pleasant tea room. The Lord
Chancellor's intricately detailed
ceremonial carriage which is
on loan from the National
Museum (see pp42–3) is an
incongruous exhibit but
considered to be one of the
best examples of carriage-
work in existence.

Footpaths wind through the
woodland, and the elegant,
rolling grounds of Newbridge,
which are landscaped in the
style of an English estate.

Ardgillan
Demesne ⑰

Balbriggan, Co Dublin. 📞 849 2212.
🚌 33 via Skerries to Balbriggan.
Castle ⭕ Apr–Sep: 11am–6pm Tue–
Sun & public hols (Jul–Aug: daily); Oct–
Mar: 11am–4:30pm Tue–Sun & public
hols. ⚫ 23 Dec–1 Jan. 📷 ♿ except
kitchen. **Park and Gardens** ⭕ daily.
🆆 www.visitdublin.com

IN BETWEEN THE very likeable
resort towns of Skerries
and Balbriggan, the Ardgillan
Demesne is set on a high
stretch of coastline and offers

The elegant façade of Newbridge House

Stately drawing room in Ardgillan Castle

a particularly pleasant vantage point for stunning views over Drogheda Bay. Its sweeping and expansive grounds, which cover 78 ha (194 acres), incorporate various ornamental gardens, including a rose garden and a walled kitchen garden, as well as rolling pasture and dense woodland (the name Ardgillan means "high wooded area").

In the grounds stands Ardgillan Castle, which was built in 1737 by the Reverend Robert Taylor. The rooms on the ground floor are all furnished in Georgian and Victorian styles and the basement kitchen also retains its original decor. Upstairs there is an exhibition space which houses a permanent collection of old maps.

Drogheda ⓲

Co Louth. 🏘 28,000. 🚊 🚌 🛈 Bus Station, Donore Rd, 041 9837070, 9:30am–5:30pm Mon–Sat. 🚌 Sat.

Iₙ ₜₕₑ 14ᴛʜ ᴄᴇɴᴛᴜʀʏ, this historic Norman port situated near the mouth of the River Boyne was one of Ireland's most important towns. It was first captured by the Danes in AD 911 and later heavily fortified by the Normans. However, the place seems never to have fully recovered from a vicious attack by the English general Oliver Cromwell in 1649, during which 3,000 citizens were killed after refusing to surrender. Although it looks rather dilapidated today, the town has retained its original street plan and has a rich medieval heritage. Little remains of Drogheda's Norman defences but **St Lawrence Gate**, a fine 13th-century barbican, has survived. The **Butter Gate** is the only other surviving gate. Near St Lawrence Gate there are two churches called **St Peter's**. The one belonging to the Church of Ireland, built in 1753, is the more striking and has some splendid gravestones. The Catholic church, on West Street and dating from 1791, is worth visiting just to see the embalmed head of Oliver Plunkett, an archbishop who was martyred in 1681. It is displayed in an elaborate glass case beside its certificate of authenticity, dated 1682.

South of the river you can climb Millmount, a Norman motte that is topped by a Martello tower. As well as providing a good view, this is the site of the **Millmount Museum**, which contains an interesting display of artifacts relating to the town and its history, as well as a number of craft workshops.

Gramophone in the Millmount Museum

🏛 Millmount Museum
Millmount Square. 📞 041 9833097. 🕐 Tue–Sun. 🕐 10 days at Christmas. 📷 🚫 🚻 Ⓦ www.millmount.net

Monasterboice ⓳

Co Louth. 🚌 to Drogheda. 🕐 daily.

Fₒᴜɴᴅᴇᴅ ɪɴ ᴛʜᴇ 5th century by an obscure disciple of St Patrick called St Buite, this monastic settlement is one of the most famous religious sites in Ireland. The ruins of the medieval monastery are enclosed within a graveyard in a lovely secluded spot to the north of Drogheda. The site includes a roofless round tower and two churches, but Monasterboice's greatest treasures are its 10th-century High Crosses, carved to help educate an illiterate populace.

Muiredach's High Cross is the finest of its kind in Ireland, and its sculpted biblical scenes are still remarkably fresh. They depict the life of Christ on the west face, while the east face features mainly Old Testament scenes. These include Moses striking the rock to get water for the Israelites and David struggling with Goliath. The cross is named after an inscription on the base which reads: "A prayer for Muiredach by whom this cross was made", which, it is thought, may refer to the abbot of Monasterboice.

The 6.5-m (21-ft) West Cross, also known as the Tall Cross, is one of the largest in Ireland. The carving has not lasted as well as on Muiredach's Cross, but scenes from the Death of Christ can still be made out. The North Cross, which is the least notable of the three, features a Crucifixion illustration and a carved spiral pattern.

Round tower and West High Cross at Monasterboice

Thatched cottage in Carlingford on the mountainous Cooley Peninsula

Carlingford ⑳

Co Louth. 🚶 650. 🚌 ℹ️ **Holy Trinity Heritage Centre** *Churchyard Rd, 042 9373454.* 🕐 *10am–12:30pm, 2–4:30pm Mon–Fri.* 🔲 *www.fjord lands.org* **Carlingford Adventure Centre** *Tholsel St.* 📞 *042 9373100.* 🕐 *9am–5:30pm daily.* ⚫ *two weeks at Christmas.* 🔲 *www.carlingfordadventure.com*

THIS IS A PICTURESQUE fishing village, beautifully located between the mountains of the Cooley Peninsula and the waters of Carlingford Lough. The border with Northern Ireland runs right through the centre of this drowned river valley, and from the village you can look across to the Mountains of Mourne on the Ulster side. Carlingford is an interesting place to explore, with its pretty whitewashed cottages and ancient buildings clustered along medieval alleyways. The ruins of **King John's Castle**, built by the Normans to protect the entrance to the lough, still dominate the village. The **Holy Trinity Heritage Centre**, which is housed in a medieval church, tells the history of the port from Anglo-Norman times.

Carlingford is the country's oyster capital, and its oyster festival in August draws large crowds. The lough is popular for watersports and in summer cruises leave from the quay.

Carlingford is well placed for hikes on the Cooley Peninsula. The **Carlingford Adventure Centre** provides information on walking and water activities.

ENVIRONS: A scenic route weaves around the **Cooley Peninsula**, skirting the coast and then cutting through the mountains. The section along the north coast is the most dramatic: just 3 km (2 miles) northwest of Carlingford, in the **Slieve Foye Forest Park**, a road climbs to give a breathtaking view over the hills and lough.

The Táin Trail, which you can join at Carlingford, is a 30-km (19-mile) circuit through some of the peninsula's most rugged scenery, with cairns and other prehistoric sites dotted over the moorland. Keen hikers can walk it in a day.

Dundalk ㉑

Co Louth. 🚶 30,000. 🚌 🚂 ℹ️ *Jocelyn St, 042 9335484.* 🛒 *Thu.*

DUNDALK ONCE marked the northernmost point of the Pale, the area controlled by the English during the Middle Ages *(see p100)*. Now, lying midway between Dublin and Belfast, it is the last major town before you reach the Northern Ireland border.

Dundalk is the gateway to the Cooley Peninsula, but there is little worth stopping for in the town itself. However, the **County Museum**, which is housed in an 18th-century distillery, gives an insight into some of Louth's traditional industries, such as beer-making.

🏛 **County Museum**
Jocelyn St. 📞 *042 9327056.* 🕐 *10:30am–5:30pm Tue–Sat, 2–6pm Sun.* ⚫ *25–26 Dec, 1 Jan.* 🈁 ♿ 🔲 *www.louthonline.com*

Mellifont Abbey ㉒

Cullen, Co Louth. 📞 *041 9826459.* 🚌 *to Drogheda.* 🚌 *to Drogheda or Slane.* 🕐 *May–Oct: 10am–6pm daily (last adm: 5:15pm).* 🈁

ON THE BANKS of the River Mattock, 10 km (6 miles) west of Drogheda, lies the first Cistercian monastery to have been built in Ireland. Mellifont was founded in 1142 on the orders of St Malachy, the Archbishop of Armagh. He was influenced by St Bernard, who was behind the success of the Cistercian Order in Europe. The archbishop introduced not only Cistercian rigour to Mellifont, but also the formal style of monastic architecture used on the continent. In 1539, the abbey was closed and turned into a fortified house. William of Orange used it as his headquarters during the Battle of the Boyne in 1690. It is now a ruin, but it is still possible to appreciate the scale and plan of the original complex. Little survives of the abbey church but, to the south of it, enclosed by what remains of the Romanesque cloister, is the most interesting building at Mellifont: a unique 13th-century lavabo where monks came to wash their hands in a

Glazed medieval tiles at Mellifont Abbey

Ruined lavabo at Mellifont Abbey

THE BATTLE OF THE BOYNE

In 1688, the Catholic King of England, James II, was deposed from his throne, to be replaced by his Protestant daughter, Mary, and her husband, William of Orange. Determined to win back the crown, James sought the support of Irish Catholics, and challenged William at Oldbridge by the River Boyne west of Drogheda. The Battle of the Boyne took place on 12 July 1690, with James's poorly trained force of 25,000 French and Irish Catholics facing William's hardened army of 36,000 French Huguenots, Dutch, English and Scots. The Protestants triumphed and James fled to France, after a battle that signalled the beginning of total Protestant power over Ireland. It ushered in the confiscation of Catholic lands and the suppression of Catholic interests, sealing the country's fate for the next 300 years.

William of Orange leading his troops at the Battle of the Boyne, 12 July 1690

---

fountain before meals. Four of the building's original eight sides survive, each with a graceful Romanesque arch. On the eastern side of the cloister stands the 14th-century chapter house. It has an impressive vaulted ceiling and a floor laid with glazed medieval tiles taken from the abbey church.

The Boyne Valley ㉓

Co Meath. 🚌 to Drogheda. 🚌 to Slane or Drogheda. 🛈 Brú na Bóinne interpretive centre, 041 9880300. 🌐 www.heritageireland.ie

Known as Brú na Bóinne, the "Palace of the Boyne", this river valley was the cradle of Irish civilization. The fertile soil supported a sophisticated society in Neolithic times. Much evidence survives, in the form of ring forts, passage graves and sacred enclosures. The most important Neolithic monuments in the valley are three passage graves: supreme among these is **Newgrange** (see pp112–13), but **Dowth** and **Knowth** are significant too. The Boyne Valley also encompasses the Hill of Slane and the Hill of Tara (see p114), both major sites in Celtic history. The whole area is rich in prehistory, and with monuments predating Egypt's pyramids, the Boyne Valley has been dubbed the Irish "Valley of the Kings".

Knowth and Newgrange can only be seen on a tour run by the interpretive centre near Newgrange, which also details the area's Stone Age heritage.

🏛 Dowth

Off N51, 3 km (2 miles) E of Newgrange. ⬤ to the public.
The passage grave at Dowth was plundered in Victorian times by souvenir hunters and has not been fully excavated since. Visitors cannot approach the tomb, but may walk around the outside of the monument.

🏛 Knowth

1.5 km (1 mile) NW of Newgrange. ⬤ as Newgrange (see pp112–13).
Knowth outdoes Newgrange in several respects, above all in the quantity of its treasures – Europe's greatest concentration of megalithic art. In addition, the site was occupied for a much longer period – from Neolithic times to about 1400.

Unusually, Knowth has two passage tombs rather than one. The excavations begun in 1962 are now complete and the site is open. The tombs can only be viewed externally to prevent further decay and visitors must sign up for tours via Brú na Bóinne (see p112).

River Boyne near the site of the Battle of the Boyne

Newgrange ㉔

Tri-spiral carving in chamber

THE ORIGINS of Newgrange, one of the most important passage graves in Europe, are steeped in mystery. According to Celtic lore, the legendary kings of Tara *(see p114)* were buried here, but Newgrange predates them. Built in around 3200 BC, the grave was left untouched by all invaders (though not by tomb robbers) and was eventually excavated in the 1960s. Archaeologists then discovered that on the winter solstice (21 December), rays of sun enter the tomb and light up the burial chamber – making it the oldest solar observatory in the world. All visitors to Newgrange and Knowth are admitted through the visitors' centre *(see p111)* from where tours of the historic sight are taken; early arrival is advised in summer to avoid long queues.

Basin stone
The chiselled stones, found in each recess, would have once contained funerary offerings and the bones of the dead.

The chamber has three recesses or side chambers: the north recess is the one struck by sunlight on the winter solstice.

Chamber ceiling
The burial chamber's intricate corbelled ceiling, which reaches a height of 6 m (20 ft) above the floor, has survived intact. The overlapping slabs form a conical hollow, topped by a single capstone.

CONSTRUCTION OF NEWGRANGE

The tomb at Newgrange was designed by people with clearly exceptional artistic and engineering skills, who had use of neither the wheel nor metal tools. About 200,000 tonnes of loose stones were transported to build the mound, or cairn, which protects the passage grave. Larger slabs were used to make the circle around the cairn (12 out of a probable 35 stones have survived), the kerb and the tomb itself. Many of the kerbstones and the slabs lining the passage, the chamber and its recesses are decorated with zigzags, spirals and other geometric motifs. The grave's corbelled ceiling consists of smaller, unadorned slabs and has proved almost completely waterproof for the last 5,000 years.

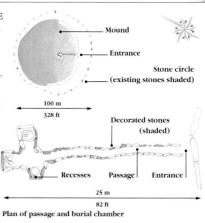

Mound
Entrance
Stone circle
(existing stones shaded)

100 m
328 ft

Decorated stones
(shaded)

Recesses   Passage   Entrance

25 m
82 ft
Plan of passage and burial chamber

VISITORS' CHECKLIST

8 km (5 miles) E of Slane, Co
Meath. 041 9880300.
to Drogheda. to Drogheda &
Drogheda to visitor's centre.
May–Sep: 9am–6:30pm (Jun–mid-
Sep: 7pm) daily; Oct–Apr: 9:30am–
5:30pm (Nov–Feb: 5pm) daily.
24–27 Dec. inside
tomb. obligatory (last tour:
1 hr 45 min before closing).
W www.heritage ireland.ie

Restoration of Newgrange
*Located on a low ridge north of the Boyne, Newgrange
took more than 70 years to build. Between 1962
and 1975 the passage grave and mound were
restored as closely as possible to their original state.*

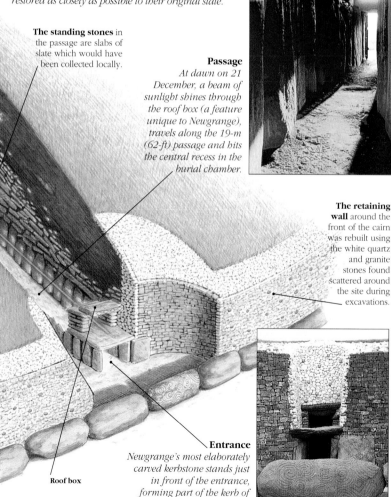

The standing stones in
the passage are slabs of
slate which would have
been collected locally.

Passage
*At dawn on 21
December, a beam of
sunlight shines through
the roof box (a feature
unique to Newgrange),
travels along the 19-m
(62-ft) passage and hits
the central recess in the
burial chamber.*

**The retaining
wall** around the
front of the cairn
was rebuilt using
the white quartz
and granite
stones found
scattered around
the site during
excavations.

Roof box

Entrance
*Newgrange's most elaborately
carved kerbstone stands just
in front of the entrance,
forming part of the kerb of
huge slabs around the cairn.*

Trim Castle, set in water meadows beside the River Boyne

Slane ㉕

Co Meath. 🚶 *950.* 🚌 ℹ️ *041 988 0305.*

Slane is an attractive estate village, centred on a quartet of Georgian houses. The Boyne river flows through it and skirts around **Slane Castle Demesne**, set in glorious grounds laid out in the 18th century by the renowned landscape gardener, Capability Brown. The castle, dating from 1785, incorporates the designs of James Wyatt, Francis Johnson and James Gandon and is famous for its Gothic Revival ballroom designed by Thomas Hopper. The castle was badly damaged by fire in 1991 but reopened in 2001 after a decade of restoration. Just to the north rises the **Hill of Slane** where, in AD 433, St Patrick is said to have lit a Paschal (Easter) fire as a challenge to the pagan High King of Tara. The local priest still marks this event by the lighting of a fire at Easter.

Hill of Tara ㉖

Nr Killmessan Village, Co Meath. 🚗 *May–Oct: 046 25903; Nov–Apr: Brú na Bóinne 041 9880300.* 🚌 *to Navan.* ⏰ *May–Oct: 10am–6pm daily (last adm: 5:15pm).* 💰 *for interpretive centre.* 🅿️ ⓦ *www.heritageireland.ie*

A site of mythic importance, Tara was the political and spiritual centre of Celtic Ireland and the seat of the High Kings until the 11th century. The spread of Christianity, which eroded the importance of Tara, is marked by a statue of St Patrick. Tara's symbolism was not lost on Daniel O'Connell *(see p14),* who chose the site for a rally in 1843, attended by more than a million people.

Tours from the interpretive centre point out a Stone Age passage grave and Iron Age hill forts though, to the untutored eye, these look like mere hollows and grassy mounds. Clearest is the Royal Enclosure, an oval fort, in the centre of which is Cormac's House containing the "stone of destiny" (*Liath Fáil*), an ancient fertility symbol and inauguration stone of the High Kings. However, all this is secondary to the views over the Boyne Valley and the site's sense of history.

Trim ㉗

Co Meath. 🚶 *6,500.* 🚌 ℹ️ *Mill St, 046 9437111.* 🚌 *Fri.* ⓦ *www.eastcoastmidlandsireland.com*

Trim is one of the most pleasing Midlands market towns. A Norman stronghold on the River Boyne, it marked a boundary of the Pale *(see p100).* Trim runs efficient heritage and genealogy centres, including a visitors' centre next door to the tourist office.

Trim Castle was founded in 1173 by Hugh de Lacy, a Norman knight, and is one of the largest medieval castles in Europe. It makes a spectacular backdrop so is often used as a film set, most recently seen in Mel Gibson's *Braveheart* (1995). The castle is currently closed for renovation, but visitors can peer in from a barbican tower that is still open. In the summer, the Nun Run, a bizarre horse race with nuns as jockeys, takes place near the castle.

Aerial view of Iron Age forts on the Hill of Tara

Over the river is **Talbot Castle**, an Augustinian abbey converted to a manor house in the 15th century. Just north of the abbey, **St Patrick's Cathedral** incorporates part of a medieval church with a 15th-century tower and sections of the original chancel.

Butterstream Gardens, on the edge of town, are the best in the county. A luxuriant herbaceous bed is the centrepiece, but equally pleasing are the woodland, rose and white gardens. The design is enhanced by pergolas, pools and bridges.

✿ **Butterstream Gardens**
Kildalkey Rd. 📞 046 36017.
🕐 Apr–Sep: 11am–6pm daily. 🅿

Mullingar ㉘

Co Westmeath. 🚶 14,000. 🚆 🚌
ℹ Market Sq, 044 48650. 🍴 Sat.

THE COUNTY TOWN of Westmeath is a prosperous market town encircled by the Royal Canal (see p83), which links Dublin with the River Shannon. Although Mullingar's main appeal is as a base to explore the surrounding area, pubs such as Con's and cheery Canton Casey's can make a pleasant interlude. In addition, the 20th-century cathedral features unusual mosaics of St Anne and St Patrick.

ENVIRONS: Recent restoration of the Dublin to Mullingar stretch of the Royal Canal has resulted in attractive towpaths for canalside walks, as well as good angling facilities.

The remains of the Jealous Wall at Belvedere House, near Mullingar

Lighting votive candles in Mullingar Cathedral

South of Mullingar, just off the road to Kilbeggan, stands **Belvedere House**, a romantic Palladian villa overlooking Lough Ennel. Built in 1740 by architect Richard Castle, Belvedere is decorated with Rococo plasterwork and set in wonderful gardens. Shortly after the house was built, the first Earl of Belvedere accused his wife of having an affair with his brother, and imprisoned her for 31 years in a neighbouring house. He sued the brother and had him jailed for life. In 1760, the Earl built a Gothic folly – the Jealous Wall – in order to block the view from another brother's more opulent mansion. The Jealous Wall still remains, as does an octagonal gazebo and other follies.

Charming terraces, framed by urns and yews, descend to the lake; on the other side of the house is a pretty walled garden, enclosed by an arboretum and rolling parkland. There is also an animal sanctuary next to the visitor centre.

🏛 **Belvedere House**
6 km (4 miles) S of Mullingar.
📞 044 49060. 🕐 May–Sep: 10:30am–6pm daily; Oct–Feb: 10:30am–4:30pm daily (last adm: 1hr before closing). 🅿 of estate by tram. 🚻 visitor centre only. 🚽 📷
W www.belvedere-house.ie

Miniature whiskey bottles at Locke's Distillery in Kilbeggan

Kilbeggan ㉙

Co Westmeath. 🚶 600. 🚌

SITUATED BETWEEN Mullingar and Tullamore, this pleasant village has a small harbour on the Grand Canal. However, the main point of interest is **Locke's Distillery**. Founded in 1757, it claims to be the oldest licensed pot still distillery in the world. Unable to compete with Scotch whisky manufacturers, the company went bankrupt in 1954, but the aroma hung in the warehouses for years and was known as "the angels' share". The distillery was reopened as a museum in 1987. The building is authentic, a solid structure complete with a water wheel and an indoor steam engine. A tour traces the process of Irish whiskey-making, from the mash tuns through to the fermentation vats and creation of wash (rough beer) to the distillation and maturation stages. At the tasting stage, workers would sample the whiskey in the can pit room. Visitors can still taste whiskeys in the bar but, unlike the original workers, cannot bathe in the whiskey vats.

🏛 **Locke's Distillery Museum** Main St. 📞 0506 32134. 🕐 Apr–Oct: 9am–6pm daily; Nov–Mar: 10am–4pm daily. 🅿 🍴
W www.lockesdistillerymuseum.com

TRAVELLERS' NEEDS

WHERE TO STAY

WHETHER YOU ARE STAYING in exclusive luxury or modest bed-and-breakfast accommodation, one thing you can be certain of in Dublin is that you will receive a warm welcome. The Irish are renowned for their friendliness and even in big corporate hotels, where you might expect the reception to be more impersonal, the staff go out of their way to be hospitable. The choice is enormous: you can stay in an elegant, refurbished Georgian house, a comfortable bed-and-breakfast, a Victorian townhouse, an old-fashioned commercial hotel or a cosy pub. Details are given here of the various types of accommodation available. The listings on pages 120–23 recommend around 50 hotels in both central Dublin and outside the city – all places of quality, ranging from basic to luxury – and should help you decide upon your choice of accommodation. Fáilte Ireland (the Irish Tourist Board) and Dublin Tourism also publish comprehensive guides to recommended accommodation in the area.

Doorman at the Conrad Hotel

A typical bedroom in the comfortable Brooks Hotel (p121)

Main entrance to the fashionable Clarence Hotel (p121)

HOTELS

AT THE TOP of the price range there are quite a few expensive, luxury hotels in the heart of Dublin. Magnificently furnished and run, they offer maximum comfort, delicious food and often have indoor facilities, such as a gym and swimming pool. As well as luxurious individual hotels there are also the modern hotel chains, such as **Jury's** and **Irish Welcome**, which offer a high standard of accommodation. However, these establishments can lack the charm and individuality of privately run hotels.

There are also numerous very moderate hotels in the centre of Dublin, providing a good standard of accommodation.

If you prefer to stay outside Dublin there are some wonderful castles and stately homes which offer the same standards as the top city hotels but which have the bonus of being set in beautiful countryside. They can often also arrange outdoor pursuits such as fishing, riding and golf.

The shamrock symbol of **Fáilte Ireland** is displayed by hotels (and other forms of accommodation) that have been inspected and approved.

BED-AND-BREAKFAST ACCOMMODATION

IRELAND HAS A reputation for the best B&Bs in Europe. Your welcome will always be friendly and the food and company excellent. Even if the house is no architectural

The entrance to the grand Shelbourne Hotel (see p121) on St Stephen's Green

beauty, the comfort and atmosphere will more than compensate. Not all of the bedrooms have bathrooms *en suite*. When one is available, you may possibly have to pay a little extra but, considering the generally cheap rates, the surcharge is negligible.

The Irish swear by their B&Bs and many stay in them by choice rather than paying to stay in the luxurious surroundings of some of the big hotels. **Town and Country Homes** will provide details of bed-and-breakfast accommodation throughout Ireland.

GUESTHOUSES

MOST GUESTHOUSES are found in cities and large towns. They are usually converted family homes and have an atmosphere all of their own. Most offer a good-value evening meal and all give you a delicious full Irish breakfast *(see p126)*. Top-of-the-range guesthouses can be just as good, and sometimes even better, than hotels. You will see a much more personal side of a town or city while staying at a guesthouse. There are plenty to choose from in the Dublin area and the prices are usually reasonable. The **Irish Hotels Federation** publishes a useful booklet with guesthouse listings that cover the whole of Ireland, including Dublin and its environs.

PRICES

Room rates advertised are inclusive of service and tax. Hotel rates can vary by as much as 40 per cent depending on the time of year. Prices in guesthouses are influenced more by their proximity to tourist sights and public transport. Dublin offers a complete range of accommodation, from youth hostels through very reasonably priced bed-and-breakfasts to lavish five-star hotels such as the Merrion, Morrison and the Clarence.

TIPPING

Tipping in dublin is a matter of personal discretion but is not common practice, even at the larger hotels. Tasks performed by staff are considered part of the service. Tipping is not expected for carrying bags to your room or for serving drinks. However, it is usual to tip the waiting staff in hotel restaurants: the standard tip is around 10–15 per cent of the bill – anything in excess of that would be considered particularly generous.

The Kinlay House youth hostel in Lord Edward Street

BOOKING

It is wise to reserve your accommodation during the peak season and public holidays *(see p27)*, particularly if your visit coincides with a local festival such as the St Patrick's Day celebrations *(see p24)* when the city can get booked up. **Dublin Tourism** *(see p148)* can offer advice and make reservations through its accommodation service. Central reservation facilities are available at the hotel chains listed here.

Fáilte Ireland accommodation sign

YOUTH HOSTELS

There are 31 youth hostels registered with **An Óige** (the Irish Youth Hostel Association), with one in the Dublin area. Accommodation is provided in dormitories with comfortable beds and basic cooking facilities. You can only use these hostels if you are a member of An Óige or another organization affiliated to the International Youth Hostel Federation.

There are also independent hostels, and places such as universities that offer similar inexpensive accommodation in Dublin. The tourist board has listings of those that are recommended.

DISABLED TRAVELLERS

A fact sheet for disabled visitors is produced by Fáilte Ireland and their accommodation guide indicates wheelchair accessibility. Dublin Tourism and **Comhairle** are also helpful. *Accommodation for Disabled Persons* and *Dublin: A Guide for Disabled Persons* are useful leaflets available at the tourist office.

DIRECTORY

CHAIN HOTELS

Irish Welcome
Bracken Court, Bracken Rd, Sandyford, Dublin 18. (*293 3000.* FAX *293 3001.*
W www.irishwelcometours.com

Jury's Doyle
Pembroke Rd, Ballsbridge, Dublin 4.
(*660 5000.* FAX *660 5540.*
W www.jurysdoyle.com

OTHER USEFUL ADDRESSES

Comhairle
Floor 7, Hume House, Ballsbridge, Dublin 4. (*605 9000.*
W www.comhairle.ie

Irish Hotels Federation
13 Northbrook Rd, Dublin 6.
(*497 6459.* FAX *497 4613.*
W www.irelandhotels.com

An Óige (Irish Youth Hostel Association)
61 Mountjoy St, Dublin 7.
(*830 4555.* FAX *830 5808.*
W www.irelandyha.org

Town and Country Homes
Beleek Rd, Ballyshannon, Co Donegal.
(*071 9822222.*
W www.townandcountry.ie

Ariel Hotel in Ballsbridge *(see p122)*

Choosing a Hotel

THESE HOTELS have been selected across a wide price range for their good value, facilities and location. The chart lists the hotels by areas, starting with central Dublin and moving on to hotels further outside the city. Many hotels have a recommended restaurant and/or bar, but for separate restaurant listings see pages 128–31. For map references, see pages 164–5.

	CREDIT CARDS	CHILDREN'S FACILITIES	PARKING FACILITIES	RESTAURANT	PUBLIC BAR
SOUTHEAST DUBLIN					
BUSWELLS Map E4. €€€€ 25 Molesworth St, Dublin 2. ☎ 614 6500. ℻ 676 2090. ⓦ www.quinnhotels.com A short walk from Grafton Street, this smart hotel is a listed Georgian building with a fine interior. ⛬ TV ⛬ ⛬ *Rooms: 69*	AE DC MC V	●	▩	●	▩
CLARION STEPHEN'S HALL Map E5. €€€€ 14–17 Leeson St Lower, Dublin 2. ☎ 638 1111. ℻ 638 1122. ⓦ www.premgroup.com All the rooms are suites and represent good value for families who want smart, comfortable accommodation in the centre of the city near St Stephen's Green. There are cooking facilities in all rooms. ⛬ TV ⛬ *Rooms: 33*	AE DC MC V	●	▩	●	▩
CONRAD HOTEL Map D5. €€€€€ Earlsfort Terrace, Dublin 2. ☎ 676 5555. ℻ 676 5424. ⓦ www.conradhotels.com This international-style hotel, by St Stephen's Green, is geared to business people and has excellent facilities. A jolly pub with a large terrace is the only concession to traditional Dublin. ⛬ TV ⛬ ⛬ ⛬ *Rooms: 192*	AE DC MC V		▩	●	▩
DAVENPORT Map F4. €€€€€ Merrion Square, Dublin 2. ☎ 607 3500. ℻ 661 5663. ⓦ www.ocallaghanhotels.ie The grand proportions of the Neo-Classical façade are carried through into the lobby – a vast, marble-floored atrium. The hotel is elegant but rather like a gentleman's club. ⛬ TV ⛬ ⛬ ⛬ *Rooms: 113*	AE DC MC V	●	▩	●	▩
FITZWILLIAM GUEST HOUSE Map E5. €€ 41 Fitzwilliam St Upper, Dublin 2. ☎ 662 5155. ℻ 676 7488. A friendly, unpretentious guesthouse in an attractive Georgian street, with simple, elegant decor and comfortable bedrooms. ⛬ TV *Rooms: 12*	AE DC MC V				
GEORGIAN HOTEL Map F5. €€ 18 Baggot St Lower, Dublin 2. ☎ 634 5000. ℻ 634 5100. @ info@georgianhotel.ie A short walk from St Stephen's Green, this hotel is a good base for exploring Dublin. The bedrooms are large and comfortable and there's a traditional restaurant in the basement. ⛬ TV ⛬ *Rooms: 47*	AE DC MC V	●		●	▩
HARCOURT Map D5. €€€ 60 Harcourt St, Dublin 2. ☎ 478 3677. ℻ 475 2013. ⓦ www.harcourthotel.ie The Harcourt hotel has modern, well-equipped rooms, a popular bar with traditional music, a restaurant and a nightclub. ⛬ TV ⛬ *Rooms: 104*	AE MC V DC	●		●	▩
KILRONAN HOUSE €€ 70 Adelaide Rd, Dublin 2. ☎ 475 5266. ℻ 478 2841. ⓦ www.dublinn.com A small cosy guesthouse in a quiet street near St Stephen's Green. Delicious breakfasts. ⛬ TV *Rooms: 15*	AE MC V	●	▩		
LEESON Map E5. €€ 26 Leeson St Lower, Dublin 2. ☎ 676 3380. ℻ 661 8273. Spread across two Georgian houses, this cheerfully decorated hotel has a relaxed, informal atmosphere and the service is good. St Stephen's Green is only a few minutes' walk away. ⛬ TV *Rooms: 20*	AE DC MC V	●	▩		▩
LONGFIELDS Map F5. €€€ 10 Fitzwilliam St Lower, Dublin 2. ☎ 676 1367. ℻ 676 1542. ⓦ www.longfields.ie Two Georgian townhouses have been knocked together to create this stylish hotel with an attractive sitting room and smart, pretty bedrooms. There is a very good restaurant in the basement. ⛬ TV *Rooms: 26*	AE DC MC V			●	▩
THE MERRION Map F4. €€€€€ Merrion St Upper, Dublin 2. ☎ 603 0600. ℻ 603 0700. ⓦ www.merrionhotel.com This top-class hotel was created from four Georgian townhouses. Its elegant interior is full of antiques and it has an outstanding art collection. It is a highly civilized but relaxing hotel. ⛬ TV ⛬ ⛬ ⛬ ⛬ *Rooms: 145*	AE DC MC V	●	▩	●	▩

<table>
<tr><td colspan="2">

Price categories for a standard double room per night, inclusive of breakfast, service charges and any additional taxes such as VAT:
€ under 100 euros
€€ 100 to 150 euros
€€€ 150 to 200 euros
€€€€ 200 to 250 euros
€€€€€ over 250 euros

</td><td colspan="2">

CHILDREN'S FACILITIES
Cots and high chairs are available and some hotels will also provide a baby-sitting service.
PARKING FACILITIES
Parking provided by the hotel in either a private car park or a private garage close by.
RESTAURANT
The hotel has a restaurant for residents which also welcomes non-residents – usually only for evening meals.
PUBLIC BAR
The hotel has a bar that is open to non-residents as well as those staying in the hotel.

</td></tr>
</table>

	CREDIT CARDS	CHILDREN'S FACILITIES	PARKING FACILITIES	RESTAURANT	PUBLIC BAR
MONT CLARE Map F4. €€€ Merrion Square, Dublin 2. 607 3800. FAX 607 3807. www.ocallaghanhotels.ie info@ocallaghanhotels.ie Not as grand as its sister The Davenport, but with the same club-like feel. A busy, traditional pub is on the ground floor. TV **Rooms: 74**	AE DC MC V		■	●	■
RUSSELL COURT Map D5. €€ 21–25 Harcourt St, Dublin 2. 478 4066. FAX 478 4994. www.russellcourthotel.ie reservations@russellcourthotel.ie Jolly, welcoming hotel with young staff and a lively atmosphere in the evenings. There's a choice of bars and a more formal restaurant. Bedrooms are neat and well-equipped. TV **Rooms: 44**	AE DC MC V	●	■	●	■
SHELBOURNE HOTEL Map D4. €€€€€ 27 St. Stephen's Green, Dublin 2. 663 4500. FAX 661 6006. www.shelbourne.ie The Shelbourne has been the city's most distinguished hotel since it opened in the 19th century. It has every facility for the business traveller, yet manages to retain a personal atmosphere. TV **Rooms: 190**	AE DC MC V	●	■	●	■
TEMPLE BAR HOTEL Map D3. €€€ Fleet St, Temple Bar, Dublin 2. 677 3333. FAX 677 3088. www.towerhotelgroup.ie reservations@tbh.ie Situated in the heart of Dublin's Temple Bar, this hotel is a popular meeting place with its theme bar "Buskers" attracting a lively crowd. Bedrooms are comfortable but lack character. TV **Rooms: 129**	AE DC MC V	●		●	■
WESTBURY HOTEL Map D4. €€€€€ Grafton St, Dublin 2. 679 1122. FAX 679 7078. www.jurysdoyle.com You couldn't get much closer to the centre of things than here, only seconds from Dublin's major shopping street. It is a smart, ritzy hotel, decorated in traditional style. TV **Rooms: 204**	AE DC MC V	●	■	●	■
SOUTHWEST DUBLIN					
AVALON HOUSE Map C4. € 55 Aungier St, Dublin 2. 475 0001. FAX 475 0303. www.avalon–house.ie This cheap and cheerful budget accommodation is centrally located and has clean bedrooms and a communal kitchen. **Rooms: 60**	AE DC MC V				
BLOOMS HOTEL Map D3. €€ Anglesea St, Temple Bar, Dublin 2. 671 5622. FAX 671 5997. www.blooms.ie This modern hotel is in a busy part of the city near Trinity College. Decor is traditional and there's a nightclub in the basement. TV **Rooms: 97**	AE DC MC V			●	■
BROOKS HOTEL Map D4. €€€€€ 59-62 Drury St, Dublin 2. 670 4000. FAX 670 4455. www.brookshoteldublin.com A very comfortable and friendly modern hotel only a few minutes walk from Grafton Street. The decor makes the spacious rooms feel very cosy. A 45-seat mini-cinema is a recent addition. TV **Rooms: 98**	AE DC MC V	●		●	■
CENTRAL HOTEL Map D5. €€ 1–5 Exchequer St, Dublin 2. 679 7302. FAX 679 7303. www.centralhotel.ie As its name suggests, this hotel is centrally located. The Exchequer Bar on the ground floor has live music at weekends, so choose your neat and functional room carefully. TV **Rooms: 70**	AE DC MC V	●		●	■
CLARENCE Map C3. €€€€€ 6–8 Wellington Quay, Dublin 2. 407 0800. FAX 407 0820. www.theclarence.ie The hotel is owned by Bono and The Edge of the rock band U2 and exudes understated elegance. A stylish restaurant sets the standard for the rest of the hotel – still one of the trendiest places to stay in town. TV **Rooms: 50**	AE DC MC V	●	■	●	■

For key to symbols see back flap

<table>
<tr><td colspan="2">

Price categories for a standard double room per night, inclusive of breakfast, service charges and any additional taxes such as VAT:
€ under 100 euros
€€ 100 to 150 euros
€€€ 150 to 200 euros
€€€€ 200 to 250 euros
€€€€€ over 250 euros

CHILDREN'S FACILITIES
Cots and high chairs are available and some hotels will also provide a baby-sitting service.
PARKING FACILITIES
Parking provided by the hotel in either a private car park or a private garage close by.
RESTAURANT
The hotel has a restaurant for residents which also welcomes non-residents – usually only for evening meals.
PUBLIC BAR
The hotel has a bar that is open to non-residents as well as those staying in the hotel.

</td></tr>
</table>

Listing	Price	Credit Cards	Children's Facilities	Parking Facilities	Restaurant	Public Bar
GRAFTON CAPITAL HOTEL Map D4. Lower Stephen St, Dublin 2. 648 1100. FAX 648 1122. W www.capital-hotels.com @ info@graftoncapital-hotel.com This neat hotel, with its Georgian façade, is decorated in Georgian style throughout. Only a few minutes' walk from Grafton Street, it makes an excellent city base. TV *Rooms: 75*	€€	AE DC MC V	●		●	■
JURY'S CHRISTCHURCH INN Map B4. Christchurch Place, Dublin 8. 454 0000. FAX 454 0012. W www.jurysdoyle.com The Jury's group "inns" offer spruce modern facilities. This hotel, 15 minutes from St Stephen's Green, has a good bar and restaurant, and neat, well-equipped rooms at reasonable prices. TV *Rooms: 182*	€€	AE DC MC V	●		●	■

NORTH OF THE LIFFEY

Listing	Price	Credit Cards	Children's Facilities	Parking Facilities	Restaurant	Public Bar
BROWNS HOSTEL Map E1. 90 Lower Gardiner St, Dublin 1. 855 0034. FAX 855 8223. W www.brownshostelireland.com @ bhostel1@eircom.net Set in a Georgian town house beside Brown's Hotel, this hostel is clean and bright, with a games room and cheap internet facilities. TV *Rooms: 13*	€	AE MC V				
GRESHAM HOTEL Map D1. 23 O'Connell St Upper, Dublin 1. 874 6881. FAX 878 7175. W www.gresham-hotels.com @ info@thegresham.com One of Dublin's oldest and best-known hotels. It is a popular rendezvous spot so the public areas are always busy. The bedrooms are comfortable and there is ample safe parking. TV *Rooms: 288*	€€€	AE DC MC V	●	■	●	■
HOTEL ISAACS Map E2. Store St, Dublin 1. 855 0067. FAX 836 5390. W www.isaacs.ie @ hotel@isaacs.ie Developed alongside an older hostel of the same name, the hotel is reasonably priced, well-run and centrally located. TV *Rooms: 58*	€€	AE MC V	●	■	●	■
THE MORRISON Map D1. Ormond Quay, Dublin 1 887 2400. FAX 878 3185. W www.morrisonhotel.ie Built in 1999 with John Rocha as design consultant, this is the ultimate cool but comfortable hotel. A favourite with the stars, it has two chic bars and the excellent Halo Restaurant *(see p129)* TV *Rooms: 84*	€€€€	AE DC MC V	●		●	■

FURTHER AFIELD

Listing	Price	Credit Cards	Children's Facilities	Parking Facilities	Restaurant	Public Bar
ANGLESEA TOWN HOUSE 63 Anglesea Rd, Dublin 4. 668 3877. FAX 668 3461. W www.63anglesea.com This Edwardian house is beautifully decorated and furnished. It has a lovely drawing room, very comfortable bedrooms and offers a superb breakfast – all within 20 minutes walk of the centre. TV *Rooms: 7*	€€	AE DC MC V		■		
BERKELEY COURT HOTEL Lansdowne Rd, Dublin 4. 660 1711. FAX 661 7238. W www.jurysdoyle.com The very smart lobby area sets the standard for this luxury hotel, which is well located for Lansdowne Road stadium. TV *Rooms: 188*	€€€€	AE DC MC V	●	■	●	■
BEWLEYS HOTEL BALLSBRIDGE Merrion Rd, Ballsbridge, Dublin 4. 668 1111. FAX 668 1999. W www.bewleyshotels.com @ bb@bewleyshotels.com This fine 19th century building used to be a school but was converted into a hotel in 1999 and is very good value. TV *Rooms: 304*	€€	AE MC V DC	●	■	●	■
CLARA HOUSE Leinster Rd, Rathmines, Dublin 6. 497 5904. FAX 497 5580. @ clarahouse@eircom.net In an attractive area, ten minutes' walk from the centre, this Georgian house is a comfortable B&B with a friendly atmosphere. TV *Rooms: 13*	€	MC V		■		

GLENOGRA GUESTHOUSE €
64 Merrion Rd, Ballsbridge, Dublin 4. 668 3661. FAX 668 3698.
W www.glenogra.com @ info@glenogra.com
Attractive, stylish guesthouse convenient for Dun Laoghaire and the centre of Dublin. Bedrooms are charming and comfortable. TV *Rooms: 12*
AE MC V

HIBERNIAN €€€€
Eastmoreland Place, Ballsbridge, Dublin 4. 668 7666. FAX 660 2655.
W www.hibernianhotel.com @ info@hibernianhotel.com
Located in a quiet street but close to the centre, this impressive turn-of-the-century building has elegant, luxurious rooms. TV *Rooms: 40*
AE DC MC V

JURY'S HOTEL AND THE TOWERS AT JURY'S €€€€€
Pembroke Rd, Ballsbridge, Dublin 4. 660 5000. FAX 660 5540.
W www.jurysdoyle.com
A modern, business hotel, a short distance from the centre with excellent facilities. The Towers is an exclusive wing with de luxe bedrooms. TV *Rooms: 400*
AE DC MC V

JURYS TARA €€€
Merrion Rd, Dublin 4. 269 4666. FAX 269 1027. W www.jurysdoyle.com
Conveniently situated for Dun Laoghaire, the hotel also has a number of rooms overlooking Dublin Bay. TV *Rooms: 113*
AE DC MC V

BEYOND DUBLIN

CARLINGFORD *McKevitt's Village Hotel* €
Market Sq, Co Louth. 042 9373116. FAX 042 9373144. W www.mckevittshotel.com
Popular village inn at the heart of the local scene. Rooms have real fires and a great atmosphere, bedrooms are pristine and pretty. TV *Rooms: 17*
AE DC MC V

CARLINGFORD *Viewpoint* €
Omeath Rd, Co Louth. 042 9373149. FAX 042 9373149.
W www.viewpointcarlingford.com @ paulwoodsviewpoint@hotmail.com
Motel-style, modern accommodation. Well-equipped bedrooms with wonderful views across Carlingford Lough. TV *Rooms: 8*
V MC

DROGHEDA *Boyne Valley Hotel and Country Club* €€€
Co Louth. 041 9837737. FAX 041 9839188. W www.boyne-valley-hotel.ie
Although the decor and furnishings are modern, this hotel preserves much of the 18th-century manor house's traditional feel. TV *Rooms: 80*
AE DC MC V

DULEEK *Annesbrook* €€
Co Meath. 041 9823293. FAX 041 9823024. W www.annesbrook.com
This 17th-century house overlooks lovely gardens. It has a welcoming atmosphere and spacious, comfortable bedrooms. *Rooms: 5*
MC V

MULLINGAR *Greville Arms Hotel* €€
Co Westmeath. 044 48563. FAX 044 48052. W www.grevillearms.com
Centrally located in Mullingar, this traditional hotel caters for both locals and tourists. It has a large and very welcoming bar. TV *Rooms: 40*
AE DC MC V

RATHNEW *Hunter's Hotel* €€€€
Co Wicklow. 0404 40106. FAX 0404 40338. W www.hunters.ie
This inn on the old Dublin coaching road dates back to 1720 and is run by the fifth generation of the Hunter family. It is comfortable and relaxing with delicious food and a lovely garden. TV *Rooms: 16*
AE MC V

RATHNEW *Tinakilly Country House and Restaurant* €€€€
Co Wicklow. 0404 69274. FAX 0404 67806. W www.tinakilly.ie
This elegant 19th-century house overlooks three ha (seven acres) of gardens and has wonderful views of the sea. TV *Rooms: 51*
AE DC MC V

SLANE *Conyngham Arms Hotel* €€
Co Meath. 041 9884444. FAX 041 9824205. W www.conynghamarms.com
This traditional family hotel is welcoming and comfortable. It makes a good base for touring the beautiful Boyne Valley. TV *Rooms: 15*
MC V

STRAFFAN *Kildare Hotel and Country Club* €€€€€
Co Kildare. 601 7200. FAX 601 7299. W www.kclub.ie @ resortsales@kclub.ie
Parts of this exclusive hotel building date back to the 17th century. Facilities include a championship golf course. TV *Rooms: 69*
AE DC MC V

RESTAURANTS, CAFÉS AND PUBS

THE DUBLIN OF today is a modern, cosmopolitan city, something which is reflected in its vast array of restaurants. The Temple Bar area is good for modern international cuisine, and also has a large number of pubs as well as a few traditional Irish restaurants. There are many Italian, Chinese and Indian restaurants, and in recent years Thai, Indonesian, Japanese, Mexican and Cuban places have proliferated. Seafood and fish is abundant in Dublin, in particular smoked salmon and oysters; the latter is famously often consumed with Guinness. Popular for a light lunch is smoked salmon on delicious dark rye bread, with a pint of Guinness. Wherever you eat, portions will be generous, especially in pubs, whose platefuls of roast meat and vegetables offer excellent value for money. Takeaway food, from fish and chips to pizzas and kebabs, is also widely available.

The Bad Ass Café, Temple Bar

IRISH EATING PATTERNS

TRADITIONALLY, the Irish have started the day with a huge breakfast: bacon, sausages, black pudding, eggs, tomatoes and brown bread. The main meal, dinner, was served at midday, with a lighter "tea" in the early evening.

Although Continental breakfasts are now available, the traditional breakfast is still included in almost all hotel and B&B rates. Most of the Irish today settle for a light lunch and save their main meal for the evening. Vestiges of the old eating patterns remain in the huge midday meals still served in pubs.

EATING OUT

ELEGANT DINING becomes considerably more affordable when you make lunch your main meal of the day. In many of the top restaurants in Dublin, the fixed-price lunch

and dinner menus offer much the same, but the bill at lunchtime will usually amount to about half the price. If you like wine to accompany your meal, the house wines are quite drinkable in most restaurants and can reduce the total cost of your meal. If you are travelling with children, look out for one of the many restaurants that offer a children's menu. Lunch in Dublin is invariably served between noon and 2:30pm, with dinner between 6:30 and 10pm, although many ethnic and city-centre restaurants stay open later. If you are staying in a bed-and-breakfast, your hosts may provide a home-cooked evening meal if given advance notice. Visa and Mastercard are the most commonly accepted credit cards in Ireland, with American Express and Diners Club also in use.

GOURMET AND ETHNIC DINING

ONCE CONSIDERABLY lacking in gourmet establishments, Dublin now offers many restaurants that rank among Europe's very best, with chefs trained in outstanding domestic and Continental institutions. Increasingly it is the hotels which house some of the city's best restaurants, with award-winning cuisine. There is a choice of Irish, French, Italian, Chinese, Indian, Cuban, Indonesian, Japanese, Mexican, Thai and even Russian cuisines to be found in and around Dublin. Locations vary as widely as the cuisine, from conventional hotel dining rooms, town-house basements and city mansions to romantic castle hotels and tiny village cafés tucked away by the sea.

Doorman at the Khyber Tandoori

In the city centre, the eating areas with the widest choice tend to be located in Temple Bar or between St Stephen's Green and Merrion Square. Outside the city, Malahide and Howth have a good selection of restaurants, and Dun Laoghaire is worth a special visit for fresh fish and seafood.

BUDGET DINING

IT IS QUITE POSSIBLE to eat well on a moderate budget in Dublin. Both in the city and outside it, there are small

La Med restaurant, one of Temple Bar's many fashionable eating places

The Steps of Rome, off Grafton Street *(p132)*

cafés, tea rooms and family-style restaurants which offer reasonably priced meals. Sandwiches are usually made with thick, delicious slices of fresh, rather than processed, cheese or meat; salad plates feature chicken, pork, beef and the ever-popular smoked salmon; and hot meals usually come with generous helpings of vegetables, with the beloved potato often showing up in different forms, including roasted and mashed, sometimes all on one plate.

Another cheap alternative is to take picnics when you go out. Farmhouse cheeses and homegrown tomatoes make delicious sandwiches, and the beautiful countryside, fine beaches and breathtaking mountains make ideal locations for a picnic. Phoenix Park and Powerscourt both have their own picnic areas.

The cosy Old Mill restaurant in Temple Bar Square *(p129)*

PUB FOOD

IRELAND'S PUBS have moved into the food field with a vengeance. In addition to bar snacks (soup, sandwiches and so on), available from noon until late, salads and hot meals are served from midday to 2:30pm. At rock-bottom prices, hot plates all come heaped with mounds of fresh vegetables, potatoes, and good portions of local fish or meat. Particularly good value are the pub carveries that offer a choice of joints, sliced to your preference. In recent years, the international staples of spaghetti, lasagne and quiche have also appeared on pub menus, along with more Mediterranean dishes such as *bruschetta* in the trendier pubs. For a list of recommended pubs, see pages 132–3.

PUB OPENING HOURS

MANY PEOPLE come to Dublin for its endless pubs and bars and its excellent stouts and whiskeys. Opening hours are the same winter and summer alike: Monday to Wednesday 10:30am until 11:30pm; Thursday to Saturday 10:30am until 12:30pm. Sunday opening times have changed to become more flexible. Pubs used to close for "holy hour" between 2pm and 4pm. Now most pubs are open on a Sunday from 12:30pm until 11pm. Late bars tend to stay open until 1am or 2am, the nightclubs even later.

FISH AND CHIPS AND OTHER FAST FOODS

THE IRISH, from peasant to parliamentarian, love their "chippers", immortalized in Roddy Doyle's novel *The Van*, and any good pub night will often end with a visit to the nearest fish-and-chip shop. At virtually any time of day, however, if you pass by Leo Burdock's in Dublin, there will be a long queue for this international institution *(see p132)*. With Ireland's long coastline, wherever you choose, the fish will usually be the freshest catch of the day – plaice, cod, haddock, whiting or ray (a delicacy). As an alternative to fish and chips, there are numerous good pasta and pizza restaurants around the city, including the Steps of Rome, Pasta Fresca and Milano, which also does takeaways. In addition Dublin has become home to the ubiquitous burger chains, including McDonald's, as well as other forms of fast food outlets such as KFC.

Picnickers enjoying the sunshine outside at Dublin Zoo *(p79)*

VEGETARIAN FOOD

AS WITH MOST western European cities, there is plenty of scope for vegetarians to eat well in Dublin. Although much traditional Irish food is meat-based, most restaurants will have vegetarian dishes on the menu, particularly in the modern international and Italian restaurants, but there are also some excellent exclusively vegetarian restaurants in the city. If you happen to go somewhere to eat and realize that there is no vegetarian option, most restaurants will be more than happy to make something up for you, such as a salad or a vegetable stir fry.

What to Eat in Dublin

IRELAND'S RICH PASTURELAND, unpolluted rivers and extensive coastline provide tender lamb, beef and pork, an array of fish and seafood and fresh fruit and vegetables. From hearty rural fare that makes the most of the ingredients available, Irish cooking has evolved into the gourmet cuisine created by internationally trained chefs. Often you will find the best of both worlds, with Irish stew or ham and cabbage on the same menu as more exotic dishes. The ideal end to a meal is an Irish coffee – coffee, cream and whiskey.

Irish coffee

Bread, invariably baked daily, comes in a variety of different guises. Traditional soda bread may be brown or white.

Brown soda bread · Soda bread · Soda farl · Potato cake

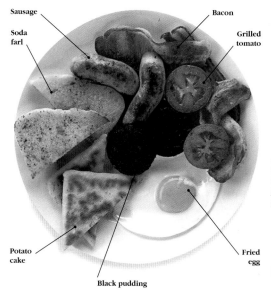

Sausage · Bacon · Soda farl · Grilled tomato · Potato cake · Fried egg · Black pudding

A traditional Irish breakfast consists of home-baked soda farls (soft bread cakes leavened with soda and butter-milk) and potato cakes (bread made from mashed potato, butter and flour), as well as the basic ingredients of a fry-up. Known as a "fry", this is a perfect way to set yourself up for the day. Without the soda farls and potato cakes, meals like this are consumed with relish at any time of day.

Mushroom soup makes a wholesome starter or snack. It is normally made with freshly picked local mushrooms and a generous amount of cream.

Smoked salmon, available all over Ireland and very popular, is generally served as simply as possible – enabling you to enjoy the full flavour of the fish.

Mussel soup is a substantial dish made with fresh local mussels in a creamy fish stock fla-voured with vegetables and herbs. Try it with brown soda bread.

Fresh oysters, here served on a bed of seaweed and cracked ice, make a light but delicious lunch – especially when accom-panied by a glass of Guinness.

Dublin coddle, a traditional Saturday night supper dish, consists of chopped sausages and ham or bacon cooked in stock with potatoes and onions.

Irish stew, *originally a peasant dish, is a thick casserole made with lamb or mutton, onions, and parsley, topped with potatoes.*

Fresh salmon *is often poached in fish stock or wine and herbs. Galway salmon is particularly sought after for its fine taste.*

Lamb cutlets *are usually served with mint sauce or jelly. Lamb from Kerry and Wicklow is renowned for its tenderness.*

Vegetables *are served in generous portions, usually as an accompaniment to the main course. It is not uncommon to be given potatoes in a number of different forms – roast, boiled, mashed, baked or chipped – together with whichever vegetables happen to be fresh and in season.*

Mashed potato
Roast potatoes
Broccoli
Boiled potatoes
Carrots

Baked ham, *coated with cloves and brown sugar, is commonly served with boiled cabbage in butter and eaten at Christmas or on other festive occasions.*

Strawberries and cream *are the archetypal summer dessert. They are sometimes sweetened with honey rather than sugar.*

Porter cake, *a classic Irish cake made with dried fruit, is most famous for the inclusion of stout, usually in the form of Guinness.*

Apple tart, *or "cake" as the Irish often call it, is eaten all year round but is traditionally associated with Hallowe'en.*

CHEESES

For centuries, cheese has been made in farms and monasteries throughout Ireland. Cheese-making has expanded in the last 25 years and Ireland now produces cheeses with a worldwide reputation, from semi-soft ones such as Cashel Blue and St Killian, which is similar to Camembert, to Gouda-like Carrigaline and smoked Durrus.

St Killian

Carrigaline

Cashel Blue

Durrus

Tea-time *favourites include sponges, fruit cakes and scones with or without fruit. Barm brack, a doughy, fruity bread, is traditionally eaten at Hallowe'en and on All Saints Day, when a ring is hidden in the cake. According to tradition, the finder of the ring will marry by the following Easter.*

Brown scone
Fruit scone
Plain scone
Barm brack

Choosing a Restaurant

THIS CHART LISTS restaurants, selected for their good value, exceptional food and/or interesting location. The chart highlights some of the factors which may influence your choice. Smoking has been banned inside all restaurants in Ireland. The entries are listed by areas, starting with the Southeast. For Dublin map references, see the Street Finder map on pages 164–5.

	CREDIT CARDS	OPEN LUNCH TIME	OPEN LATE	FIXED-PRICE MENU	GOOD WINE LIST

SOUTHEAST DUBLIN

AYA Map D4. Clarendon St, Dublin 2. **℄** 677 1544. **FAX** 677 1607. **W** www.aya.ie A welcome addition to ethnic cuisine in Dublin is this contemporary Japanese restaurant, sushi bar and deli. Bright, light and neat with delicious food. Smoking area. **⛾** limited **♿ V** €€	AE MC V	●		●	▦
BOULEVARD CAFÉ Map D4. 27 Exchequer St, Dublin 2. **℄** 679 2131. Continental ambience with Oriental influences and highly professional service marks this out from the usual pizza/pasta places. **♿ V** €€€	AE MC V	●	▦		
CAFÉ BAR DELI 12 South Great Georges St, Dublin 2. **℄** 677 1646. **FAX** 677 6044. **W** www.cafebardeli.ie This former Bewley's café is home to a quality Mediterranean restaurant, which serves good-value meals in a friendly, lively atmosphere. Good location, close to shopping areas. **⛾ ♿ V** €€€	AE DC MC V	●	▦		
DOBBIN'S WINE BISTRO Map F5. 15 Stephen's Lane, Mount St, Dublin 2. **℄** 676 4679. **FAX** 661 3331. An intimate, friendly bistro in a WW2 Nissan hut, with an innovative monthly menu and one of Dublin's best wine lists. **V** €€€€	AE DC MC V	●		●	▦
EAMONN O'REILLY'S ONE PICO RESTAURANT 5–6 Molesworth Lane, Dublin 2. **℄** 676 0300. **FAX** 676 0411. This award-winning restaurant offers the unusual combination of Irish food with Asian, Mediterranean and Pacific cuisine. **V** €€€€	AE DC MC V	●	▦		▦
L'ECRIVAIN Map F5. 109 Baggot St Lower, Dublin 2. **℄** 661 1919. **FAX** 661 0617. **W** www.lecrivain.com In the heart of Georgian Dublin, this stylish, restaurant serves modern Irish food with a French twist. **♿ V** €€€€	AE DC MC V	●	▦		
THE FADO Map D4. Mansion House, Dawson St, Dublin 2. **℄** 676 7200. **FAX** 676 7530. **W** www.fado.ie Part of the Mansion House, the stunning dining room is in the Belle Époque Style. The cuisine is Irish with French influence. **⛾ ♿ V** €€€€	AE DC MC V	●	▦	●	▦
GOTHAM CAFÉ Map D4. 8 Anne St South, Dublin 2. **℄** 679 5266. **FAX** 679 5280. The American-style menu at this bright, funky café includes "Bowery", "Upper East Side" and "Central Park" gourmet pizzas. **⛾ ♿ V** €€€	AE MC V	●	▦		
KILKENNY SHOP RESTAURANT Map E4. The Kilkenny Shop, 5–6 Nassau St, Dublin 2. **℄** 677 7066. **W** www.kilkennygroup.com A busy restaurant, overlooking Trinity College playing fields, offering traditional Irish cooking, homemade quiches and salads. **♿ V** €€€	AE DC MC V	●		●	
CAFÉ MAO Map D5. 2–3 Chatham Row, Dublin 2. **℄** 670 4899. **FAX** 670 4893. **W** www.cafemao.com Situated a short stroll from Grafton Street, this young, cool, clean restaurant serves Asian fusion food. **⛾ V** €€€	AE DC MC V	●	▦	●	
PEARL BRASSERIE Map D4. 20 Upper Merrion St, Dublin 2. **℄** 661 3627. **FAX** 661 3629. **W** www.pearl-brasserie.com A classical French Brasserie serving traditional French cuisine and combining charm, friendly service and affordable prices. **V** €€€€	AE MC V	●	▦		▦
RAJDOOT TANDOORI Map D4. 26–28 Clarendon St, Dublin 2. **℄** 679 4274. **FAX** 679 4274. **W** www.rajdoottandoori.com This authentically decorated North Indian restaurant serves mildly spiced curries and, from the clay oven, tandoori barbecued dishes. **⛾ V** €€€€	AE DC MC V	●	▦		

		CREDIT CARDS	OPEN LUNCH TIME	OPEN LATE	FIXED-PRICE MENU	GOOD WINE LIST

Average prices for a three-course meal for one, half a bottle of house wine and unavoidable charges such as service and cover:
€ under 15 euros
€€ 15 to 25 euros
€€€ 25 to 35 euros
€€€€ over 35 euros

OPEN LUNCH TIME
Many restaurants open only in the evening, but those in large towns and attached to pubs often open at lunch time.

OPEN LATE
Restaurant remains open with the full menu available after 10pm.

FIXED-PRICE MENU
A good-value fixed-price menu on offer at lunch, dinner or both, usually with three courses.

GOOD WINE LIST
Denotes a wide range of good wines, or a more specialized selection of wines.

	CREDIT CARDS	OPEN LUNCH TIME	OPEN LATE	FIXED-PRICE MENU	GOOD WINE LIST
SANDBANK BISTRO CAFE Map D4. €€€€ Westbury Hotel, Grafton St, Dublin 2. ☎ 646 3353. W www.jurysdoyle.com Completely refurbished, this is a smart but simple bistro with beech tables and a minimalist feel to the decor. The menu is Mediterranean in style and specialises in seafood. ⬛ 🚹 V	AE DC MC V	●	■	●	■
LA STAMPA Map D4. €€€€ 35 Dawson St, Dublin 2. ☎ 677 8611. W www.lastampa.ie This up-market restaurant in the heart of Dublin is noted for its sumptuous, highly ornate Georgian decor. The atmosphere is lively and the food is Mediterranean and World cuisine. Booking advised. V	AE DC MC V		■		
TIGER BECS Map D4. €€€€ Dawson St, Dublin 2. ☎ 677 4444. This high-quality Thai restaurant offers a diverse range of delicious dishes in a dark, stylishly designed Moroccan setting. V	AE MC		■	●	
SOUTHWEST DUBLIN					
ELEPHANT AND CASTLE Map D3. €€€ 18 Temple Bar, Dublin 2. ☎ 679 3121. FAX 679 1399. This boisterous American-style restaurant serves food cooked to order from tortillas to hamburgers. The spicy chicken wings are superb. 🚹 V	AE DC MC V	●	■		
LEO BURDOCK'S Map C4. € 2 Werburgh St, Dublin 8. ☎ 454 0306. Dublin's oldest fish-and-chip takeaway attracts a mix of patrons. The fish is fresh, and the chips made from top-grade Irish potatoes. 🚹		●	■		
LORD EDWARD Map B4. €€€€ 23 Christchurch Place, Dublin 8. ☎ 454 2420. FAX 454 2420. Dublin's oldest seafood restaurant serves lunch in the ground-floor pub and evening meals in the upstairs restaurant. Courteous service. V	AE DC MC V	●		●	■
LA MED Map D3. €€€€ 22 East Essex St, Temple Bar, Dublin 2. ☎ 670 7358. FAX 670 7358. W www.lamed.ie This bright and airy restaurant serves a range of Mediterranean dishes and has a lively atmosphere. There is no lunchtime opening from Monday to Wednesday. 🚹 V	AE MC V	●	■		■
MERMAID CAFÉ Map C3. €€€€ 69–70 Dame St, Dublin 2. ☎ 670 8236. FAX 670 8205. W www.mermaid.ie This popular restaurant near Dublin Castle serves a variety of trendy European dishes. The decor is simple but smart with highly polished handmade tables. ⬛ V	MC V	●	■		■
THE OLD MILL Map D3. €€€ 14 Temple Bar, Merchants' Arch, Dublin 2. ☎ 671 9262. This cosy French restaurant with its low, beamed ceilings has a romantic atmosphere. The menu is changed daily. V	AE DC MC V	●	■	●	■
YAMAMORI NOODLES Map C3 €€€ 71–72 South Great George's St, Dublin 2 ☎ 475 5001. FAX 475 5001. This bright and buzzing restaurant has an extensive menu, but specializes in sushi. Decor is a fusion of traditional and modern. V	AE MC V	●	■		
NORTH OF THE LIFFEY					
CHAPTER ONE RESTAURANT Map C1. €€€€ Below Dublin Writers' Museum, Parnell Square, Dublin 1. ☎ 873 2266. FAX 873 2330. The decor features pictures of Irish writers. Cuisine is modern European using a lot of organic produce. There is also an oyster and champagne bar on the premises. 🚹 V	AE DC MC V	●	■	●	■

For key to symbols see back flap

		CREDIT CARDS	OPEN LUNCH TIME	OPEN LATE	FIXED-PRICE MENU	GOOD WINE LIST

Average prices for a three-course meal for one, half a bottle of house wine and unavoidable charges such as service and cover:
€ under 15 euros
€€ 15 to 25 euros
€€€ 25 to 35 euros
€€€€ over 35 euros

OPEN LUNCH TIME
Many restaurants open only in the evening, but those in large towns and attached to pubs often open at lunch time.
OPEN LATE
Restaurant remains open with the full menu available after 10pm.
FIXED-PRICE MENU
A good-value fixed-price menu on offer at lunch, dinner or both, usually with three courses.
GOOD WINE LIST
Denotes a wide range of good wines, or a more specialized selection of wines.

Restaurant	Price	Credit Cards	Open Lunch Time	Open Late	Fixed-Price Menu	Good Wine List
FLANAGAN'S RESTAURANT Map D2. 61 O'Connell St Upper, Dublin 1. ℂ 873 1388. FAX 872 9344. Flanagan's is great value for money with an extensive menu ranging from steaks, burgers, pizzas and salads to vegetarian and pasta dishes. 🚻 V	€€€	MC V	●	▦	●	▦
THE HALO RESTAURANT Map C3. The Morrison Hotel, Ormond Quay, Dublin 1. ℂ 887 2421. FAX 874 4039. Chic, minimalist design restaurant serving outstanding organic dishes Modern European with Asian influence. ♿ V	€€€€	AE DC MC V	●	▦	●	▦
THE ITALIAN CONNECTION Map D2. 95 Talbot St, Dublin 1. ℂ 878 7125. FAX 624 7185. A friendly, relaxed atmosphere makes dining at this restaurant a pleasure. The menu offers a range of classic Italian dishes. ♿ 🚻 V	€€€	AE DC MC V	●	▦	●	▦
SHERIES RESTAURANT Map D2. 3 Lower Abbey St, Dublin 1. ℂ 874 7237. FAX 874 7237. Serving both traditional Irish dishes and modern European food, Sheries is open from breakfast time onwards but closes at 8pm. 🚻 V	€€€	AE DC MC V	●			▦
101 TALBOT Map E2. 100–102 Talbot St, Dublin 1. ℂ 874 5011. FAX 878 1053. W www.101talbot.com A cheerful and relaxed restaurant close to The Abbey Theatre – good for pre-theatre meals. Excellent choice of vegetarian dishes. V	€€€	AE DC MC V		▦	●	

FURTHER AFIELD

Restaurant	Price	Credit Cards	Open Lunch Time	Open Late	Fixed-Price Menu	Good Wine List
ABBEY TAVERN Abbey St, Howth. ℂ 839 0307. FAX 839 0284. W www.abbeytavern.ie A 16th-century tavern complete with original stone walls, gas lights and open turf fires, just off Howth Harbour and specializing in seafood. Its Irish music sessions are an institution. Book ahead. 🚻 V	€€€€	AE DC MC V	●		●	▦
BELLA CUBA 11 Ballsbridge Terrace, Dublin 4. ℂ 660 5539. FAX 660 5539. W www.bella-cuba.com Dublin's first Cuban restaurant is an unusual place with atmosphere and music to match the genuine Cuban cuisine. V	€€€	AE MC V		▦	●	▦
BON APPETIT 9 St James Terrace, Malahide. ℂ 845 0314. W www.bonappetite.ie A superb range of seafood, meat dishes and game, when in season, are offered here. The wine list is extensive and the staff efficient. V	€€€€	DC MC V	●	▦	●	▦
AL BOSCHETTO 1a Beattys Avenue, Ballsbridge, Dublin 4. ℂ 667 3784. This relaxed and informal restaurant run by an Italian family, serves delicious Italian dishes at reasonable prices. ♿ 🚻 V	€€€	AE DC MC V	●	▦	●	▦
BRASSERIE NA MARA 1 Harbour Rd, Dun Laoghaire. ℂ 280 6767. FAX 284 4649. This delightful restaurant in the old Georgian train station, overlooking the harbour, serves the best just-caught seafood in the area. Non-fish dishes are also available. Smoking area outside. ♿ V	€€€	AE DC MC V	●		●	▦
CAVISTON'S 58 Glasthule Rd, Sandycove. ℂ 280 9120. FAX 284 4054. W www.cavistons.com Treat yourself for lunch – open noon to 5pm only (last orders 3pm). This excellent fish restaurant serves fresh mouthwatering dishes. ♿ 🚻 V	€€€	AE DC MC V	●		●	▦
KING SITRIC FISH RESTAURANT East Pier, Howth. ℂ 832 5235. FAX 839 2442. W www.kingsitric.ie Howth crab and lobster star on the menu of this well-known, recently refurbished restaurant. Reserve for dinner. V	€€€€	AE MC V	●	▦	●	▦

PALMCOURT CAFÉ €€€€
Berkeley Court Hotel, Lansdowne Rd, Ballsbridge, Dublin 4. 📞 660 1711. ☏ 661 7238.
In this bright, conservatory-style room in one of the city's most luxurious
hotels, meals from the extensive menu are excellent value for money.
Very popular with Dubliners. 🚻

	AE				
	DC				
	MC				
	V				

ROLY'S BISTRO €€€€
7 Ballsbridge Terrace, Ballsbridge, Dublin 4. 📞 668 2611. 🌐 www.rolysbistro.ie
Extremely popular up-market bistro with plenty of atmosphere and
excellent service. Seasonal dishes a speciality. Book ahead.

	AE				
	DC				
	MC				
	V				

BEYOND DUBLIN

CARLINGFORD *Slieve Foy Restaurant* €€€€
Newry St. 📞 042 9373223.
A renovated 17th-century fisherman's cottage overlooking the harbour is
the setting for culinary gems with organically grown ingredients.

	AE				
	MC				
	V				

CARLOW *The Beams Restaurant* €€€€
59 Dublin St. 📞 059 9131824.
A family-run restaurant in a 17th-century building with beamed ceilings.
Dishes include wild Atlantic salmon with white wine sauce, plus a huge
choice of Irish cheeses. Closed Sunday and Monday.

	MC				
	V				

CARRICKMACROSS *Nuremore Hotel* €€€€
Carrickmacross. 📞 042 9661438. ☏ 042 9661853. 🌐 www.nuremore-hotel.ie
This beautiful restaurant has an imaginative menu, including French
and Irish cuisine, served in a tranquil setting.

	AE				
	DC				
	MC				
	V				

DUNDALK *Quaglino's Restaurant* €€€€
88 Clanbrassil St. 📞 042 9338567. ☏ 042 9351333.
This bright restaurant features superb Continental and Modern Irish
cuisine using local produce. Lunch on Sunday only.

	AE				
	DC				
	MC				
	V				

DUNLAVIN *Rathsallagh House & Restaurant* €€€€
Dunlavin. 📞 045 403112. ☏ 045 403343. 🌐 www.rathsallagh.com
The award-winning restaurant in this sumptuous country house serves
game in season and fresh fish from the Wexford coast.

	AE				
	DC				
	MC				
	V				

GOREY *Marlfield House* €€€€
Courtown Rd. 📞 055 21124. ☏ 055 21572. 🌐 www.marlfieldhouse.ie
This Regency mansion houses one of the southeast's premier dining
rooms. Organically grown vegetables are used.

	AE				
	DC				
	MC				
	V				

KILDARE *Silken Thomas* €€
The Square. 📞 045 522232. ☏ 045 520471. 🌐 www.silkenthomas.com
Located near the Norman castle keep in the town centre, this restaurant
includes beef stroganoff and Gaelic steak on its menu.

	DC				
	MC				
	V				

MULLINGAR *Crookedwood House* €€€
Crookedwood. 📞 044 72165. ☏ 044 72166. 🌐 www.crookedwoodhouse.com
This 200-year-old building has beautiful views over the lake. The restaurant
specializes in Modern Irish cuisine. Lunch on Sunday only.

	AE				
	DC				
	MC				
	V				

NAAS *Killashee House Hotel* €€€€
Killashee, Naas. 📞 045 879277. ☏ 045 879266. 🌐 www.killasheehouse.com
The exquisite dining room is matched by the mouth-watering Irish and
Mediterranean dishes created by award-winning chefs.

	AE				
	DC				
	MC				
	V				

RATHNEW *Hunter's Hotel* €€€€
Rathnew. 📞 0404 40106. ☏ 0404 40338. 🌐 www.hunters.ie
Cheerful hotel dining room attracting patrons from Dublin and nearby,
with its friendly ambience and superb meat and fish dishes.

	AE				
	MC				
	V				

RATHNEW *Tinakilly Country House and Restaurant* €€€€
Co Wicklow. 📞 0404 69274. ☏ 0404 67806. 🌐 www.tinakilly.ie
There is a delicious, daily-changing menu at this elegant restaurant,
which also enjoys the advantage of a welcoming country house setting.

	AE				
	DC				
	MC				
	V				

TULLAMORE *Moorhill Country House* €€€
Clara Rd. 📞 0506 21395. ☏ 0506 52424. 🌐 www.moorhill.ie
Traditional but imaginative restaurant in renovated stables, with stone
walls, oak beams and open fires. Lunch on Sunday only.

	AE				
	DC				
	MC				
	V				

For key to symbols see back flap

Pubs, Bars and Cafés

Dublin's pubs are a slice of living history, famous as the haunts of literary figures, politicans and rock stars alike. Today, as well as the memorabilia on the walls, it is the singing, dancing, talk and laughter that make a pub tour of Dublin a necessity *(see p142)*.

There are nearly 1,000 pubs inside the city limits. Some excel in entertainment, others in the quality of their Guinness and their pub food, but there are also many modern bars to match the best in Europe.

In recent years Dublin has become very cosmopolitan and, as well as the pubs, there is a wide range of cafés offering quick and inexpensive food. The ones listed here are good for those on a busy sightseeing schedule.

TRADITIONAL PUBS

Each Dublin pub has its own character and, while many of them are rather touristy, they retain a trade-mark clientèle: **Doheny & Nesbitt** and the **Horseshoe Bar** attract politicians, journalists and lawyers while **Neary's** pulls in a theatrical crowd. Others have a strong literary connection; Brendan Behan drank at **McDaid's** while **Davy Byrne's** was featured in Joyce's *Ulysses*. Some of the best and most ornate interiors include **The Brazen Head**, the **Stag's Head**, the **Long Hall** and **Kehoe's** with its great snugs. **Mulligan's**, founded in 1782, claims to have the best Guinness. If you fancy something different, **Porter House** in Parliament Street brews its own, including an excellent oyster stout.

MUSIC PUBS

Regular traditional music sessions take place all over Dublin. **The Brazen Head**, **O'Donoghue's** and the **Cobblestone** are popular venues. The **International Bar** focuses on singers and comedians, while **Whelan's** has a proper venue room next door with an eclectic range of acts for a cover charge of under 10 euros.

MODERN BARS

Recently, a number of Continental-style bars have cropped up which cater to a young and fashionable crowd. **Hogan's**, and the **Globe** are on the edge of Temple Bar. The main bar at the **Clarence Hotel** does great cocktails. Inventive drinks are also on the menu at the trendy **Chocolate Bar**. **Café en Seine** near Trinity College has a wide choice of food and offers a live jazz brunch on Sunday.

PUB FOOD

Many of Dublin's grand old pubs offer tasty and good-value pub lunches. Just off Grafton Street are **O'Neill's** and the very traditional **Old Stand**. In Temple Bar, **Oliver St John Gogarty** is probably the best option.

MUSEUM AND SHOP CAFÉS

Many of Dublin's tourist attractions offer good-quality cafés and snack bars. One of the best is at the **National Gallery**: it serves mainly Mediterranean food and is operated by the Fitzer's chain. Food at the **National Museum** has more of a traditional Irish choice while **Irish Film Institute** offers an eclectic range. Food at **Avoca** is modern and delicious: go early if you want to get in. For a unique place to eat, try the upstairs café at the **Winding Stair Bookshop**.

BREAKFAST

Most hotels and B&Bs in the city serve reasonable breakfasts, an essential start to a full day's sightseeing. A particular favourite of Dubliners is **Café Java**, while the great

Billboard Café stays open 24 hours a day from Thursday at 7:30am to Sunday at 8pm and serves breakfast throughout. **Café Kylemore** also makes a good breakfast.

COFFEE AND CAKES

In an attractive setting among the stalls at Powerscourt Townhouse, **Chompy's** offers generous portions of cheesecake and other gateaux as well as a good selection of tea and coffee.

PIZZA AND PASTA

Irish-Italian cafés and restaurants offer some of the best-value meals in the city. Two very popular ones, the family-oriented **Little Caesar's Palace** and the tiny **Steps of Rome**, lie off Grafton Street, as does the excellent **Pasta Fresca**. Temple Bar's **Bad Ass Café** has a youthful feel and serves pizza, pasta and salads. Sinéad O'Connor worked here before making it in music. **Milano**, currently with two branches in the city, is a branch of the popular British chain Pizza Express.

TRADITIONAL FOOD

For traditional food with a modern slant, **Gallagher's Boxty House**, specialising in Irish pancakes, is a popular choice. However, some might prefer the even simpler fare at **Café Kylemore** which is run by a major city bakery. For good honest fish and chips try the venerable **Leo Burdock's**.

VEGETARIAN

One of the great favourites is the long-running café, **Cornucopia**, also open for breakfast and lunch. **Café Fresh** is a fun place to eat in the Powerscourt Townhouse while **Juice** offers a cool, modern feel. The **Alamo Café** is the pick of the city's Mexican restaurants and offers lots of choice for vegetarians but also serves meat dishes. Temple Bar's Saturday market has a good organic selection.

DIRECTORY

TRADITIONAL PUBS

The Brazen Head
20 Bridge St Lower.
Map A3.
679 5186.

Davy Byrne's
21 Duke St.
Map D4.
677 5217.

Doheny & Nesbitt
5 Lower Baggot St.
Map F5.
676 2945.

Horseshoe Bar
Shelbourne Hotel,
27 St Stephen's Green.
Map E4.
663 4500.

John Kehoe's
9 Anne St South.
Map D4.
677 8312.

The Long Hall
51 South Great George's
St. **Map** C4.
475 1590.

McDaid's
3 Harry St.
Map D4.
679 4395.

Mulligan's
8 Poolbeg St.
Map E3.
677 5582.

Neary's
1 Chatham St.
Map D4.
677 8596.

Porter House
16-18 Parliament St.
Map C3.
679 8847.

Stag's Head
1 Dame Court, off Dame St.
Map C3.
679 3701.

MUSIC BARS

Cobblestone
77 North King St.
Map A2.
872 1799.

International Bar
23 Wicklow St.
Map D3.
677 9250.

O'Donoghue's
15 Merrion Row.
Map C5.
660 7194.

Whelan's
25 Wexford St.
Map C5.
478 0766.

MODERN BARS

The Café Bar
Morrison Hotel
Ormond Quay.
Map C3.
887 2400.

Café en Seine
40 Dawson St.
Map D4.
677 4567.

Chocolate Bar
Harcourt St, at Hatch St
Lower. **Map** D5.
478 0225.

Octagon Bar
Clarence Hotel
6-8 Wellington Quay.
Map C3.
670 9000.

The Globe
11 South Great George's St.
Map C4.
671 1220.

Hogan's
35 South Great George's St.
Map C4.
677 5904.

PUB FOOD

The Old Stand
37 Exchequer St.
Map D3.
677 7220.

**Oliver St John
Gogarty**
57 Fleet St.
Map D3.
671 1822.

O'Neill's
2 Suffolk St.
Map D3.
679 3656.

MUSEUM AND SHOP CAFÉS

Avoca Café
11-13 Suffolk St.
Map D3.
286 7466.

Irish Film Institute
6 Eustace St,
Temple Bar.
Map C3.
677 8788.

National Gallery
Merrion Square West.
Map E4.
661 5133.

National Museum
Kildare St.
Map E4.
677 7444.

**Winding Stair
Bookshop & Café**
40 Ormond Quay Lower.
Map C3.
873 3292.

BREAKFAST

Billboard Café
43 Lower Camden St.
Map C5.
475 5047.

Café Java
5 Anne St South.
Map D4.
670 7239.
145 Leeson St.
Map E5.
660 0675.

COFFEE AND CAKES

Chompy's
Powerscourt Townhouse,
South William St.
Map D4.
679 4552.

PIZZA AND PASTA

Bad Ass Café
9 Crown Alley,
Temple Bar.
Map D3.
671 2596.

**Little Caesar's
Palace**
1-3 Balfe St. **Map** D4.
670 4534.

Milano
38 Dawson St.
Map D4.
670 7744.
19 Essex St East.
Map C3.
670 3384.

Pasta Fresca
4 Chatham St.
Map D4.
679 2402.

Steps of Rome
Unit 1, Chatham Court,
Chatham St.
Map D4.
670 5630.

Boticelli
3 Temple Bar
Map C3
672 7289

TRADITIONAL FOOD

Café Kylemore
1 Upper O'Connell St.
Map D2.
878 0498.

**Gallagher's Boxty
House**
Temple Bar.
Map D3.
677 2762.

Leo Burdock's
2 Werburgh St.
Map C4.
454 0306.

VEGETARIAN

Alamo Café
22 Temple Bar.
Map C3.
677 6546.

Cafe Fresh
Powerscourt Townhouse,
South William St.
Map D4.
671 9669.

Cornucopia
19 Wicklow St.
Map D3.
677 7583.

Juice
9 Castlehouse
South Great George's St.
Map C4.
475 7856.

SHOPS AND MARKETS

DUBLIN IS A paradise for shoppers, with its wide streets, indoor markets, craft stores and out-of-town shopping centres. Popular buys include chunky Aran sweaters, Waterford crystal, Irish linen, hand-loomed tweed from Donegal and tasty farmhouse cheeses. The thriving crafts industry is based on traditional products with an innovative twist. Typical of contemporary Irish crafts are good design, quality craftsmanship and a range spanning Celtic brooches and bone china, knitwear and designer fashion, carved bogwood and books of Irish poetry. Kitsch souvenirs also abound, from leprechauns and shamrock emblems to Guinness tankards and garish religious memorabilia. Irish whiskeys and liqueurs are always popular and very reasonable to buy in Dublin. In the directory on page 137, a map reference is given for each address that features on the Dublin Street Finder map on pages 164–5.

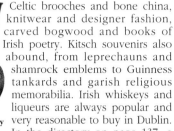

Modern Irish pottery

Johnson's Court alley behind Grafton Street in southwest Dublin

WHERE TO SHOP

THERE ARE two major shopping quarters in Dublin. The north side of the Liffey, centred on O'Connell and Henry streets, has several shopping centres and department stores. The famous Moore Street fruit and vegetable market is held Monday to Saturday just off Grafton Street. More upmarket shops can be found on the south side, around Grafton and Nassau streets. The Temple Bar area contains a number of trendy craft shops.

WHEN TO SHOP

MOST SHOPS are open from Monday to Saturday, 9am to 5:30 or 6pm. Shops open late on Thursday nights. Shops are closed at Easter and Christmas and on St Patrick's Day but are open on most other public holidays.

HOW TO PAY

MAJOR CREDIT cards such as VISA and MasterCard are accepted in most large stores, but smaller shops may prefer cash. Traveller's cheques are accepted in major stores with a passport as identification. Eurocheques are generally no longer acceptable.

SALES TAX AND REFUNDS

MOST PURCHASES are subject to VAT (sales tax) at 21 per cent, a sum included in the sales price. However, visitors from outside the European Union (EU) can reclaim VAT prior to departure. If you are shipping goods overseas, refunds can be claimed at the point of purchase. If taking your goods with you, look for the CashBack logo in shops, fill in the special voucher, then visit the CashBack offices at Dublin airport.

SHOPPING CENTRES

DUBLIN HAS several large shopping centres – some in the city centre and some outside. The **Dun Laoghaire Shopping Centre** is on several floors and has a huge range of clothes shops, bookshops and electronics shops. In central Dublin is the **St Stephen's Green Shopping Centre**, the **Jervis Shopping Centre** and the **Ilac Centre**, all offering the comfort of covered shopping. A more unusual centre is the **Powerscourt Townhouse** *(see p58)*, more of an indoor market than a shopping centre, selling various Irish crafts.

BOOKS

BOOKSHOPS ABOUND in Dublin. **Eason and Son**, on O'Connell Street, is the biggest bookseller in the city with a wide range of Irish literature and national and

The Ha'penny Bridge Galleries on Bachelors Walk

Brown Thomas department store on Grafton Street

international newspapers. For antiquarian books, **Cathach Books** on Duke Street has an excellent selection.

Foreign-language books are available in Dublin – try **International Books** for the best range. **Hodges Figgis** specializes in Irish literature and academic publications. They also have a coffee shop in the store. One of the best for general books is the **Dublin Bookshop** on Grafton Street (part of the Dubray Books chain). On two floors, they have an extensive Irish section and a good range of tourist guides as well as general fiction and children's books. **Waterstone's** and **Hughes & Hughes** are also both good general booksellers.

Sign outside Eason and Son

MUSIC

TRADITIONAL MUSICAL instruments are made in many regions of Ireland, but Dublin has a history of specializing in hand-made harps. Several shops sell musical instruments, such as hand-crafted bodhráns (traditional goatskin hand-held drums) and uilleann pipes (bagpipes). **Waltons** sells traditional instruments and sheet music, while **Claddagh Records** is a specialist folk shop, selling Irish folk and ethnic music. For a standard range of pop and classical music there are two branches of the **HMV** music store in Dublin.

ANTIQUES

DUBLIN HAS its own antiques centre, in the form of Francis Street in the south west of the city. **Lantern Antiques** specializes in old pub fittings such as mirrors and old advertisements. For rugs and carpets try **Forsyth's Antiques**. For 20th-century decorative arts visit **Johnston Antiques**. The **Ha'penny Bridge Galleries** sell everything from furniture through to cast iron and marble. **Courtville Antiques** in the Powerscourt Townhouse has a beautiful collection of antique jewellery, silver, paintings and objets d'art. On Grafton Street, **McCormack** is particularly good for antique jewellery.

CRAFTS

THE **Whichcraft Gallery** in Cow's Lane and the **Irish Celtic Craftshop** in Lord Edward Street have a great

Bodhráns of perfect pitch for sale in Dublin

range of contemporary Irish crafts. The Crafts Council also recommends other good outlets for Irish crafts, and the tourist offices have lists of local workshops, where you can often watch the production process. **The Kilkenny Shop** sells tiles, rugs, metal-, leather- and woodwork.

JEWELLERY

IN ITS GOLDEN AGE, Celtic metalwork was the pride of Ireland. Many contemporary craftspeople are still inspired by traditional designs on Celtic chalices and ornaments. Silver and gold jewellery is made all over Ireland in many designs and widely available in Dublin. The Claddagh ring is the most famous of all – the lovers' symbol of two hands cradling a heart with a crown. In the Powerscourt Townhouse, shops have handmade and antique jewellery on display and gold- and silversmiths can be seen at work. **McDowell** jewellers specialize in handcrafted gold and silver Irish jewellery.

CHINA, CRYSTAL AND GLASSWARE

IRELAND'S MOST FAMOUS make of crystalware is Waterford Crystal. Still made today in the town of Waterford, south of Dublin, this beautiful crystal and glassware is known all over the world for its outstanding quality.

Dublin Crystal, in Blackrock, south of the city, makes and sells on the premises fine-quality hand-cut crystal.

There are many producers of fine china in Ireland. Royal Tara China in Galway is Ireland's leading fine bone china manufacturer, with designs incorporating Celtic themes. The best place to buy china and glassware is in department stores, such as Clery's and Brown Thomas.

LINEN

D AMASK LINEN was brought to Armagh in Northern Ireland by Huguenot refugees fleeing French persecution. Linen is widely available all over Ireland today, and fine Irish linen can be bought at many outlets in Dublin, including the **Brown Thomas** department store, which has an excellent linen shop. Another good supplier is **Murphy, Sheehy and Co**, who are located behind the Powercourt Townhouse. As well as being famous for fine-quality Irish linen, they also sell tweeds.

Sign for the linen department at Brown Thomas store

KNITWEAR AND TWEED

A RAN SWEATERS are sold all over Ireland, but originate in County Galway and the Aran Islands themselves, off the west coast of Ireland. One of Dublin's best buys, these oiled, off-white sweaters used to be handed down through generations of Aran fishermen. Legend has it that each family used its own motifs so that, if a fisherman were lost at sea and his body unidentifiable, his family could recognize him by his sweater. Warm and rain-resistant clothes are generally of good quality, from waxed jackets and duffel coats to sheepskin jackets. **House of Ireland** offer an excellent selection of quality Irish clothing. Knitwear is sold everywhere in Dublin.

Good buys include embroidered waistcoats and handwoven scarves. **The Sweater Shop** has woollens and tweeds at reasonable prices. The Suffolk Street branch of **Avoca** has a good mix of traditional and trendy.

Donegal tweed is noted for its texture and subtle colours (originally produced by local plant and mineral dyes). Tweed caps, scarves, ties, jackets and suits are sold in outlets such as **Kevin & Howlin** in Dublin. For menswear specialists, try **Kennedy & McSharry**.

FASHION

I NSPIRED BY a predominantly young population, Ireland is fast acquiring a name for fashion. Conservatively cut tweed and linen suits continue to be models of classic good taste, while younger designers are increasingly experimental, using bold lines and mixing traditional fabrics.

A-Wear is an Irish chain store that has a branch in Dublin. In the Design Centre in Powerscourt Townhouse Shopping Centre are clothes by the best Irish designers including John Rocha, Paul Costelloe, Louise Kennedy, Quin and Donnelly and Mariad Whisker. The department stores **Brown Thomas** and **Clery's** have an excellent selection of men's, women's and children's clothing. Shoe and clothing sizes are identical to British fittings.

Fresh cheeses in Meetinghouse Square

FOOD AND DRINK

S MOKED SALMON, home-cured bacon, farmhouse cheeses, preserves, soda bread and handmade chocolates make perfect last-minute gifts. **Butlers Chocolate Café,** sells particularly delicious handmade Irish chocolates. Several shops will package and send Irish salmon overseas.

Bewley's teas and coffees are sold in supermarkets like Tescos, **Dunnes** and Super Value all over Ireland. Guinness travels less well and is best drunk in Ireland. Irish whiskey is hard to beat as a gift or souvenir. Apart from the cheaper Power and Paddy brands, the big names are Bushmills and Jameson. Irish liqueurs to enjoy include Irish Mist and Bailey's Irish Cream.

Fresh fruit stall off O'Connell Street

DIRECTORY

SHOPPING CENTRES

Dun Laoghaire Shopping Centre
Marine Rd, Dun Laoghaire.
(280 2981.

Ilac Centre
Henry St.
Map D2.
(704 1460.

Jervis Shopping Centre
125 Abbey St Upper.
Map C2.
(878 1323.

Powerscourt Townhouse Shopping Centre
South William St.
Map D4.
(679 5718.

St Stephen's Green Shopping Centre
St Stephen's Green West.
Map D4.
(478 0888.

BOOKS

Cathach Books
10 Duke St.
Map D4.
(671 8676.
W www.rarebooks.ie

Dublin Bookshop
36 Grafton St.
Map D4.
(677 5568.

Eason and Son
80 Middle Abbey St.
Map D2.
(873 3811.
W www.eason.ie

Hodges Figgis
56–58 Dawson St.
Map D4.
(677 4754.

Hughes & Hughes
St Stephen's Green Shopping Centre.
Map D4.
(478 3060.
Also at
Dublin Airport.
(704 4034.

International Books
18 Frederick St South.
Map E4.
(679 9375.
W www.interbookirl.com

Waterstone's
7 Dawson St.
Map D4.
(679 1415.
Also at
Jervis Shopping Centre.
Map C2.
(878 1311.
W www.waterstones.co.uk

MUSIC

Claddagh Records
2 Cecilia St, Temple Bar.
Map C3.
(677 0262.

HMV
18 Henry St.
Map D2.
(873 2899.
Also at
Grafton St.
Map D4.
(679 5334.

Waltons
3–5 Frederick St North.
Map C1.
(874 7805.

JEWELLERY

McDowell
3 Upper O'Connell St.
Map D2.
(874 4961.

ANTIQUES

Courtville Antiques
Powerscourt Townhouse Shopping Centre.
Map D4.
(679 4042.

Forsyth's Antiques
108 Francis St.
Map B4.
(473 2148.

The Ha'penny Bridge Galleries
15 Bachelors Walk.
Map D3.
(872 3950.

Lantern Antiques
56 Francis St.
Map B4.
(453 4593.

McCormack
51 Grafton St.
Map D4.
(677 3737.

Johnston Antiques
69–70 Francis St.
Map B4.
(473 2384.
W www.johnston antiques.net

CRAFTS

The Whichcraft Gallery
Cow's Lane, Temple Bar.
Map C3.
(474 1011.
W www.whichcraft.com

The Irish Celtic Craftshop
10–12 Lord Edward St.
Map C3.
(679 9912.

The Kilkenny Shop
6 Nassau St.
Map E4.
(677 7066.
W www.kilkenny group.com

CERAMICS, CHINA AND CRYSTAL

Dublin Crystal
Brookfield Terrace
(off Carysfort Avenue),
Blackrock, Co Dublin.
(298 7302.
W www.dublincrystal.com

LINENS

Brown Thomas Linen Department
Grafton St.
Map D4.
(605 6666.

Murphy, Sheehy and Co
14 Castle Market.
Map D4.
(677 0316.
W www.murphysheehy fabrics.com

KNITWEAR AND TWEED

Avoca
11-13 Suffolk St.
Map D3.
(677 4215.
W www.avoca.ie

House of Ireland
37–38 Nassau St.
Map D4.
(671 1111.
W www.houseof ireland.com

Kennedy and McSharry
39 Nassau St.
Map D3.
(677 8770.

Kevin and Howlin
31 Nassau St.
Map D3.
(677 0257.

The Sweater Shop
9 Wicklow St.
Map D3.
(671 3270.
W www.sweatershop.ie

FASHION

A-Wear
26 Grafton St.
Map D4.
(671 7200.
W www.awear.ie

Brown Thomas
88–95 Grafton St.
Map D4.
(605 6666.

Clery's
18–27 O'Connell St Lower.
Map D2.
(878 6000.
W www.clerys.ie

FOOD AND DRINK

Butlers Chocolate Café
51a Grafton St.
Map D4.
(671 0599.

Dunnes
Henry St.
Map D2.
(671 4629.

What to Buy in Dublin

St Brigid's cross

THE MANY GIFT and craft shops scattered throughout Dublin make it easy to find Irish specialities to suit all budgets. The best buys include linen, tweeds and lead crystal. Local crafts make unique souvenirs, from delicate handmade silver jewellery and hand-thrown ceramics to traditional musical instruments. Religious artifacts are also widely available. Irish food and drink, especially whiskey, are evocative reminders of your trip.

Traditional hand-held drum
(*bodhrán*) and beater

Connemara marble
"worry stone"

Traditional
Claddagh ring

Enamel brooch

Modern jewellery and metalwork draw on a long and varied tradition. Craftspeople continue to base their designs on sources such as the Book of Kells (see p38) and Celtic myths. Local plants and wildlife are also an inspiration. Claddagh rings – traditional betrothal rings – originated in County Galway but are widely available in Dublin.

Fuchsia earring
from Dingle

Celtic design
enamel brooch

Celtic design
silver pendant

Donegal tweed jacket and waistcoat

Tweed jacket and skirt

Clothing made in Ireland is usually of excellent quality. Tweed-making still flourishes in Donegal where tweed can be bought ready-made as clothing or hats or as lengths of cloth. Knitwear is widely available throughout Dublin in department stores and local craft shops. The many hand-knitted items on sale, including Aran jumpers, are not cheap but should give years of wear.

Tweed cap

Aran jumper

Tweed fisherman's hat

Irish linen is world-famous and the range unparalleled. There is a huge choice of table and bed linen, including extravagant bedspreads and crisp, formal tablecloths. On a smaller scale, tiny, intricately embroidered handkerchiefs make lovely gifts as do linen table napkins. Tea towels printed with colourful designs are widely available. You can also buy linen goods trimmed with fine lace, which is still handmade in many parts of the country.

Set of linen placemats and napkins

Fine linen handkerchiefs

Nicholas Mosse plate

Belleek teapot

Nicholas Mosse cup

Irish ceramics come in traditional and modern designs. You can buy anything from a full dinner service by established factories, such as Royal Tara China or the Belleek Pottery, to a one-off contemporary piece from a local potter's studio.

Irish crystal, hand-blown and hand-cut, can be ordered or bought in many shops in Dublin. Pieces from the principal manufacturers, such as Waterford Crystal, Tyrone Crystal and Jerpoint Glass, from glasses and decanters to elaborate chandeliers, are widely sold.

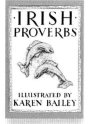

Book of Irish Proverbs

Books and stationery are often beautifully illustrated. Museums and bookshops stock a wide range.

Celtic design cards

Waterford crystal tumbler and decanter

Food and drink will keep the distinctive tastes of Dublin fresh long after you arrive home. Whiskey connoisseurs should visit the Old Jameson Distillery (see p73) to sample their choice of whiskeys. The Guinness Storehouse (see p80) is a must for aficionados of the dark stout. Good regional food can be found all over the Dublin area.

Jameson whiskey

Bushmills whiskey

Fruit cake made with Guinness

Jar of Irish marmalade

Packet of dried seaweed

ENTERTAINMENT IN DUBLIN

A LTHOUGH DUBLIN is well served by theatres, cinemas, night-clubs and rock venues, what sets the city apart from other European capitals is its pubs. Lively banter, impromptu music sessions and great Guinness are the essential ingredients for an enjoyable night in any one of dozens of lively, atmospheric hostelries in Dublin.

One of the most popular entertainment districts is the Temple Bar area. Along this narrow network of cobbled streets you can find

Traditional Irish dancer

everything from traditional music in grand old pubs to the latest dance tracks in a post-industrial setting. The variety of venues makes the centre south of the Liffey the place to be at night, although the north side does boast the two most illustrious theatres, the largest cinemas and the 7,000-seater Point Theatre, a converted 19th-century rail terminal beside the docks. It is now the venue for all major rock concerts and stage musicals as well as some classical music performances.

The listings magazine, *In Dublin*, published every other week

ENTERTAINMENT LISTINGS

T HE MAIN LISTINGS magazine, *In Dublin*, comes out every two weeks and is readily available from all newsagents. *Hot Press*, a national bimonthly newspaper that covers both rock and traditional music, has comprehensive listings for Dublin. The *Dublin Event Guide* is a free sheet available from pubs, cafés, restaurants and record shops. Like *In Dublin*, it is published every two weeks, and is particularly strong on information about the city's music and nightclubs.

BOOKING TICKETS

T ICKETS FOR many events are available on the night, but it is usually safer to book in advance. The principal venues accept payment over the telephone by all the major credit cards. The **Ticket Shop** accepts phone bookings by credit card for many of the major shows and events in

and around Dublin, while **HMV** and **Dublin Tourism** (Suffolk Street) sell tickets for theatres and rock gigs.

THEATRE

A LTHOUGH DUBLIN has only a limited number of theatres, there is almost always something worth seeing and the productions are of a very high standard. Most of Dublin's theatres are closed on Sunday.

The most famous venue is Ireland's national theatre, the **Abbey** *(see p68)*, which concentrates on major new Irish productions as well as revivals of works by Irish playwrights such as Brendan Behan, Sean O'Casey, JM Synge and WB Yeats. The smaller **Peacock Theatre** downstairs covers more experimental works.

Street entertainer in central Dublin

Colourful façade of the Olympia Theatre on Dame Street

Also on the north side is the **Gate Theatre** *(see p70)*, founded in 1929 and noted for its interpretations of well-known international plays. The main venue south of the Liffey, the **Gaiety Theatre**, stages a mainstream mix of plays, emphasizing the work of Irish playwrights. Some of the best fringe theatre and modern dance in Dublin can be seen at **Project** arts centre in Temple Bar and the **City Arts Centre**, which sometimes has midnight performances. **Andrews Lane Theatre** provides a forum for up-and-coming new writers and directors. The **Olympia Theatre** on Dame Street has the feel of a Victorian music hall. Specializing in comedy and popular

Buskers playing near Grafton Street in Southeast Dublin

drama, the Olympia also occasionally attracts some of the top performers to stage rock and Irish music concerts in the theatre's intimate setting.

Every October the **Dublin Theatre Festival** takes over all the venues in the city with a mix of mainstream, fringe, Irish and international plays.

CLASSICAL MUSIC, OPERA AND DANCE

DUBLIN MAY not have the range of classical concerts of other European capitals, but it has a great venue in the **National Concert Hall**. In the 1980s, this 19th-century exhibition hall was redesigned and acoustically adapted, and is where the National Symphony Orchestra plays most Friday evenings. The programme also includes jazz, dance, opera, chamber music, and some traditional music.

The **Hugh Lane Municipal Gallery of Modern Art** *(see p71)* has regular Sunday lunchtime concerts. Other classical venues include the **Royal Hospital Kilmainham** *(see p82)*, the **Bank of Ireland Arts Centre** on Dame Street and the **Royal Dublin Society (RDS)**. International opera is staged in the **Point Theatre**. The DGOS (Dublin Grand Opera Society) performs every April and November at the Gaiety Theatre on King Street South.

TRADITIONAL MUSIC AND DANCE

TO MANY IRISH PEOPLE the standard of music in a pub is just as important as the quality of the Guinness. Central

Dublin has a host of pubs reverberating to the sound of bodhráns, fiddles and uilleann pipes. One of the most famous is **O'Donoghue's**, where the legendary Dubliners started out in the early 1960s. The long-established **Auld Dubliner** and **Cobblestone** are also renowned venues for local and foreign bands. Established acts play venues such as **Mother Redcap's Tavern**, which is a fun place occupying a spacious old factory and appealing to all ages. **Jury's Hotel** and the **Castle Inn** stage Irish cabaret featuring dancing, singing and lively, toe-tapping music.

ROCK, JAZZ, BLUES AND COUNTRY

DUBLIN HAS HAD a thriving rock scene ever since local band Thin Lizzy made it big in the early 1970s. U2's international success acted as a further catalyst for local bands, and there's a gig somewhere

in the city on most nights. **Whelan's** features the best new Irish bands nightly; the likeable **International Bar** caters mostly for acoustic acts and singer-songwriters; while the **Ha'penny Bridge Inn** has folk and blues on Friday and Saturday nights. Big names play at either the Point Theatre or, in summer, local sports stadia. **Slane Castle** hosts a big rock event every summer.

The **Temple Bar Music Centre** and **The Sugar Club** offer jazz, blues, salsa, swing and latin throughout the year with the **Heineken Green Energy Festival** in May. Country music also has a big following throughout Ireland.

HOTEL BARS

THE PUBS of Dublin have started to overflow and, as a result, a new breed of bar has taken off. The hotel bars are the city's sophisticated watering holes, appealing to those who wish to escape the "craic" of the more traditional pubs.

The **Inn on the Green**, located in the Fitzwilliam Hotel has Nineties cool metal decor. At the Merrion Hotel, you can hide from the hubbub of the city in the **Cellar Bar**. Trendy media types hang out at the mellow **Octagon Bar** at The Clarence, or the **Lobo Bar** at the Morrison, but if it's glamour you seek, head for a shot of whiskey in **The Horseshoe Bar** at the famous Shelbourne Hotel.

The Laughter Lounge

Crowds enjoying the Temple Bar Blues Festival

Comedian at The Ha'Penny Bridge Inn on Wellington Quay

COMEDY

T HE **LAUGHTER LOUNGE** is one of Dublin's top comedy venues, attracting big names from the world of stand-up comedy. Other venues include the **Olympia Theatre** for international stars and **The Ha'penny Bridge Inn**, Tuesday to Thursday, for local talent.

NIGHTCLUBS

U NTIL A CLUSTER of new dance venues opened in the early 1990s, Dublin's club-life was fairly unremarkable; nowadays there is plenty of choice. **POD** (Place of Dance) attracts visiting stars taking time out from their film or video shoots in the city. Also trendy is **Lillie's Bordello**, a magnet for celebrities, models and wannabes. It caters for a mainstream dance sound, while the more laid back venue **Rí-Rá** (Irish for uproar), is at the cutting edge of R&B and dance music.

For a lounge atmosphere, head for **The Sugar Club**, which always offers live music and cocktails. **The River Club** is theoretically only open to members, but dress smart and you should get in. Most clubs close at 2am but some stay open until 5am.

PUB CRAWLS AND TOURS

T HERE ARE numerous pub crawls in Dublin, most of which cover the character pubs and those with a long and colourful history. The **Dublin Literary Pub Crawl**, which starts in The Duke pub on Duke Street, is perhaps the most famous of these. The two-and-a-half-hour tours feature pubs once frequented by Ireland's most famous authors and playwrights.

Viking Splash Tours operate a land and water sightseeing tour of Dublin. This tour is carried out in an amphibious military vehicle decorated as a Viking ship and complete with Viking costumed driver.

A handful of tours around the city offer an insight into Dublin's dark and spooky history. **The Walk Macabre** visits scenes of murder and intrigue in the city. If you prefer to be driven around, the **Dublin Ghost Bus Tour** offers on-board entertainment as well as lessons in bodysnatching and the story behind Stoker's *Dracula*.

If tracing Dublin's musical heritage is of more interest, join the **Music Hall of Fame**. This takes you to the sites where bands such as U2 and Thin Lizzy first found fame. The **Musical Pub Crawl** is another tour that traces the history of Irish music, with musicians performing from pub to pub.

The **Historical Walking Tour** of Dublin takes in many of the significant locations of the city's colourful past.

The National Concert Hall on Earlsfort Terrace

Record shop and ticket office in Crown Alley, Temple Bar

CINEMA

D UBLIN'S CINEMAS have had a boost thanks to the success of Dublin-based films such as *My Left Foot* (1989), *The Commitments* (1991) and *Michael Collins* (1996) and a subsequent growth in the country's movie production industry. The **Irish Film Institute** *(see p56)* opened its doors in 1992 and was a most welcome addition to the city's entertainment scene. Housed in an original 17th-century building in Temple Bar, the centre shows mostly independent and foreign films, along with a programme of lectures, seminars and masterclasses. It boasts two screens, a bar, a restaurant and an archive of old film material.

"Mr Screen" cinema sign

Another cinema whose repertoire is mostly art house is the **Screen**, near Trinity College. The large first-run cinemas, such as the **Savoy** and the multiplex **UGC Cinemas**, are all located on the north side of the river. These usually offer reduced prices for their afternoon screenings and show late-night movies at the weekend.

Temple Bar's summer-long **Diversions** festival offers regular outdoor screenings of Irish and international films at Meeting House Square. Tickets are free and available from Temple Bar Properties.

DIRECTORY

BOOKING TICKETS

HMV
18 Henry St. **Map** D2.
(872 2095.
65 Grafton St. **Map** D4.
(679 5334.

Ticketmaster
(1890 925 100.
w www.ticketmaster.ie

THEATRE

Abbey Theatre
Abbey St Lower. **Map** E2.
(878 7222.

Andrews Lane Theatre
9–11 St Andrew's Lane.
Map D3. (679 5720.

City Arts Centre
23–25 Moss St. **Map** E2.
(677 0643.

Dublin Theatre Festival
44 East Essex St. **Map** C3.
(677 8439.

Focus Theatre
6 Pembroke Place. **Map** E5.
(676 3071

Gaiety Theatre
King St South. **Map** D4.
(677 1717.
w www.gaietytheatre.com

Gate Theatre
Cavendish Row. **Map** D1.
(874 4045.

Olympia Theatre
Dame St. **Map** C3.
(677 1020.

Project
39 East Essex St.
Map C3. (881 9613/14.
w www.project.ie

CLASSICAL MUSIC, OPERA AND DANCE

Bank of Ireland Arts Centre
Foster Place, College Green.
Map D3. (671 1488.
w www.bankofireland.ie

Hugh Lane Municipal Gallery of Modern Art
Charlemont House, Parnell
Sq North. **Map** C1.
(222 5550.
w www.hughlane.ie.

Royal Hospital Kilmainham
Kilmainham, Dublin 8.
(612 9900.
w www.modernart.ie

National Concert Hall
Earlsfort Terrace. **Map** D5.
(417 0077.
w www.nch.ie

Point Theatre
East Link Bridge, North
Wall Quay. **Map** F2.
(836 3633.
w www.thepoint.ie

Royal Dublin Society (RDS)
Ballsbridge. (668 0866.
w www.rds.ie

TRADITIONAL MUSIC & DANCE

Auld Dubliner
24–25 Temple Bar.
Map D3. (677 0527.

Castle Inn
5–7 Lord Edward St.
Map C3. (475 1122.

Cobblestone
77 King St North.
Map A2. (872 1799.

Jury's Hotel
Pembroke Rd, Ballsbridge.
(660 5000.

Mother Redcap's Tavern
Back Lane, Christchurch.
Map B4. (453 8306.

O'Donoghue's
15 Merrion Row.
Map E5. (676 2807.

ROCK, JAZZ, BLUES, SALSA AND COUNTRY

The Ha'penny Bridge Inn
Wellington Quay.
Map C3. (677 0616.

Heineken Green Energy Festival
(284 1747.
w www.mcd.ie

International Bar
23 Wicklow St. **Map** D3.
(677 9250.

Slane Annual Rock Concert
Slane Castle, Co. Meath
(041 982 4207.
w www.slanecastle.ie

Temple Bar Music Centre
Curved St, Temple Bar.
Map E4. (677 0647.
w www.tbmc.ie

Whelan's
25 Wexford St. **Map** C5.
(478 0766.
w www.whelanslive.com

COMEDY

Murphy's Laughter Lounge
4–6 Eden Quay. **Map** D2.
(874 4611.

NIGHTCLUBS

Lillie's Bordello
Adam Court, off Grafton St.
Map D4. (679 9204.

POD
Old Harcourt St. **Map** D5.
(478 0225.

Rí-Rá
11 South Great George's St.
Map C3.
(671 1220.

River Club
Merchants' Arch, Temple
Bar. **Map** D3.
(677 2382.

The Sugar Club
8 Lower Leeson St.
Map E5.
(678 7188.

PUB CRAWLS AND TOURS

Dublin Bus Ghost Tour
(873 4222.

Dublin Literary Pub Crawl
(670 5602.

The Walk Macabre
(087 6771512.

Historical Walking Tour
(878 0227.

Musical Pub Crawl
(475 3313.

Music Hall of Fame
(878 3345.

Viking Splash Tours
(707 6000.

HOTEL BARS

Cellar Bar
Merrion Hotel, 24 Merrion
St Upper. **Map** E5.
(603 0600.

The Horseshoe Bar
The Shelbourne Hotel, 27
St Stephen's Green North.
Map E4. (663 4740.

Inn on the Green
Fitzwilliam Hotel, 12 St
Stephen's Green West.
Map D4. (478 7000.

The Lobo Bar
The Morrison, Ormond
Quay. **Map** C3. (878 2999.

Octagon Bar
The Clarence, 6–8
Wellington Quay.
Map C3. (407 0800.

CINEMA

Diversions festival
Meeting House Square.
Map C3. (671 5717.
w www.templebar.ie

Irish Film Institute
6 Eustace St, Temple Bar.
Map C3. (679 5744.
w www.fii.ie

Savoy
O'Connell St. **Map** D2.
(874 8487.

Screen
D'Olier St. **Map** D3.
(672 5500.

UGC Cinemas
Parnell Centre, Parnell St.
Map C2. (872 8444.

Outdoor Activities

THE CITY OF DUBLIN is only minutes away from open countryside, and Ireland has many activities to tempt all lovers of the outdoors. The beautiful Wicklow Mountains are within easy reach for scenic walks, and the coastline from Dublin Bay to Dun Laoghaire offers a range of sports including sailing, fishing and windsurfing. There are plenty of opportunities to go horse riding and cycling in the Dublin area. Entire holidays can be based around outdoor activities. In addition to the contacts on page 145, Fáilte Ireland and Dublin Tourism *(see pp148–9)* have information on all sports and recreational activities in and around the city.

Backpackers walking in the Dublin area

Fishing in the canal at Robertstown, County Kildare

The beautiful gardens of Powerscourt House *(see pp106–7)*

WALKING

WALKING IN IRELAND puts you in the very midst of some glorious countryside. The network of waymarked trails takes you to some of the loveliest areas, inaccessible by car. Information on long-distance walks is available from Fáilte Ireland. Routes include the Wicklow Way which leads from the south of Dublin into the heart of the beautiful Wicklow Mountains *(see p105)*. All the walks may be split into shorter sections for less experienced walkers or those short of time.

Hill walking, rock climbing and mountaineering holidays are also available in Ireland. For specialized information, contact the **Mountaineering Council of Ireland**. When walking or climbing always make sure that you go well-equipped for the notoriously changeable Irish weather.

HORSE RIDING AND PONY TREKKING

MANY RIDING CENTRES, both residential and non-residential, offer trail riding and trekking along woodland trails, deserted beaches, country lanes and mountain routes. **Equestrian Holidays Ireland** organizes holidays for riders of various abilities. There are two types of trail riding – post-to-post and based. Post-to-post trails follow a series of routes with accommodation in a different place each night. Based trail rides follow different routes in one area and you stay at the same place for the whole holiday. Lessons are available at many riding centres for beginners to more advanced riders. Fáilte Ireland publish details of riding centres and courses.

Horseriding in Phoenix Park

FISHING

THE CLAIM that Ireland is a paradise for anglers is no exaggeration. Coarse, game and sea fishing all enjoy widespread popularity. Coastal rivers yield the famous Irish salmon, and, among other game fish, sea trout and brown trout also offer a real challenge.

Flounder, whiting, mullet, bass and coalfish tempt the sea angler; deep-sea excursions chase abundant supplies of dogfish, shark, skate and ling. You can organize sea-angling trips from many places.

Maps and information on fishing locations are provided by the **Central Fisheries Board** and the **Irish Federation of Sea Anglers**.

CYCLING

CYCLING is very popular both in central Dublin and in the countryside. If you prefer to bring your own bike, you can transport it fairly cheaply by train or bus. If not, you can always rent one from **Cycleways** or **Belfield Bike Shop** on the campus of University College Dublin. Also based here, **Irish Cycling Safaris** concentrate on trips outside Dublin, so you can enjoy the quiet country roads. The paths along Dublin Bay offer fun routes, while the Wicklow Mountains are more of a challenge. They also offer guided cycling tours of the city centre for groups.

WATER SPORTS

WITH A COASTLINE of over 4,800 km (3,000 miles), it is small wonder that water sports are among Ireland's favourite recreational activities. Surfing, windsurfing, water-skiing, scuba-diving and canoeing are the most popular, and there are facilities for all of these along the Dublin coast and in Dublin Bay itself

Windsurfing is a popular sport throughout Ireland and there are a number of clubs and schools operating around Dublin Bay. **Surfdock** at Grand Canal Dock Yard and **Wind & Wave** in Monkstown both offer advice, tuition and the latest equipment.

There is a wide range of diving conditions off the coast of Ireland and the **Irish Underwater Council** will give you details of courses and their facilities.

Dun Laoghaire harbour at dusk

CRUISING AND SAILING

A TRANQUIL CRUISING holiday is an ideal alternative to the stress and strain of driving, and Ireland's many rivers and lakes offer a huge variety of conditions for those who want a waterborne holiday. Stopping over at waterside towns and villages puts you in touch with the Irish on their home ground. Hiring a boat and drifting down the Grand Canal (see p83) from Dublin to the Shannon gives you a unique view of the countryside.

Another popular sailing area is the scenic Howth peninsula, and the harbour of Dun Laoghaire southeast of Dublin, where you will find sailing schools offering tuition at all levels. For details of these schools, contact the **Irish Sailing Association**.

SPORTS FOR THE DISABLED

SPORTS ENTHUSIASTS with a disability can obtain details of facilities for the disabled from the **Irish Wheelchair Association**. Central and local tourist boards, and many of the organizations listed in the directory under each sport, will be able to offer facilities for disabled visitors. To be sure of this, it is advisable to call the venue first to check what is available.

Cycling in the Irish countryside

DIRECTORY

WALKING

Mountaineering Council of Ireland
House of Sport, Longmile Rd, Dublin12
(625 1115.
[w] www.mountaineering.ie

HORSE RIDING

Association of Irish Riding Establishments
11 Moore Park, Newbridge, Co Kildare. (045 431584. [w] www.aire.ie

Equestrian Holidays Ireland
1 Sandyford Office Park, Foxrock, Dublin 18.
(295 8928.

FISHING

Central Fisheries Board
Balnagowan House, Mobhi Boreen, Glasnevin, Dublin 9.
(884 2600.
[w] www.cfb.ie

Irish Federation of Sea Anglers
Mr Hugh O'Rorke, 67 Windsor Drive, Monkstown, Co Dublin.
(280 6873.
[w] www.ifsa.ie

CYCLING

Cycleways
185–186 Parnell St, Dublin 1. (873 4748.
[w] www.cycleways.com

Irish Cycling Safaris
Belfield Bike Shop, University College Dublin, Dublin 4. (706 1697.
[w] www.cyclingsafaris.com

WATER SPORTS

Irish Underwater Council
78a Patrick St, Dun Laoghaire, Co Dublin.
(284 4601.
[w] www.scubaireland.com

Surfdock Windsurfing
Grand Canal Dockyard, South Dock Rd, Ringsend, Dublin 4.
(668 3945.
[w] www.surfdock.ie

Wind & Wave
16a the Crescent, Monkstown, Co Dublin.
(284 4177.
[w] www.windandwave.ie

SAILING

Irish Sailing Association
3 Park Rd, Dun Laoghaire, Co Dublin.
(280 0239.
[w] www.sailing.ie

SPORTS FOR THE DISABLED

Irish Wheelchair Association
Áras Chúchulain, Blackheath Drive, Clontarf, Dublin 3.
(818 6400.
[w] www.iwa.ie

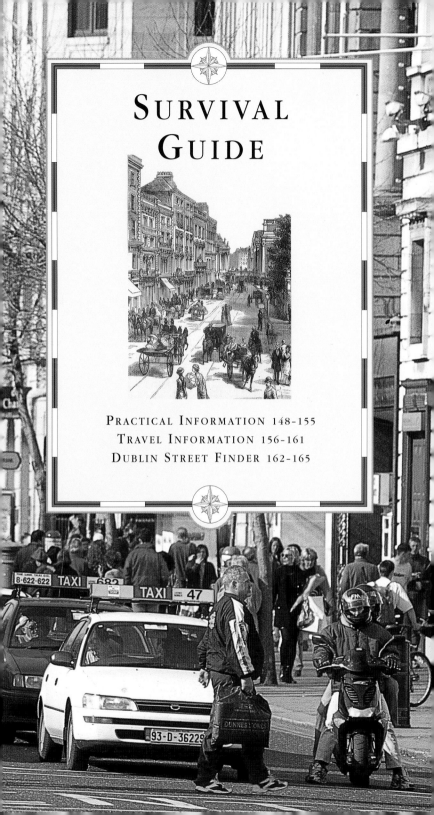

SURVIVAL
GUIDE

PRACTICAL INFORMATION

IN THE PAST FEW YEARS, Dublin has enjoyed a dramatic renaissance. The renovation of the vibrant Temple Bar area, combined with the city's numerous museums, galleries and shops, attracts visitors in their thousands all year round. The best time to visit the region is probably late spring, before the peak summer season. Dublin is generally a safe place, but it does have a wide mixture of districts. You can very quickly find

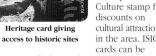

Dublin Tourism logo

yourself out of a tourist area and in a less desirable part of town. It is wise to avoid the rougher areas to the north of the Liffey, away from O'Connell Street, especially at night. Transport around the city is good and taxis are readily available in the town centre. Dublin Tourism has geared itself up to the increasing demands of the tourist, and their office (in a converted church) is well organized with helpful and friendly staff.

Sign to Ardgillan Demesne

VISAS

VISITORS FROM the EU, US, Canada, Australia and New Zealand require a valid passport but not a visa for entry into Ireland. All others, including those wanting to study or work, should check with their local embassy first. UK nationals do not strictly need a passport to enter Ireland but should take it with them for identification.

TOURIST INFORMATION

THE TOURIST BOARD for all of Ireland, north and south, is **Tourism Ireland**, incorporating Faílte Ireland and the Northern Ireland Tourist Board. Its network of overseas offices offer brochures and information.
    Dublin Tourism is the regional authority for the Dublin area. The main office is in a converted church on Suffolk Street. There are also walk-in information offices at 14 Upper O'Connell Street, Baggot Street and Dublin Airport. Tourist offices sell maps and guide books, provide local information and can arrange car rental and reserve

accommodation. Their accommodation lists include only hotels and guesthouses approved by the tourist board. Museums and libraries often stock useful tourist literature.

ADMISSION CHARGES

SOME OF DUBLIN's major sights have an admission fee but many are free. For each place of interest in this guide, we specify whether or not there is a charge. Entrance fees are usually between 1 and 10 euros with discounts for students and the elderly. **The Heritage Service** maintains Ireland's parks, museums, monuments and gardens and issues a Heritage Card which allows unlimited access to more than 70 sites for a year.

Students at Trinity College, Dublin

STUDENT INFORMATION

STUDENTS WITH a valid ISIC card (International Student Identity Card) benefit from numerous travel discounts as well as reduced admission to museums and concerts. Buy a Travelsave stamp from any branch of **USIT** and affix it to your ISIC card to get a discount on various rail and bus services operated by Iarnród Éireann and Dublin Bus. You can also get a Temple Bar Culture stamp for discounts on cultural attractions in the area. ISIC cards can be obtained easily from any branch of USIT in Dublin.
    USIT will also supply non-students under 26 with an EYC or IYC (European or International Youth Card) for discounts on airfares, and in restaurants, shops and theatres.

Heritage card giving access to historic sites

DUTY-FREE GOODS

IN 1999 the duty-free allowances on goods bought by adults travelling between the Republic of Ireland and other countries were abolished.
    However, a wide range of items may still be purchased at airport shops and on ferries, including goods that were previously duty-free, such as beers, wines, spirits, perfume and cigarettes. These shops can also be a useful source of souvenirs and last-minute gifts.

A selection of daily newspapers

RELIGIOUS SERVICES

FOR MANY PEOPLE in Ireland churchgoing is a way of life. The Republic is 95 per cent Roman Catholic. Tourist offices, hotels and B&Bs keep lists of church service times.

IRISH TIME

THE WHOLE of Ireland is in the same time zone as Great Britain; five hours ahead of New York and Toronto, one hour behind Germany and France, and ten hours behind Sydney. Clocks go forward one hour for summer time.

NEWSPAPERS AND MAGAZINES

THE REPUBLIC of Ireland has six national daily papers and five Sunday papers. Quality dailies include the *Irish Independent,* the *Examiner* and *The Irish Times.* The broadsheets are useful for information on theatre and concerts. Ireland's daily tabloid is the *Star.*

British tabloids are on sale throughout Dublin. Broadsheets such as *The Times* are also available and cost less than the quality Irish press. Local papers give details of what is on where, and when.

OPENING TIMES

INCREASING NUMBERS of shops are now open on Sunday afternoons. Some museums are shut on Monday. Opening hours are generally between 10am and 5pm but phone to check before your visit.

METRICATION

THIS HAS been taking place over several years now. Although most road signs are now shown in kilometres, speed limits are still displayed in miles. Fuel is sold in litres but beer is still sold in pints.

RADIO AND TELEVISION

IRELAND HAS FOUR TV channels, RTE 1, RTE 2, TV3 and TG4, which is an Irish-language service. There are six national radio stations and many local ones. The five British television channels can also be picked up in most parts of Ireland. Cable and satellite TV is quite common and is offered by most hotels.

FACILITIES FOR THE DISABLED

MOST SIGHTS in Ireland have access for wheelchairs. However it is always worth phoning to check details. The Access Department of the **National Disability Association** provide useful information on amenities.

DIRECTORY

TOURIST INFORMATION

In Ireland
C 1850 230 330 (information).
C 1800 363 626 (reservations).
W www.ireland.ie

In the UK
C 0800 039 7000 (info).
W www.tourismireland.com

In the USA and Canada
C 1800 223 6470 (info).
C 1800 398 4376 (res).
W www.tourismireland.com

EMBASSIES AND CONSULATES

Australia
Fitzwilton House, Wilton Terrace, Dublin 2. C 664 5300.
W www.australianembassy.ie

Canada
65–68 St Stephen's Green, Dublin 2. C 417 4100.
W www.canada.ie

UK
29 Merrion Rd, Dublin 4.
C 205 3700.
W www.britishembassy.ie

United States
42 Elgin Rd, Ballsbridge, Dublin 4. C 668 7122.
W www.usembassy.ie

USEFUL ADDRESSES

Dublin Tourism Centre
Suffolk St, Dublin 2.
C 605 7700 or 1850 230330.
W www.visitdublin.com

The Heritage Service
6 Upper Ely Place, Dublin 2.
C 647 3000 or 1890 321421.
W www.heritageireland.ie

National Disability Association
25 Clyde Rd, Ballsbridge, Dublin 4. C 668 4181.
W www.nda.ie

USIT
19/21 Aston Quay, Dublin 2.
C 602 1777. W www.usit.ie

LANGUAGE

The Republic of Ireland is officially bilingual – almost all road signs have names in English and Irish. English is spoken everywhere except for a few parts of the far west, an area known as the Gaeltacht, but now and then you may find signs only in Irish. On the right are some of the words you are most likely to come across when travelling around the Republic.

Sign using old form of Gaelic

USEFUL WORDS

an banc – **bank**
an lár – **town centre**
an trá – **beach**
ar aghaidh – **straight on**
bealach amach – **exit**
bealach isteach – **entrance**
dúnta – **closed**
fáilte – **welcome**
fir – **men**
gardaí – **police**
leithreas – **toilet**
mná – **women**
oifig an phoist – **post office**
oscailte – **open**
óstán – **hotel**
siopa – **shop**
sláinte! – **cheers!**
stop/stad – **stop**
ticéad – **ticket**
traein – **train**

Personal Security and Health

Although crime in Ireland has long been a relative rarity, in recent years bag-snatching, pickpocketing and car break-ins have become more and more prevalent on the streets of Dublin. Levels of crime are still low by international standards, but Dublin is a modern city with most of the accompanying problems, and visitors should not allow the fabled Irish friendliness to lull them into complacency. Tourist offices and hoteliers will gladly point out the areas to be avoided, but anyone who takes simple precautions should enjoy a trouble-free stay.

Police motorcyclist patrolling the busy Dublin streets

Garda station situated on Pearse Street, near the centre of Dublin

PERSONAL SECURITY

The police in Dublin and the rest of the Republic, should you ever need them, are called the **Gardaí**. Until recently, street crime was very rare in Dublin but, because of poverty and a degree of heroin addiction in certain areas of the city, it is now on a steady increase. However, if you use common sense when wandering around, there should be little cause for concern: avoid the backstreets or poorly lit areas at night; don't draw attention to yourself by wearing flashy jewellery; sit near the driver on buses; use a bag that can be held securely; be alert in crowded places.

You may be approached in the street by people asking for money. This rarely develops into a troublesome situation, but it is still best to avoid eye contact and leave the scene as quickly as possible. In general, safety in the city is about being alert to your surroundings. If you feel uncomfortable anywhere, especially at night, walk away confidently and head for well-lit, populated areas.

Light outside Garda station

PERSONAL PROPERTY

Before you leave home, make sure your possessions are insured, as it can be expensive and difficult to do so in Ireland. Travel insurance for the UK will not cover you in the Republic, so ensure your policy is adequate.

As pickpocketing and petty theft can be a problem in Dublin, it is best not to carry your passport, air tickets or large amounts of cash around with you, or even leave them in your room. Most hotels have a safe and it makes sense to take advantage of this facility. Visitors carrying large amounts of money around should use traveller's cheques rather than cash (*see p152–3*). When sitting in pubs and restaurants, keep your bag on your lap, if possible, and don't leave your wallet lying on the table. A money belt that can be worn under clothing is a good investment, as is a shoulder bag that can be carried across the chest with the opening facing inwards. When withdrawing money from cash machines, put the notes away as quickly as possible; don't stand around counting them.

Also, if there is a cash machine inside the bank, use that one in preference to one in the street.

If travelling by car, ensure that all valuables are out of sight and the car is locked, even when leaving it for just a few minutes. When you arrive at a hotel, ask the receptionist about secure parking in the area and, on trips out of Dublin to other towns, use guarded parking areas rather than street parking.

LOST PROPERTY

Report all lost or stolen items at once to the police. To make an insurance claim, you will need to get a copy of the police report. Most rail and bus stations in Dublin and the surrounding towns operate a lost property service.

Male and female Garda officers in ordinary uniform

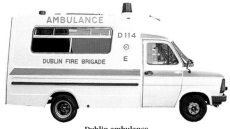

Dublin ambulance

Dublin fire engine

Garda patrol car

Pharmacy in the city showing old-fashioned snake and goblet symbol

In smaller towns, however, you may discover pharmacists opposed to contraception who do not sell condoms.

MEDICAL TREATMENT

Residents of countries in the European Union can claim free medical treatment in Ireland by getting form E111 before setting out. To avoid having to pay for any treatment or prescribed medicines, you will need to show your E111 and a form of identification, such as a driver's licence or passport. Also, be sure to let the doctor know that you want treatment under the EU's social security regulations. Travellers from outside the EU should either have their own accident and health insurance or be willing to pay for any treatment received.

In an emergency, either call an ambulance (by dialling 999 or 112) or head for 24-hour accident and emergency departments at **Beaumont, St James** or **St Vincent's** hospitals. **Dublin Dental Hospital** serves emergency dental needs. They are closed at weekends but provide numbers of dentists on call.

PHARMACIES

A WIDE RANGE of medical supplies is available over the counter at pharmacies. However, many medicines are available only with a prescription from a local doctor. If you are likely to require specialized drugs during your stay, take your own supplies or ask your doctor to write a letter specifying the generic name of the medicine you require. Always obtain a receipt for insurance claims. For after-hours medical requirements, try **O'Connell's**, a chain of pharmacies with extended opening hours.

Until recently, condoms were not freely available in Dublin or the rest of the Republic but are now fairly easy to obtain.

DIRECTORY

USEFUL ADDRESSES

Police, Fire, Ambulance and Coastguard Services
📞 Dial 999 or 112.

O'Connell's Late Night Pharmacy
55 O'Connell St. 🕐 7:30am–10pm Mon–Sat, 10am–10pm Sun.
Map D2. 📞 873 0427.

Beaumont Hospital
Beaumont Rd, Dublin 9.
📞 809 2714

Dublin Dental Hospital
Lincoln Place, Dublin 2.
Map E4. 📞 612 7200.

Pharmacy in the fashionable Temple Bar area

Banking and Currency

BANKS IN DUBLIN provide a very good service and will often exchange traveller's cheques without charging commission. They will also change currency, and many have a cash dispenser, or automated teller machine (ATM), for use outside banking hours. Most of the banks are VISA/Delta affiliated, so as long as you have a card bearing the VISA or Cirrus logo, you should be able to withdraw cash at these machines, although a fee may be charged. Outside the city you will find that the banks do not always have cash machines, and opening hours may vary from those in the city centre. Traveller's cheques are by far the safest way to carry money around, but credit cards are more convenient and are widely accepted in the city.

Thomas Cook on Grafton Street in central Dublin

Drawing money from an Allied Irish Bank cash dispenser

USING BANKS

THE FIVE RETAIL BANKS in the Republic of Ireland are the Bank of Ireland, the Allied Irish Bank (AIB), the Ulster Bank, the National Irish Bank and the Permanent-TSB Bank.

The usual banking hours in Dublin are Monday to Wednesday and Friday from 10am to 4pm and Thursday 10am to 5pm. In rural areas banks often stay open late on market day instead. Some of the smaller branches further out of the city centre may shut at lunch time. Branches of the Permanent-TSB Bank remain open from 10am to 5pm Monday to Friday, but open at 10:30am on Wednesday. All the banks are closed on public holidays *(see p27)*.

BUREAUX DE CHANGE

IN ADDITION to the banks, there are some private *bureaux de change* in Dublin. As with most other exchange facilities, *bureaux de change* open later than banks. However, rates of exchange vary considerably and commission charges can be high, so it's worth looking around before undertaking any transactions. Some department stores also offer *bureaux de change* facilities.

Allied Irish Bank logo

National Irish Bank logo

CREDIT CARDS

THROUGHOUT DUBLIN you can pay by credit card in nearly all hotels, petrol (gas) stations, large shops and supermarkets. The hotels *(see pp120–23)* and restaurants *(see pp128–31)* listings indicate which establishments accept which credit cards. VISA and MasterCard (also known as Access) are the most widely accepted credit cards. Fewer businesses are also prepared to accept American Express and Diners Club cards. In more rural areas you may not always be able to use your credit card, so be sure to carry cash or traveller's cheques with you as an alternative.

TRAVELLER'S CHEQUES

TRAVELLER'S CHEQUES are the safest way to carry around large amounts of money. These are best changed at one of the main banks but, failing this, many shops and restaurants accept them in place of cash although they usually charge commission. Hotel receptions are often willing to change cheques.

Traveller's cheques can be bought before setting out at American Express, Thomas Cook or at your own bank at home. In Ireland, traveller's cheques can be purchased at banks or from *bureaux de change*, which can be found in Dublin and other large towns, as well as at airports.

Façade of the Bank of Ireland on College Green in central Dublin

THE EURO

INTRODUCTION OF the single European currency, the euro, is taking place in 12 of the 25 member states of the EU. Austria, Belgium, Finland, France, Germany, Greece, Ireland, Italy, Luxembourg, Netherlands, Portugal and Spain chose to join the new currency; the UK, Denmark and Sweden stayed out, with an option to review their decision. The euro was introduced on 1 January 1999, but only for banking purposes. Notes and coins came into circulation on 1 January 2002. A transition period has allowed euros and the punt (the Irish pound) to be used simultaneously. After July 2002, all currencies of the participating member states were phased out, although there was some local variation.

Bank Notes

Euro bank notes have seven denom-inations. The 5-euro note (grey in colour) is the smallest, followed by the 10-euro (pink), 20-euro (blue), 50-euro (orange), 100-euro (green), 200-euro (yellow) and 500-euro (purple). All notes show the 12 stars of the EU and a specific style of European architecture.

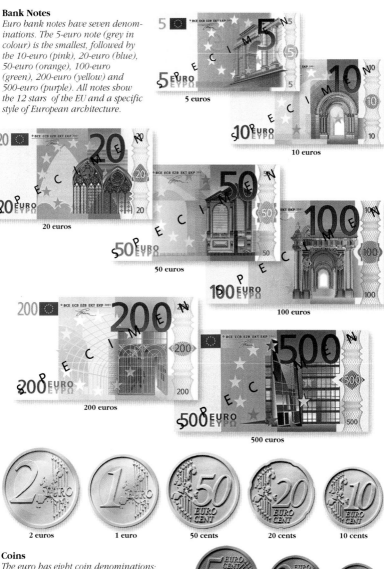

5 euros

10 euros

20 euros

50 euros

100 euros

200 euros

500 euros

2 euros   1 euro   50 cents   20 cents   10 cents

Coins

The euro has eight coin denominations: 2 euros and 1 euro (gold and silver); 50 cents, 20 cents, 10 cents (gold); 5 cents, 2 cents and 1 cent (bronze). The reverse sides of all coins are the same in all euro-zone countries, while the obverse sides are different in each state.

5 cents   2 cents   1 cent

Mail Services

Irish Post Office logo

IN ADDITION TO the main Post Office branches that offer all the mail services available there are a large number of Post Office outlets throughout Dublin incorporated into newsagents and general stores. Although it is improving all the time, the mail service in the Republic is still quite slow; allow four days when sending a letter to Great Britain or anywhere else in Europe and at least six days for North America and other destinations. Sending mail by Swiftpost or Recorded Delivery costs about 5 euros extra but guarantees delivery in a specified number of days.

A typical post office in rural Ireland

The modern St Andrews Post Office, in central Dublin

MAILBOXES AND POSTE RESTANTE

MAILBOXES in the city and in the rest of the Republic are green. In Dublin, some have two slots, marked *Dublin Only* and *All Other Places*. Many of the Republic's mailboxes are quite historic. Some even carry Queen Victoria's monogram on the front, a relic from the days of British rule. Even the smallest towns have a mailbox, and the mail is collected regularly: anything from once to four times daily.

The easiest way to receive mail in Dublin is to have it sent to your hotel. Otherwise, a Poste Restante service is available at major post offices. In the city centre the General Post Office on O'Connell Street is the most convenient, with longer opening hours than any other post office.

MAILING A LETTER

MAIN POST OFFICES in Dublin are usually open from 9am to 5:30pm during the week and from 9am to 1pm on Saturdays. Some smaller post offices do not open on Saturdays and close for lunch on weekdays. The General Post Office on O'Connell Street (*see p69*) is well placed for tourist sights and is open at lunch-time on weekdays. It has extended opening hours of 8am to 8pm from Monday to Saturday and 10am to 6pm on Sunday. Standard-value stamps can also be bought from selected newsagents around the city. The Republic of Ireland has only one class of mail, with 90 per cent of

mail delivered within Ireland the next working day. The rate for mail to Great Britain and the rest of Europe is slightly higher than within Ireland and can take between two and six days, depending on whether the economy or priority service is used. All airmail letters (including ones heading for Great Britain) should carry a blue *Priority Aerphost* sticker, available at all post offices for no cost.

List of the daily collection times

Monogram of Queen Victoria

A variety of standard issue Irish stamps

Standard mailbox

Rural mailbox

Communications

EIRCOM IS THE REPUBLIC'S national telephone company. Although it no longer has the monopoly on the telephone services in the country, the majority of the city's telephone booths are still controlled by eircom. Their modern, efficient service includes coin, card and credit card telephones, distinguished by the wording around the top of each phone booth. Eircom phonecards are available from newsagents, post offices, supermarkets and other retail outlets.

eircom phone booth

Another company, Smart Telecom, also provides coin and credit card phones. Calls on their phones cost the same as those on eircom phones and are charged at a fixed rate of approximately 40c for 2 minutes.

MAKING A PHONE CALL FROM DUBLIN

CHEAP RATE CALLS within the Republic and to the UK are from 6pm to 8am weekdays and all day at weekends. Off-peak times for international calls vary from country to country, but are generally as above. Calls from hotels are expensive at all times.
• To make a call within the Dublin area, dial the seven-digit number, dropping the general Dublin area code 01.
• To make a call to an area outside Dublin, dial the area code which begins with a 0 and then the local number.
• To call Northern Ireland, dial 048, then the area code, followed by the number.
• To call other countries, dial 00, followed by the country code (for example, 44 for the UK), the area code (minus the leading 0), then the number.

USING AN EIRCOM PHONE

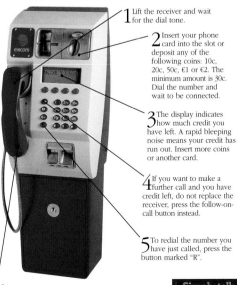

1 Lift the receiver and wait for the dial tone.

2 Insert your phone card into the slot or deposit any of the following coins: 10c, 20c, 50c, €1 or €2. The minimum amount is 30c. Dial the number and wait to be connected.

3 The display indicates how much credit you have left. A rapid bleeping noise means your credit has run out. Insert more coins or another card.

4 If you want to make a further call and you have credit left, do not replace the receiver, press the follow-on-call button instead.

5 To redial the number you have just called, press the button marked "R".

6 After you have replaced the receiver, retrieve your card or collect your change. Only wholly unused coins are refunded.

eircom phone card, available in various amounts

ACCESSING THE INTERNET

DUBLIN, LIKE MOST major cities, has plenty of public access to computers and the Internet. Public facilities are available for free from libraries, but you may have to book in advance. One way to access the Internet is at one of the many Internet cafés found all over Dublin and throughout the country in major towns and cities. The cafés generally charge by the hour or half-hour for computer use, so costs build up quickly. Internet access is often cheaper during off-peak times. Another way to access the Internet and email is through broadband-enabled eircom payphones.

Coffee and computers at the Central Cyber Café

TRAVEL INFORMATION

As DUBLIN BECOMES an increasingly popular tourist destination, the city becomes even easier to get to, with extremely frequent flights from the UK and good connections from elsewhere in the world. Ferry services are an alternative method of travel from the UK, docking at Dun Laoghaire harbour or Dublin Port. From both the airport and the har-

Aer Lingus Airbus in flight

bours it is a short ride by car or bus into central Dublin. If you are planning to stay in the centre, it is not necessary to rent a car – most of the sights are within easy walking distance of one another and the roads in the city centre can become very congested, particularly O'Connell Street. Should your feet require a rest, the bus services are frequent, and there are plenty of taxis available.

The modern exterior of Dublin International Airport

FLYING TO DUBLIN

FLIGHTS from most of the major cities in Europe arrive at **Dublin Airport**, which is the Republic of Ireland's busiest airport. Regular services to Dublin depart from all five of the London airports (Heathrow, City, Gatwick, Luton and Stansted) and from 15 other cities in Britain, such as Leeds and Manchester, as well as the Isle of Man and the Channel Islands.

The major airline operating scheduled flights from Britain and Europe to Dublin is Ireland's national airline **Aer Lingus**, although since deregulation their low-cost rival, **Ryanair**, has grown fast. From the United States, Aer Lingus and **Delta Air Lines** fly direct to Dublin Airport. However, there are no direct flights to Dublin from Australia and New

Zealand, so popular connecting points used by travellers include London, Singapore and Amsterdam.

AIR FARES

AIRLINES OFFER a host of options on air fares to Ireland from Britain. Usually, the amount you pay is determined by how flexible you are prepared to be and how far in advance you book your flight. The best bargains tend to be on flights for which the dates are not changeable. Flights from the United States can double in price in the summer and around Christmas when the fares are most expensive. Mid-week flights are often cheaper than weekend ones. The cheapest place to fly from in the UK is usually London, although the low-cost airline Ryanair flies from other locations in the UK and occasionally has very competitive

Airport sign in English and Gaelic

deals. Ticket prices from the UK are generally fairly consistent throughout the year except at Christmas and during the summer when there are comparatively few discounted fares available. During these periods, due to the increased demand by visiting friends and relatives – usually referred to by airline companies as "VFR" – seats are taken well in advance so it is advisable to book as early as possible if you are intending to travel at these times. Many airlines offer discounts to those under 25, while USIT *(see p148)* and other agencies specializing in student travl often have cheaper rates for students and under-26s.

GETTING TO AND FROM THE AIRPORT

AN EXPRESS service, the Airlink bus, runs between Dublin Airport and the city's main rail and bus stations, from early morning to midnight. Tickets are purchased on board. A cheaper alternative are the number 16A and 41 city buses, which run to the city centre. Also, an efficient DART and bus connection runs via Howth Junction. Ask at your DART station for details. There is a taxi stand outside the airport and car rental companies inside. If you are flying from Dublin and wish to leave your car there or are collecting someone, there are long- and short-stay parking facilities.

The frequent-running Airlink bus

Irish Ferries ship loading up in the harbour

FERRIES TO DUBLIN AND DUN LAOGHAIRE

THERE IS A GOOD CHOICE of ferry services from Wales to Ireland. **Irish Ferries**, the country's largest shipping company, sails on the Holyhead-Dublin route and has two crossings a day on the conventional ferry, which takes about 3¼ hours to reach Dublin Port. They also operate the Jonathan Swift high-speed service, which takes 1 hour 49 minutes. Irish Ferries does not operate on Christmas Day and St Stephen's Day (26 Dec).

The service from Holyhead to the south Dublin suburb of Dun Laoghaire – traditionally the busiest port in Ireland – is served by **Stena Line**'s Stena HSS (High-speed Sea Service). The HSS has the same passenger and vehicle capacity as conventional ferries but its jet-engine propulsion gives it twice the speed, cutting journey times in half. Vehicle loading and unloading times on the Stena HSS are also

Directions for ferry passengers

shorter than on other ferries – the loading time for cars is about 20 minutes as opposed to a minimum of 30 minutes with most other ferries. Passengers requiring special assistance at ports or on board the ship should contact the company they are booked with at least 24 hours before the departure time. Like most other ferry companies, Irish Ferries and Stena Line take bicycles for a charge, and this should be mentioned when you make a reservation. The fast ferries may not run in rough weather. Stena Line's conventional ferries run from Dublin Port.

The **Isle of Man Steam Packet Company** operates the SeaCat Rapide service once a day between Liverpool and Dublin. The crossing takes four hours. Their Isle of Man crossing takes two hours, forty-five minutes.

PORT CONNECTIONS

ALL OF IRELAND'S PORTS have adequate bus and train connections. At Dublin Port, available buses (with an extra fare) take ferry passengers into the city centre. From Dun Laoghaire, DART trains run into Dublin every 10 to 15 minutes, calling at Pearse Street, Tara Street and Connolly stations. These depart from the railway station near the main passenger concourse. Buses also run from outside Dun Laoghaire DART station to the city centre every 10 to 15 minutes. At all ports, taxis are readily available to meet arriving passengers.

Stena HSS on the Dun Laoghaire to Holyhead crossing

Getting Around Dublin

D<small>UBLIN IS A</small> fairly easy city to get around. The centre is relatively compact, so most of the sights are within walking distance of one another, and much of it, particularly south of the Liffey, is pedestrianized. If you are travelling into the city centre there is an excellent bus service and the local DART railway runs an efficient, if crowded, service to three city centre stations. The Luas line links the north and south of the city, the main railway stations and the centre to the suburbs. If you prefer to be driven around, taxis are available but are fairly expensive.

Parliament Street viewed from City Hall

Passengers boarding a Dublin Bus near Trinity College

GETTING AROUND BY BUS

D<small>UBLIN BUS</small> runs all the bus services in central Dublin and the Greater Dublin area. Bus stops for **Dublin Bus** are blue or yellow, and the numbers on them indicate which buses stop there. Buses in the city centre run approximately every 10 to 20 minutes from about 6am until 11:30pm, but do allow plenty of time if you have an appointment as they can run late. There is also a night bus service called Nitelink, which departs every hour from 12:30am to 2am Mon to Wed, 12:30am to 4.30am Thurs to Sat. If you are using the bus two or three times in a day, it is worth getting a one-day pass, costing around 5 euros. There are also four-day, weekly and monthly passes. The main bus station is **Busáras** in Store Street, a short walk from O'Connell Street. You can catch the buses operated by **Bus Éireann** from here to destinations all over the country.

DART SERVICE

T<small>HE CONVENIENT</small> local electric rail service in Dublin known as the **DART** (Dublin Area Rapid Transit) serves 30 stations between Malahide in County Dublin and Greystones in County Wicklow with several stops in Dublin city centre. A Three Day Bus and Rail ticket costs 15 euros and allows three consecutive days' travel on DART trains and also covers Dublin Bus and local suburban rail. A Day Rambler ticket covers the same methods of transport but just for one day and costs around 8 euros. Family tickets for two adults and up to four children under the age of 16 are very good value. Tickets can be perchased at any of the DART stations. Major works have been carried out along the DART line, including extensions northwards to Malahide and southwards to Greystones. There are some spectacular views along the southern section, particularly at Killiney and from Bray to Greystones.

The DART is very crowded and to be avoided at peak times during the week. The rush hours are between 7am and 9am and 5pm and 7pm.

DART station sign

LUAS

L<small>UAS, THE IRISH</small> word for speed, is the new on-street light rail network, the first stage of which was completed in June 2004. The network will provide an easy and convenient way to reach areas of the city and the suburbs previously only connected to the city centre by bus. The first phase of the project saw the completion of two new tram lines. One runs west from Connolly Station along the north side of the Liffey. It then heads south at Heuston and terminates further south and west at Tallaght. The other line starts at St Stephen's Green and runs south to Sandyford. The **Luas** lines will eventually intersect with the DART and proposed Metro line, providing Dublin with an efficient and comprehensive transport system.

Logo on Bus Éireann local and express buses

TAXIS IN DUBLIN

IN DUBLIN, cruising taxis are around but the best places to find cabs are at taxi stands, hotels and rail or bus stations. Prices are based on metered mileage and the minimum charge is around 4 euros. There are a whole range of taxi companies in the city. If you want any information about taxis, the **Irish Taxi Federation** is happy to supply details and information about taxi companies.

Taxis lined up outside the arrivals building at Dublin Airport

FARES AND TICKETS

IN THE REPUBLIC, long-distance buses are about half the price of the equivalent rail journey. If you are making the return trip on the same day, ask for a day-return ticket, which is much cheaper than the normal return fare. Also, between Monday and Thursday you can buy a "mid-week" return ticket for the price of a single journey. Under 16s pay half the adult

fare. Students with a Travel-save stamp *(see p148)* get a 30 per cent reduction. For those intending to do a lot of travelling it is cheaper to buy a "Rambler" ticket. This allows unlimited bus travel throughout the Republic for a certain number of days in a set period, for example, 15 days' travel out of 30 consecutive days.

The distinctively marked Dublin City Tour bus

BUS TOURS

BUS ÉIREANN and some local companies run half- and one-day excursions in Dublin. Dublin Bus (Bus Átha Cliath) runs the Dublin City Tour, which leaves from O'Connell Street Upper and takes in the city's most famous sights, including St Stephen's Green, the Bank of Ireland and the Parliament as well as some more obscure sights, such as Oscar Wilde's home. The witty commentary alone makes the tour well worth doing.

DRIVING

IF YOU DO NOT take your own car, there are plenty of car rental firms to choose from. Car rental can be expensive in peak season and the best rates are often obtained by booking in advance. Broker companies, such as **Holiday Autos**, use the major rental companies and will shop around to get the best deal. Car rental usually includes unlimited mileage plus passenger indemnity insurance and

cover for third party, fire and theft, but not vehicle damage.

To rent a car, you must show a full driver's licence, which you have held for two years without violations. Cars are usually rented only to those aged between 23 and 70, but some companies may make exceptions. For a list of suggested car rental companies in Dublin see p161.

PARKING

DUBLIN HAS "pay and display" areas, parking meters and car parks. Parking on the street is allowed, although a single yellow line along the edge of the road means there are some restrictions (there should be a sign nearby with permitted parking times). Double yellow lines indicate no parking at any time.

Disc parking – a version of "pay and display" – also operates in Dublin. Discs can be bought from local newsagents, petrol (gas) stations, tourist offices and many small shops.

A busy Hertz car rental desk at Dublin Airport

Travelling Outside Dublin

O NE OF THE BEST WAYS to see the magnificent scenery in the countryside around Dublin is by car. The roads have improved greatly in the last few years but the number of cars has also increased. One of the quickest ways to get to more distant destinations is by train. Ireland's national rail network is fast and efficient and also provides an ideal way to see the country's dramatic landscape. Alternatively, you can enjoy the countryside at your own pace by touring on a bicycle, although a certain degree of fitness is advisable if you are going to tackle the beautiful Wicklow Mountains.

Rural petrol pump

Purchasing a rail ticket at a station ticket office

TRAIN SERVICES IN IRELAND

T HE TWO MAIN rail stations in Dublin are Connolly, for trains to the north, northwest and Rosslare; and Heuston, which serves the west, midlands and southwest. These two stations are connected by the No. 90 bus service which runs every 10 to 15 minutes and takes a quarter of an hour, but can take about 30 minutes at rush hour. Irish Rail (Iarnród Éireann) operates a service out of Dublin to most large cities and towns. Going by rail is probably the fastest and most convenient way of travelling

to other major places. Most trains have standard and super-standard (first-class) compartments. Bicycles can be taken on trains for a supplement of around 10 euros.

TICKETS AND FARES

T HROUGHOUT IRELAND, train tickets are generally quite expensive, but there are lots of good-value incentive or concessionary passes. Most of these include bus travel, so you can travel to virtually anywhere in Ireland in just one ticket.

The most comprehensive ticket available, the Emerald Card, can be used on Irish Rail, Dublin Bus and Bus Éireann services. For around 180 euros it gives eight days' unlimited travel in a 15-day period. An 8-day Irish Explorer ticket is slightly cheaper and is valid on all Irish Rail and Bus Éireann transport. The Irish Rover ticket can also be good value. It is valid on all rail and bus journeys from three days within an 8-day

Yield (give way) road sign in Gaelic

period. For 15 euros students can buy a National Student Travelcard for a discount on all Irish Rail single and return journeys, as well as on DART and Dublin Bus services. Older travellers can get InterRail Plus 26 cards costing 7 euros.

DRIVING YOUR OWN CAR

I F YOU INTEND to use your own car, check your insurance to find out how well you are covered. To prevent a comprehensive policy being downgraded to third-party cover, ask your insurance company for a Green Card. Carry your insurance certificate, Green Card, proof of ownership of the car and, importantly, your driver's licence. If your licence was issued in the UK, bring your passport with you for identification.

Membership of a reputable breakdown service is advisable unless you are undaunted by the prospect of breaking down in remote countryside. Non-members can join up for the duration of their holiday only. Depending on the type of cover you have, breakdown organizations may offer only limited services in Ireland so check before you travel.

If you are renting a car, make sure the insurance cover meets your needs. You will need to show your driver's licence – if you are a US citizen you will need an International Driving Permit, available from the **AAA**.

Platform of Heuston Station in Dublin

RULES OF THE ROAD

EVEN FOR THOSE unused to driving on the left, driving in Ireland is unlikely to pose any great problems. For many visitors, the most difficult aspect of driving on Ireland's roads is getting accustomed to passing other vehicles on the right and giving way to traffic on the right at round-abouts. The wearing of safety belts is compulsory for drivers and for all passengers whether they are sitting in the front or rear seats. All children must be secured with a suitable restraint system. Motorcyclists and their passengers are obliged by law to wear crash helmets.

Junction ahead

Unprotected quay or river ahead

Dangerous bends ahead

Children or school ahead

ROAD SIGNS

MOST ROAD SIGNS in Ireland are in both Gaelic and English. Most are also now in kilometres although some signs may still appear in miles. The sign "Yield" is the same as the UK "Give Way". Brown signs with white lettering indicate places of historic or cultural interest.

BUYING FUEL

UNLEADED FUEL and diesel fuel are available just about everywhere in Ireland. Although prices vary, fuel is relatively cheap by European standards. Almost all the petrol (gas) stations accept VISA and MasterCard, though check before filling up, particularly in rural areas.

View of Dun Laoghaire from the road around Killiney Hill *(p89)*

SPEED LIMITS

THE MAXIMUM speed limits in Ireland, which are shown in miles, are more or less the same as those in Britain:
• 30 mph (50 km/h) in built-up areas.
• 60 mph (95 km/h) outside built-up areas.
• 70 mph (110 km/h) on highways.
On certain roads, which are marked, the speed limits are 40 mph (65 km/h) or 50 mph (80 km/h). Where there is no indication, the speed limit is 60 mph (95 km/h). Vehicles towing caravans (trailers) must not exceed 55 mph (90 km/h) on any road.

CYCLING

THE QUIET ROADS of Ireland help to make touring by bicycle a real joy. **Belfield Bike Shop** and **Cycleways** are good rental outlets in Dublin. If you are venturing further afield, local tourist offices will give you details of bike rental in their area. You can often rent a bike in one town and

Road signs in the Republic in Gaelic and English

drop it off at another for a small charge, or put it on the train. Many dealers also provide safety helmets, but bring your own waterproof clothing to help cope with the weather.

Street Finder Index

KEY TO THE STREET FINDER

▪ Major sight	🚌 Coach station	✝ Church
▪ Place of interest	🚕 Taxi rank	⊠ Post office
▪ Railway station	🅿 Main car park	═ Railway line
▪ DART station	ℹ Tourist information office	One-way street
▪ Luas stop	✚ Hospital with casualty unit	▬ Pedestrian street
▪ Main bus stop	🚓 Police station	

0 metres 200
0 yards 200

1:11,500

KEY TO STREET FINDER ABBREVIATIONS

Ave	Avenue	**E**	East	**Pde**	Parade	**Sth**	South
Br	Bridge	**La**	Lane	**Pl**	Place	**Tce**	Terrace
Cl	Close	**Lr**	Lower	**Rd**	Road	**Up**	Upper
Ct	Court	**Nth**	North	**St**	Street/Saint	**W**	West

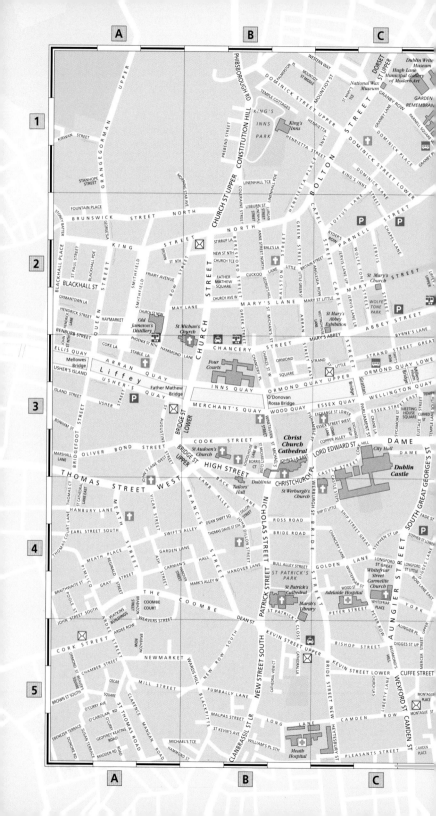

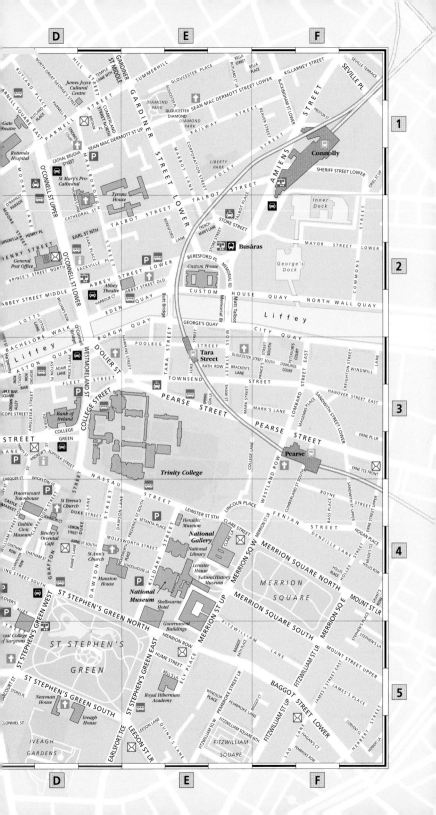

General Index

Acknowledgments

DORLING KINDERSLEY would like to thank the following people whose contributions and assistance have made the preparation of this book possible.

MAIN CONTRIBUTOR
TIM PERRY, from Dungannon, County Tyrone, writes on travel and popular music for various publishers in North America and the British Isles. He was also a contributor to the *Eyewitness Travel Guide to Ireland*.

EDITORIAL AND DESIGN ASSISTANCE
Gillian Allan, Douglas Amrine, Tessa Bindloss, Jo Blackmore, Vivien Crump, Fay Franklin, Annette Jacobs, Kathryn Lane, Nonie Luke, Ian Midson, Christina Park, Victoria Peel, Polly Phillimore, Lee Redmond, Andrew Sanger and Rachel Symons.

MAPS
Richie Toomey (ERA-Maptec Ltd, Dublin, Ireland)
MAP CO-ORDINATOR David Pugh

INDEXER
Hilary Bird.

PROOFREADER
Stewart Wild.

ADDITIONAL PICTURE RESEARCH
Monica Allende, Brigitte Arora, Anna Grapes.

ADDITIONAL ILLUSTRATIONS
Joy Fitzsimmons.

SPECIAL ASSISTANCE
Particular thanks go to Niall Kennedy at Dublin Tourism for his invaluable help throughout this project.

Thanks also to everyone at the National Museum, especially Dr Felicity Devlin, Damien Debarra and Aoife O'Shea, to Adrian le Harivel at the National Gallery, to Telecom Eireann and the General Post Office.

PHOTOGRAPHY PERMISSIONS
THE PUBLISHER would like to thank all those who gave permission to photograph at various cathedrals, churches, museums, restaurants, hotels, shops, galleries and other sights that are too numerous to list individually.

PICTURE CREDITS
tl = top left; tc = top centre; tr = top right; cla = centre left above; ca = centre above; cra = centre right above; cl = centre left; c = centre; cr = centre right; clb = centre left below; cb = centre below; crb = centre right below; bl = bottom left; bc = bottom centre; br = bottom right.

The Publisher would like to thank the following individuals, companies and picture libraries for permission to reproduce their photographs:

AER LINGUS/AIRBUS INDUSTRIE: 156t.

AKG London: 12cb, 20c.

AN POST, THE IRISH POST OFFICE: 154bl.

BORD FAILTE/IRISH TOURIST BOARD: 112tr, 112tl; Brian Lynch 17t, 27clb.

BRUCE COLEMAN LTD: George McCarthy 104tl.

BUS EIREANN: 158b.

CENTRAL BANK OF IRELAND: 153.

CENTRAL CYBER CAFÉ, DUBLIN: Finbarr Clarkson 155br.

CHESTER BEATTY LIBRARY, DUBLIN: 55t.

COLLECTIONS: Image Ireland 24t, 83b; Slide File 28crb;

CORBIS UK LTD: Bettmann/Reuters 17b; Hulton-Deutsch Collection 21t, 21crb; Library of Congress 20bl; National Gallery, London 20t.

DAVISON & ASSOCIATES LTD, IRELAND: 63cra.

DUBLIN TOURISM: 148tc.

EIRCOM: 155 tl, 155bl, 155bc.

MARY EVANS PICTURE LIBRARY: 7c, 11c, 13c, 15tr, 29c, 55cl, 68b, 117c, 146c.

GUINNESS IRELAND LTD: 80bc, 80br, 81bl, 81tl, 81tr, 81br.

HULTON GETTY: 16bc, 36bl, 91t.
THE IRISH ANTIQUE DEALERS FAIR: Louis O'Sullivan 26cr.

THE IRISH PICTURE LIBRARY: 13t.

IRISH TIMES: 106br.

JAROLD COLOUR PUBLICATIONS: 36bc.

TIMOTHY KOVAR: 56b, 141b.

MANSELL/TIME INC: 63bl.

HUGH MCKNIGHT PHOTOGRAPHY: 83t.

JOHN MURPHY: 96cb.

JOHN MURRAY: 27c, 78c.

NATIONAL CONCERT HALL, DUBLIN: Frank Fennell 142b.

NATIONAL GALLERY OF IRELAND, DUBLIN: 59tr, 71b, 82cr, 100b; *For the Road,* JB Yeats 46cl; *The Houseless Wanderer,* JH Foley 46tl; *Pierrot,* Juan Gris 46tr; *Judith with the Head of Holofernes,* Andrea Mantegna 47crb; *The Castle of Bentheim,* Jacob van Ruisdael 47c; *The Sick Call,* Matthew James Lawless 47b; *The Taking of Christ,* Caravaggio 47tr; *Convent Garden, Brittany,* c. 1913, William John Leech, ADAGP, Paris and DACS, London 1998 48ca; *A View of Powerscourt Waterfall,* George Barret the Elder 48bl; A *Group of Cavalry in the Snow,* Ernest Meissonier 49tl; *Virgin and Child Hodigitria,* Constantinople 49cra; *Guards at the Door of a Tomb,* Jean-Léon Gérôme 49cla; *Peasant Wedding,* Pieter Brueghel the Younger 49br; *Portrait of James Joyce,* Jacques Emile Blanche/ADAGP, Paris and DACS, London 1998 70bl.

NATIONAL MUSEUM OF IRELAND, DUBLIN: 19tl, 33crb, 42tr, 42cl, 42b, 43c, 43tr, 43bc, 43crb, 84clb, 85tl, 85cra, 85bl.

NATIONAL LIBRARY OF IRELAND: 6/7, 10, 103t, 111t.

NORTON ASSOCIATES: 52clb.

OFFICE OF PUBLIC WORKS, IRELAND: 112cl, 113cr, 113t, 114b.

POWERSCOURT ESTATE: 107tl.

RETROGRAPH ARCHIVE LTD: Martin Ranicar-Breese 44c.

REX FEATURES: 20b.

SLIDE FILE: 16br, 17cl, 24crb, 24bl, 25ca, 26cl, 26b, 27b, 60tl, 97c, 104cl, 104b, 110t, 114t, 140t; STENA LINE: 157b.

TEMPLE BAR PROPERTIES: 56c; BROWN THOMAS: Kieran Harnett 32t; TRINITY COLLEGE, DUBLIN:, 37cr, 38c, 38b, 38crb, 38cra; *The Marriage of Princess Aoite and the Earl of Pembroke,* Daniel Maclise 12t; TRIP ART DIRECTORS: 102c.

JACKET
Front – CORBIS: Dave Bartruff clb; DK PICTURE LIBRARY: Clive Streeter bc; Alan Williams crb; THE IRISH IMAGE COLLECTION; Tim Hannan main image. Back – CORBIS; Richard Cummins t; DK PICTURE LIBRARY: Alan Williams b. Spine - THE IRISH IMAGE COLLECTION: Tim Hannan

All other images are © Dorling Kindersley. For further information see www.dkimages.com

Dublin Transport Map

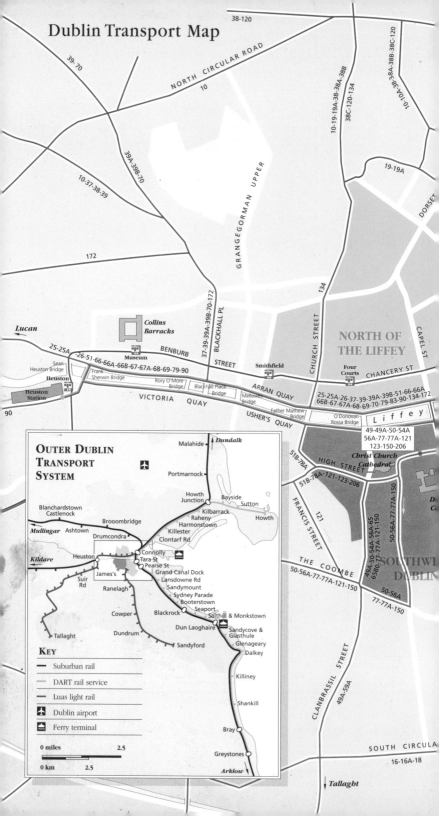

38-120

NORTH CIRCULAR ROAD

39-70

10

10-19-19A-38-38A-38B

38C-120-134

10-10A-38-38A-38B-38C-120

19-19A

39A-39B-70

172

10-37-38-39

GRANGEGORMAN UPPER

134

DORSET

Lucan →

25-25A

-26-51-66-66A-66B-67-67A-68-69-79-90

BENBURB STREET

37-39-39A-39B-70-172

BLACKHALL PL

*Collins
Barracks*

Museum

CHURCH STREET

CAPEL ST

**NORTH OF
THE LIFFEY**

Sean
Heuston Bridge

Frank
Sherwin Bridge

Rory O'More
Bridge

Blackhall Place
Bridge

Smithfield

ARRAN QUAY

Four
Courts

CHANCERY ST

25-25A-26-37-39-39A-39B-51-66-66A
66B-67-67A-68-69-70-79-83-90-134-172

Heuston

Heuston
Station

90

VICTORIA QUAY

Mellows
Bridge

Father Mathew
Bridge

USHER'S QUAY

O'Donovan
Rossa Bridge

L i f f e y

49-49A-50-54A
56A-77-77A-121
123-150-206

51B-78A

HIGH STREET

*Christ Church
Cathedral*

D

C

OUTER DUBLIN TRANSPORT SYSTEM

Malahide

Dundalk

Portmarnock

Howth
Junction

Bayside

Sutton

51B-78A-121-123-206

FRANCIS STREET

50-56A-77-77A-121-150

49A-50-54A-56A-65
65B-77-77A-121-150

SOUTHW
DUBLIN

Blanchardstown
Castleknock

Ashtown

Brooombridge

Drumcondra

Kilbarrack

Raheny

Harmonstown

Killester

Clontarf Rd

Howth

121

50-56A-77-77A-150

Mullingar

Heuston

Connolly

Tara St

Pearse St

Kildare →

James's

Suir
Rd

Ranelagh

Grand Canal Dock
Lansdowne Rd
Sandymount
Sydney Parade
Booterstown
Seaport

THE COOMBE

50-56A

77-77A-150

Cowper

Blackrock

Salthill & Monkstown

Dundrum

Dun Laoghaire

Sandycove &
Glasthule

Tallaght

Sandyford

Glenageary

Dalkey

Killiney

CLANBRASSIL STREET

49A-59A

Shankill

KEY

— Suburban rail

— DART rail service

— Luas light rail

✈ Dublin airport

⚓ Ferry terminal

Bray

SOUTH CIRCULA

Greystones

Arklow

↓ *Tallaght*

16-16A-18

| 0 miles | 2.5 |
| 0 km | 2.5 |